The Ongoing Renewal of
CATHOLICISM

Dedication

To all my undergraduate, graduate, and adult learners, who over many years have shared their lives, questions, and insights with me. This book is my legacy to upcoming college students, who are the hope of the future Church.

Author Acknowledgments

I want to thank my wife, Marie, for her assistance in so expertly editing the text.

Gratitude also to Katie Sellers for organizing and leading focus groups of college students, which were a rich resource for me in dealing with many of the questions in this text.

Publisher Acknowledgments

Thank you to the following individuals who advised the publishing team or reviewed this work in progress:

Paul Wadell, PhD, Saint Norbert College, Wisconsin

Donna Teevan, PhD, Seattle University, Washington

Shannon Schrein, OSF, PhD, Lourdes College, Ohio

Christopher McMahon, PhD, Saint Vincent College, Pennsylvania

Peter Feldmeier, PhD, University of Saint Thomas, Minnesota

The Ongoing Renewal of
CATHOLICISM

Brennan R. Hill

ANSELM ACADEMIC

Created by the publishing team of Anselm Academic.

Printed in the United States of America

7005

ISBN 978-0-88489-954-9

Library of Congress Cataloging-in-Publication Data

Hill, Brennan.

   The ongoing renewal of Catholicism / Brennan R. Hill.
   p. cm.

ISBN 978-0-88489-954-9 (pbk.)

   1. Church renewal—Catholic Church. 2. Catholic Church—Doctrines. I. Title.

BX1746.H495 2008
262´.02—dc22

                                                      2007041546

CONTENTS

1

Jesus of Nazareth

It all began with people following

a young carpenter from Nazareth. His name was Jesus
(Yeshua, Joshua), and he was born into a poor Jewish family
in a small village in Galilee, a northern province of Palestine.
His parents were Mary and Joseph, who had been married
as teenagers, in a union arranged by their parents. Like most
Palestinian Jews of the first century, Jesus and his family
probably lived in a tiny clay-brick house with two levels.
The lower level was for the protection of their animals at
night (perhaps a goat for milk, a sheep for wool, and some
chickens); the upper level, raised several feet, was for the
family meals and sleeping. A lean-to outside served as a
carpenter's shop where Joseph did his work and instructed
Jesus in the trade. The rooftop provided space for family
sharing and prayer at the end of the day.

Life in Nazareth was simple but arduous. As sharecroppers on land owned by the wealthy, families grew their own

food. They also daily carried water from a common well, made their own clothes, and eked out a living working at trades. Their workday was long, beginning at dawn and ending at sundown.

Jesus' family members were devout Jews. Prayer, discussion of the Scriptures, and acts of mercy and kindness were integral to their lives. On the Sabbath they would gather with neighbors in a central synagogue for prayer and instruction by the elders. The elderly, the sick, and the diseased had to be cared for, and no doubt Jesus learned compassion and the healing power of God by sharing in this service.

Though our knowledge of the particulars of Jesus' life is quite limited, imagining a biographical sketch such as this, based on what we do know of the families of his time, can be helpful in understanding his story.

A Pilgrimage to Jerusalem

Occasionally, once they had saved enough money, the family might join a caravan and make the difficult hundred-mile journey south to Jerusalem for Passover or one of the other big feasts. They would face many dangers: poisonous snakes, wild animals, and hostile people, including thieves waiting to pounce on vulnerable pilgrims. In Jerusalem they would stay with friends or relatives and then mingle with the million or more pilgrims to celebrate one of the great Jewish feasts at the magnificent Temple built by Herod.

Jerusalem must have been a culture shock for the country boy, Jesus. The Romans had taken over his country half a century before, so he would have seen the fearsome and brutal Roman mercenaries marching about just waiting for someone to step out of line. On a hill outside the city were lines of crosses, where those convicted of rebellion writhed in pain or slumped over already dead. Wild dogs leaped for their flesh and birds of prey zoomed down to tear at their bodies.

For the first time, Jesus would catch a glimpse of the Jewish leaders. Outside their academy, the learned and wealthy scribes would be instructing their privileged students on the intricacies of Jewish theology. Jesus himself had received only simple instruction at synagogue and from his parents. His own skills in reading the Hebrew scrolls were quite modest, and he had never learned to write. But he had learned the core Jewish beliefs about a God who was a loving Creator. Of the hundreds of Jewish laws on purification and ritual, his hard-working community knew little, nor had they much interest in learning about all the punishments demanded by the Jewish authorities on behalf of a judging and avenging God. Jesus had learned from his people that God was love and that loving God and one's neighbor as oneself was the heart of the Jewish faith.

Jesus would have encountered many others on pilgrimage. There were the Pharisees, hustling about doing social work among the poor and modeling how to obey all the Jewish laws to a T. Some had a reputation for being much too legalistic and others were known to be hypocrites, teaching one thing and doing another. At the Temple were the wealthy high priests, men who led royal lives with their multiple wives in magnificent mansions. They lived off the monies they collected from farmers tilling the many acres they owned, the sale of millions of birds and lambs for Temple sacrifices, and the taxes they collected from their people. They had sold out to the conquering Romans; a small price they thought for the sumptuous lifestyle they received in return.

Pressing through the crowded streets, Jesus would have seen the tall, slender Essenes, dressed in white robes and hurrying to their secluded monasteries where they lived in communities that rejected the Judaism known to Jesus. He might even have glimpsed someone preaching revolution against the Roman occupiers or starting a riot by stabbing a Roman soldier or someone who sympathized with the Romans.

Jesus would have seen some of the countless merchants arriving in the city with camel caravans carrying a vast array of goods, including precious glassware from Tyre and magnificent linens from Babylon. Jesus had seen such caravans pass near his own village, but had never seen the camels or the merchants up close. He must have wondered where those buying such exotic goods came up with all that money! On a poor carpenter's wages, he could barely afford a new pair of sandals or a set of earthen bowls for his mother.

There were many other sights as well: the fishermen selling their dried fish from the Sea of Galilee, slaves being sold on the auction block, and chariot races and wild animal shows in the hippodrome. There were musicals and plays in the theater for those who could afford them. Outside homes of the wealthy, Jesus might have glimpsed sumptuous banquets and seen exotic dancers overflowing into the streets. Along the roads were many beggars looking for a coin or two and prostitutes trying to drum up business.

Jerusalem must have been a world that excited the young Jesus and at the same time deeply disturbed him. Was there anything he could do to help bring his people back to their treasured values of love, humility, compassion, and forgiveness? Could he somehow show that the poor were blessed and that there was no such thing as an outcast, because each person was a child of God, with the precious gift of life within and called to love forever? Children of God should not be enslaved or brutalized by violence. There was too much greed, corruption, and hypocrisy. There should be no outcasts! The diseased were not cursed by God and should be given healing and proper care. The prostitutes, many of whom were sexually abused at home or cast out by their husbands for other women, should be given back their dignity. Goods and food should be shared, for God provides enough for all. If Jesus embarked on such a mission, would he himself be cast out, or even find himself nailed to one of those crosses on the hill outside the city?

Back in Nazareth

Jesus spent most of his life in the tiny village of Nazareth. He spent his childhood playing on the hillsides, watching sheep, and helping his parents with the many daily chores of rural life. Nazareth, though a Jewish ghetto, was not isolated. Nearby was the sophisticated city of Sepphoris. The Romans had destroyed this city after a Jewish rebellion, but during Jesus' lifetime it had been rebuilt into a prosperous and cultured place. About twenty-five miles northwest was the lovely area of Mt. Carmel, overlooking the Mediterranean Sea. This was the area where the great prophet Elijah preached. About the same distance northeast was the fishing village of Capernaum, where Jesus seems to have moved as a young adult, and which was the hometown of some of his original followers. It is quite possible that Jesus would have gone to these areas to bring back wood for his carpentry projects or for work on construction jobs.

We often see Jesus portrayed as a tall, thin, blue-eyed preacher in a snow-white robe. In actuality, if he were average in height for that time, Jesus would have been just over five feet tall. Many years of hard physical work outdoors would have hardened his muscles and calloused his hands. As a Semite, he would have been dark skinned, with dark eyes and hair. Standing in his rough, unbleached wool robe, his feet dusty from hiking and his face leathered by the sun, Jesus might have been a rugged-looking individual indeed.

Student Reflection

"This description makes Jesus more real to me. Now I realize that he was just like me and had to experience growing up, learning, and trying to find out what he should do with his life, just like I do."

It seems as though Jesus might have had brothers and sisters, for they are mentioned in the Gospels. Although the theological and historical questions surrounding this are complex, the references to Jesus' siblings can be considered here. Jesus' most notable likely sibling was James, who later would be chosen to lead the church in Jerusalem. Jesus' father, Joseph, seems to have died when Jesus was young. Though it was customary for Jews at that time to marry and raise children, Jesus does not seem to have been married. At least, no mention of his having had a wife or children is made in the Gospels. Could it be that after his brothers and sisters married, he chose to remain home to take care of his widowed mother? Possibly, just like many young people today, he was too busy with

Jesus might have had brothers and sisters

work and then his ministry to have time to marry. Whatever the case may be, Jesus appears to have stayed at home in Nazareth working at his trade until he was nearly thirty. Then he moved to Capernaum to begin a new phase of his life, one that would be more public.

A Call to Renew His Religion

Mark, the earliest gospel, recounts Jesus' step into public life with his baptism in the river Jordan. There, John the Baptizer, who may have been a relative and mentor to Jesus, called his fellow Jews to change their lives and symbolically wash away their sins in the river shallows. Although the relationship between the two men isn't entirely clear, their meeting carries importance.

John was a craggy desert dweller, a recluse who wore camel skins and ate locusts and wild honey that he found in the wilderness. He prayed for his people and occasionally came forth as a fearsome prophet to warn them of God's punishment. In part, he seems to have seen his mission as one of setting the stage for his younger, more laid-back, and less-experienced protégé, Jesus.

It must have been a proud day for John the Baptizer when his young student, Jesus, came into the river to become part of this great symbolic washing and celebration of God's forgiveness. Mark's gospel tells us that when Jesus came up from his baptism, he had a moving experience of being beloved by his God and filled with the Spirit.

How It All Got Started

The "Jesus movement" all began when this young construction worker, Jesus, left his home and family and began a mission to reform his own religion of Judaism. Like all religions, his had veered off track from its best teachings and traditions. In his home life in Nazareth and in his prayer life, he had experienced God as Abba (dear parent) and had come to strongly believe that love, compassion (especially for outcasts), healing, and justice were at the heart of his religion. The legalism, hypocrisy, harsh judgment, and fear of God that he had so often seen in his religion were simply not acceptable to this young reformer from the rural north.

A People Divided

There were serious divisions among Jesus' people, each with its own take on what it meant to be a good Jew. There were the Pharisees, with their emphasis on the scrupulous following of all the hundreds of laws on food, dress, worship, and daily life; the Sadducees, who gave themselves to power and luxury and did not believe in God's providence or even life after death; and the scribes, learned intellectuals who wrote commentaries on the law but who often took their positions too seriously and expected always to be given the best places at events. There was the beginning of a movement of Jews (sometimes called Zealots) who wanted to use violence to throw off the Roman yoke. There were the Essenes, who did not recognize the official Temple or priesthood, but kept to themselves in monasteries, preparing for the final coming to their communities alone. There were the hated Samaritans in the central province, who had their own temple, priesthood, and beliefs. And there were the Herodians, who ruled ruthlessly as puppet leaders for the Romans.

A People Oppressed

Every Passover, Jesus celebrated how God had rescued the Jewish people from slavery in Egypt and given them a land they could call their own. They had become a great nation, only to become divided and then constantly conquered by other kingdoms: Babylonia, Persia, Greece, and now the Roman Empire. Jesus' people had been exiled, dominated, and oppressed for centuries. He knew the iron hand of the Roman occupiers: they had pushed his family back into the hinterlands, where they were forced to eke out a living and pay heavy taxes on rented land, on what little they earned, and on their crops, herds, boats—even the fish they caught. Any refusal to pay taxes, any attempt to rebel or stir up trouble would be punished by either selling the offender into slavery or subjecting him to crucifixion. Jesus had become convinced that violence begot violence and that only nonviolence would produce true peace.

A Retreat to the Desert

In the East it has been customary for monks and prophets to prepare themselves for their mission by spending some time in the desert. During Jesus' time, there was a large monastery of Essenes dedicated to prayer, fasting, chastity, and ascetical living located in the harsh desert near Qumran by the Dead Sea. At this point in his life, Jesus seemed to be experiencing a deep call to leave home and take to the road as a prophet. Not far from the Qumran area, near Jericho, Jesus entered the wilderness for an extended time to pray and prepare himself for the difficult mission of bringing reform to his fellow Jews.

The desert is a stark and dangerous place, and yet a landscape that has its own unique beauty. It was a symbolic place for Jesus to pray, as his people had wandered there for many years looking for the land that Yahweh had promised them. In the desert one is alone with the self, stripped of all protection and security and deprived of interaction with others. Here there is just the self and God, and few distractions other than one's own imaginings, which have to be kept under close control. The sounds of howling animals at night could conjure up images that could bring panic. The hissing and rustling of snakes and scorpions could induce terror. And thirst, the burning sun, and the occasional dust-up from the wind could depress, discourage, and even cause one to hallucinate.

The desert is a place to learn about the true self, the purpose of one's life, the meaning of suffering and death, and where one stands with God. Jesus was now thirty, rather old in those days to just be leaving home and setting out on his own. From the time he was a child, he had felt an intense intimacy with his God. At times it was as though God spoke to him when he rose at sunrise to recite a psalm or when his mother held him before he went to sleep. He felt God's power work through him when he cared for and brought healing to the elderly, the sick, and the diseased in his village. He had felt the Creator's power when he built a house for a newly married couple, made furniture for a newborn, and built a bridge across a dangerous wadi near the well. He had felt close to his God on his trip to Carmel by the sea for lumber, on his hikes to Mt. Tabor, and during his walks along the beautiful Sea of Galilee.

Jesus had come to believe within the very fibers of his being that God was found in love, humility, compassion, and forgiveness. Greed, hatred, violence, and oppression were all the absence of God. He must go and tell his people to come back to the faith of Abraham and Moses. He must confront the hypocrisy of some of his Jewish leaders and the brutality of some of the Romans occupying his country. He must raise up the masses that were left as frightened outcasts, and teach them and their oppressors that everyone is a beloved child of God. He must help his people realize that the power of God, the reign of God, was with each of them and that with such power they could bring about peace and justice.

In the desert Jesus had to face his own demons. If he left the security of his home and trade, he would risk homelessness and hunger and face the temptation to abandon his mission and become a con man or magician to survive. In reflecting on his new call, he could see himself blindly throwing himself into his work with neither discernment nor prayer, foolishly believing that God would miraculously save him from harm. He would have to rely on the bread of God's care and revelation through discernment and prayer. As Jesus stretched out under the burning desert sun, he realized he would face opposition from both the Jewish and Roman leaders that he was about to challenge. There would be the strong temptation to become part of their corrupt leadership and sell out for a comfortable position in Jerusalem. Within his heart he could feel the fear and vulnerability, the danger that he might fail in his mission. He felt the strong drive toward security and the possibility that he might become part of the corrupt system he was challenging. Was it possible that this mission would bring him to torture and death? Would he have the courage to stay the course, or would he back off and run like a coward?

The Mission Begins

At first, Jesus was not sure when to start. He was almost thirty, which was well along in age at that time. Upon hearing of John's beheading for exposing Herod's immorality, Jesus saw that it was time for him to preach the reign of God, the loving and saving presence of God among his people.

Luke tells us that Jesus began his mission in his native Galilee, where at first his preaching in the synagogues was received with great enthusiasm. As he became famous and honored, he must have thought: "This is going to be easy. Why was I so worried and so slow to get started." But then one Sabbath, Jesus stopped at his own synagogue in Nazareth, which he had attended since childhood. He was asked to read, and opening the scroll to Isaiah, he read a moving passage:

> The Spirit of the Lord is upon me, because he has anointed me to bring glad tidings to the poor. He has sent me to proclaim liberty to captives and recovery of sight to the blind. (Lk 4:18)

When he finished the reading, Jesus sat down and told the congregation that all of this was being fulfilled today. At first, they were in awe, but when he started comparing himself to the prophets and chiding them for their lack of faith, they became angry. They ran him out of town and some even threatened to throw him off a hill. He was nearly killed on his first venture out, and by his very own Nazarenes!

Jesus then moved to the fishing village of Capernaum where the people seemed more open to his teaching. In Capernaum, Jesus decided he was going to need some help, some close followers who could travel with him and carry on his mission should something happen to him. The first group he approached was the fishermen. They were a rough and rugged lot, working from sunrise, rowing their heavy boats and throwing their soggy nets into the sea, often at risk of drowning as the wild storms rose over the hills without warning. Jesus knew that as tradesmen like him, they were subject to heavy Roman taxes on the purchase of nets and boats, on use of docks, and on every fish they caught and sold. Like him, they had worked for years under these oppressive taxes, paying through the nose while the wealthy in Jerusalem raked in their share of the revenues and then sent the rest to the Romans. Many Romans lived sumptuously off these tariffs, and in Rome so much wealth flowed in from the provinces that citizens did not have to pay taxes at all.

Jesus had known the oppression of the greedy and corrupt Herodians, high priests, and Romans all his life. And he was well aware that if anyone spoke up or rebelled, they would be sold into slavery or even crucified. Facing these risks, Jesus wanted to start a community of people who would drop out of the system, leave their trades, stop paying the taxes, and preach love, healing, and forgiveness. Like the prophets of old, Jesus would start a movement that would challenge the evils and injustices around them and try to lead people onto another path, another way of life based on love, compassion, and concern about those who were cast out.

The Call of the Disciples

Jesus first approached a rugged fisherman known for his quick temper and impetuous nature, a man named Simon. Jesus called Simon and also his brother Andrew and then two other powerful fishermen known as "Sons of Thunder"—James and John. A little later, Jesus startled his little band by calling someone they hated, someone who actually collected their taxes, keeping much for himself, and then betrayed his own Jewish people by sending the rest of their hard-earned money to the Romans. His name was Levi, and Jesus further upset his followers by going to Levi's house to share a meal with him and a whole group of tax collectors. Jesus' followers grew further dismayed at the group Jesus was assembling. There was Philip, who was personally called by Jesus and who brought along his friend Nathaniel. Jesus also called Bartholomew, Thaddeus, and Thomas, the latter always a hard sell. There was another James and another Simon, who had been with the Zealots, and Judas Iscariot, who had been dagger man for the revolutionaries.

Women Disciples

Jesus also called women to join his community of disciples. To our knowledge, no Jewish leader had ever done this. Often in Jesus' religion, women were held to be regularly unclean as a result of their menstruation and seductive through their supposed wily ways and emotional weakness. Thus women were kept in the background: they were not allowed near the Temple sanctuary, were segregated in the synagogue, and were not formally instructed in the Torah. They were seldom to be in public, but if they had to be, they were to be completely covered and were not to speak to men. Girls came of age at twelve and a half. They would then be married and become, in some ways, the property of their husband. Their value in many families depended much on the production of children and service to their husband. Failure in these areas sometimes meant that women were set aside through divorce and forced to live in poverty; some fell into slavery or even prostitution. Widows had few rights of inheritance and were subject to the authority of male in-laws.

Jesus was quite radical in his position on women. He saw all people as children of Abba, as brothers and sisters. He was familiar with the male images of God—father, warrior, and husband. But Jesus was equally aware that God was imaged in his Scriptures as a seamstress, a nurse, a midwife, and a loving mother. He often ignored the taboos of his religion: Jesus talked with women in public and even took them by the hand and healed them. He opposed the unjust divorce laws and reached out to widows and prostitutes. He drew all children, boys and girls, to his heart.

So many stories in the Gospels carry memories of Jesus' care for women. He saved the life of the woman who was about to be stoned to death for adultery; he raised up the prostitute who washed his feet at Simon the Pharisee's house as a repentant woman of love and hospitality. He accepted the often-married Samaritan woman, talked with her publicly, and sent her into her village to preach his gospel. He taught Martha and Mary in their own home; cured Peter's mother-in-law; healed a woman from her constant hemorrhaging; raised from the dead the widow's son and the little daughter of Jairus. He cured Mary Magdalene of serious illness.

But Jesus' most radical decision regarding women was to call them to be his disciples and travel with him in his little band.

Mary of Magdala was one of his favorites. There is no evidence whatsoever that Mary had been a prostitute. Indeed, Mary was a woman of means who wanted to be part of the group and help provide them with food and other necessities. He also chose Joanna, whose husband was the minister of finance for Herod and who had left the luxury of the palace to become a disciple. And, of course, there were other women who were closely associated with the community, including Mary, Jesus' mother; Martha and Mary, Jesus' close friends from Bethany; Susanna, and according to Luke, "many others." For all, it meant a new way of life with this young preacher and healer who taught with his own authority and seemed bent on challenging the religious and political structures of his time. It was indeed a motley crew and Jesus would have to have strong leadership qualities to mold this diverse group into a movement.

 Student Reflection

"I have always felt kind of left out in the Catholic Church. It seems like a male operation! I am so glad to hear that Jesus had different ideas about women and wanted them to be disciples."

Miracles

As the small band took its first hesitant steps with Jesus through Galilee, they were amazed at how intimate he seemed to be with God and how divine power seemed to work through him. He would rise before the rest from his mat on the ground, go aside, and be lost in prayer. After breakfast, he would lead them along dusty roads into the small towns and villages. Along the way, in isolated areas, they would encounter the much-feared lepers, outcasts who were considered by many to be punished by God with their affliction. Jesus would stop, befriend them, offer them respect and love, and even touch their open wounds and heal them. Jesus always found it impossible to believe that disease and deformity were sent by God to punish sin. He experienced God as a loving Creator who blessed and healed. This was the God that seemed to be working through Jesus' rough and calloused hands.

In the villages Jesus would encounter people overcome by convulsions and mad screaming so that they seemed possessed, and yet he would tenderly approach them and bring them peace. At one point he was at a home in Capernaum and when word got out, people crowded into the little house until it was jammed. Outside four men carrying their paralyzed friend couldn't get in, so they took off the roof and lowered their friend down. Jesus forgave the paralyzed man's sins, cured him of his paralysis, and then stood him up to walk on his own.

People were amazed, for they had never seen anything like this. The disciples had heard about a few such miracles in their Scriptures: Abimelech and his family had been healed of their afflictions, Saul had been healed of an evil spirit, and Elijah and Elisha had both restored life to people. But these were a very long time ago and were rarities, nothing like this, with nearly every day people healed of illnesses, the blind given their sight, the deaf their hearing restored, cripples able to walk again, evil spirits driven out, even the dead brought back to life. It was as though God's power was exploding all around them through this rugged and compassionate young man. It was awesome and yet at the same time frightening, because Jesus was beginning to attract a lot of attention, even making enemies among the religious leaders who thought he was acting through the power of Satan, not God. Those in charge of the Temple insisted that any such cures be verified by them and accompanied by offerings to Moses. Here was a young upstart peasant, dabbling on his own with powers that must be evil, and outside of Temple control!

people had never seen anything like this

A New Kind of Teacher

Jesus had seen some of the teachers of his day. On occasion a Pharisee would visit his village and give discourses on the hundreds of Jewish laws that had to be obeyed with regard to washing, eating, and Sabbath observance. Being simple rural people, Jesus' family found it difficult to obey all these laws, but they did the best they could. The main Jewish law, one that they were very serious about following, was the law of love—the dedicated love for their God and love for themselves and their neighbor.

Along the trade route that passed near Nazareth, Jesus had likely seen the Cynics following the caravans. They were ascetic teachers who preached about detachment, living close to nature, and resistance to oppression and hypocrisy. Jesus might have liked their message and their simple style, but found them too philosophical for his taste.

Jesus had also likely heard of some of the great sages of his time. His village elders would have told him of the beloved Hillel, who had died when Jesus was a boy. Hillel was known to be a gentle, liberal, and open teacher, who taught his followers to be flexible with regard to the laws and to not be judgmental or overly concerned about the future. People remembered his teaching about loving one's neighbor as one's self. Jesus had also likely heard about Shammai, whose teachings were more strict and legalistic, and Philo, who brought the Jewish people learning from Egypt and Greece.

On visits to Jerusalem, Jesus certainly observed the formal and learned scribes, standing on the corners, surrounded by their handpicked students, and orating on the latest scholarly opinions about the law. He had seen the white-robed and aloof Essenes scurrying to their monasteries. He had heard that they had rejected the Temple and Jesus' own form of Judaism for their version, which taught that the messiah was coming to the Essenes.

Jesus knew that his style of teaching would have to reflect his own background. He had never had the opportunity to attend any of the scribal academies in Jerusalem. After all, he had grown up in a poor, rural village in the north and could barely read or write. His understanding of his religion had come in part from a loving family and from the elders of his village. Mostly his religious convictions had come in his time at prayer, in his experience of his God in his heart, as well as in people and in the beautiful natural scenes in Galilee. He had a profound sense that he was a beloved son of God and that every person he encountered was also a child of God and therefore his sister or brother. This was good news indeed and stood as a contradiction to the hypocrisy, hatred, revenge, and violence that he so often saw around him.

Jesus chose to begin his teaching with the message of John the Baptizer. He proclaimed: "This is the time of fulfillment. The kingdom of God is at hand. Repent, and believe in the gospel" (Mk 1:15). This would be the heart of his message: the reign of God, or the loving, saving presence of the Creator is in your midst. Repent, change your direction, and get in touch with that loving, saving presence of God. If God reigns in your heart and in the world, there will be no place for hatred, prejudice, revenge, greed, lust, violence, or oppression. Jesus did not have to quote scholarly scribal opinions to make this point. He knew that this was the core of the Jewish experience, of his own experience.

Jesus could teach this truth on his own authority! This was the good news that his God had revealed to him, and he felt impelled to call his people back to the treasures in their tradition.

Jesus' God was a God of love, and he decided to spend the rest of his years showing through his life and teachings the power and presence of this God, whom he familiarly called *Abba* ("dear parent"). Revealing the will of Abba would mean teaching about the blessings given to those who chose to be children of Abba. At one point, standing on a mountaintop, he proclaimed that Abba's blessings were given to the poor, the meek, those seeking justice and peace, the merciful, the clean of heart, and those who were persecuted for seeking justice.

Love was Jesus' central teaching. In fact, to share his vision of a reformed Judaism, he put together two teachings from the Torah. One was from Deuteronomy—the commandment to love God with one's whole heart, soul, and mind. The other was from Leviticus—the commandment to love one's neighbor as oneself.

Jesus was convinced that these two commandments summed up the whole of the law and the prophets.

Love was to be extended not only to friends and relatives but to enemies as well. Those who followed Jesus' teachings were to turn the other cheek and pray for those who persecuted them. They were to be nonviolent and thoroughly dedicated to peacemaking.

Teaching in Parables

Jesus chose to express his teachings about God's kingdom in parables, stories that are also found in the Hebrew Scriptures and in the rabbinic writings after Jesus' time.

Jesus developed many original parables, which were based on his experience of God's presence in sowing seeds, harvesting fruit trees, tending to sheep, fishing, baking bread at home, and feeling the warm sun on his face. All of these he experienced as God's power within creation, revealing, gathering in, caring for, rescuing, transforming, and sharing love. Jesus had to tell his people that the God of love reigned and that there were signs of the divine presence in moments of tenderness, times of peace, and in victories over sin and evil. As a Jew, Jesus was devoted to a savior God who had freed his people from slavery in Egypt and who now called the Jews to be liberators of all people. Often in the tiny clapboard synagogue of his village, Jesus heard Isaiah's good news that peace and salvation flow when God's power reigns. Often he prayed the psalm: "Your love is before my eyes; I walk guided by your faithfulness" (Ps 26:3).

In this kingdom there were to be no outcasts, no oppression, no violence. Yet, Jesus was a realist and knew that many who lived off the domination and control of others would see his message as dangerous. There were the Romans, who had brutally conquered his people, taken their land and their freedom, and made them live in fear under heavy taxation. A public word about the evil of such oppression could mean being sold into slavery or crucifixion. Then there were the high priests in Jerusalem. They were appointed by the Romans and lived in luxury and comfort as payment for their loyalty to their imperial invaders. There were some of the members of the Sanhedrin, the supreme court of Israel, who preached and demanded strict obedience to the law, but had little love in their hearts for the many Jews who worked like slaves and had very little to show for it. There was the Herodian family, who ruled their people as corrupt puppet rulers for Rome. In the Mediterranean area, where honor and shame were so important, Jesus saw many of the "honorable" as hypocrites and traitors to their own people, while he saw many good Jews dishonored and put to shame by their own leaders and by the Roman tyrants who ruled over them.

Jesus knew that in this environment, his law of love and nonviolence would be a hard sell and would threaten those in power. After all, he was telling those who constantly heard they were nobodies who must submit and obey that they were children of God and therefore free and worthy of human dignity. He was telling his people, who were required to submit to the "divine" Caesar, not to go beyond paying their taxes. He warned that the greedy rich would have a difficult time entering the kingdom, and he urged them to share their goods with the poor. He condemned those who laid heavy burdens on the people. And on one historic afternoon, he attacked the corrupt moneychangers and merchants at the Temple and condemned the corrupt system for which they worked.

At a time of repression, treachery, and corruption, Jesus called for freedom and equality. He called for conversion. He called for an end to violence, teaching his followers to turn the other cheek and to love and pray for their enemies. Jesus led his little band in a way that was countercultural. They were to live simply, detached from material things, given to the service of the poor and oppressed, and ready to put their lives on the line to stand up for justice and peace. The freedom of their people was to be the goal, and he told them: "If a Son frees you, then you will truly be free" (Jn 8:36). But this freedom would be brought about by love, compassion, and forgiveness, not by violence.

Jesus told many parables to help his followers understand the nature of God's kingdom. The kingdom was like a mustard seed, small—even hidden—but with great power to spread quickly. Those in the kingdom are like prodigal sons who can expect unconditional love and forgiveness from the Abba God. The parable of the persistent widow shows the power of prayer in revealing the kingdom. The story of the Pharisee and the tax collector praying in church shows that humility and not self-righteousness is required to enter the kingdom. The story of the Good Samaritan reveals that everyone is our neighbor and worthy of our service. And stories of people cast out into the darkness and sheep being separated from goats reveal that we can choose to reject the presence of God and the kingdom of love and peace.

Prayer

Jesus seems to have received his insight and energy from his prayer, his intimate communication with Abba. From the time he was a boy, his mother, Mary, taught him the Hebrew psalms. He liked to recite them when watching the sheep in the evening or while working at his trade by day. He liked to climb to the top of mountains, where he somehow felt closer to Abba, and just listen to the silence amidst the clouds and in the warm rays of the sun. He enjoyed going into the desert, where he could be alone and test his strength and survival skills. There, he had no one to turn to but his God, who came in the power of love and tenderness. In synagogue, Jesus enjoyed listening to the readings of the Torah and was thrilled to join his community in prayers of praise and thanksgiving.

Jesus carried this dedication into his public mission. When his disciples awoke at sunrise, they would see his empty mat and know that already he had gone off on his own to contemplate and prepare for his day. They watched him at table in the Jewish fellowship meals as he joined in prayer with both friends and enemies. And on Sabbath, the peace that came over him made them feel that being in his presence was experiencing time and space as sacred.

The disciples learned a great deal about prayer from Jesus. He taught them not to pray ostentatiously, but quietly and humbly, using few words. He taught them to give praise to their Abba and ask that the kingdom of love and peace be on earth as it is in heaven. He told them to ask for material and spiritual nourishment, their "daily bread," and showed them how to pray for forgiveness as well as protection from temptation and sin. Their Abba was generous, openhanded, and all they had to do was ask and blessings would be given them.

A New Way of Life

Jesus preached a renewed way of being Jewish, of being a human person. He taught a way of life with an about-face: repentance and commitment to following the true path of goodness. They should begin by treating others the way they themselves wished to be treated. He taught them to live simply and not hoard material things because one cannot serve God while serving things. Wealth could be a real serious obstacle to living in the kingdom of God, where love and kindness reign. He taught his disciples to give access to the poor and to be without worry about their basic needs. Abba, Jesus said, knows their needs and will provide if they stay focused on seeking the kingdom of peace and justice. Just as Abba looks after all of nature, including the smallest bird or lily, God will look after each of them. He told them not to judge others and used one of his famous exaggerations to make his point: don't try to take the speck out of your neighbor's eye and miss the plank in your own eye!

Jesus called his disciples to a life of service to others, especially to the outcasts of the world. Indeed, he told them, their ultimate place in God's kingdom would depend on their choices with regard to feeding the hungry, giving drink to the thirsty, taking in the homeless, clothing the naked, and visiting the sick and those in prison. Whatever they did to the least among them, they did to the Lord himself!

Like the Prophets of Old

Jesus must have seemed like a prophet to many of those who heard him preach on the hillsides. The Jewish people had not seen many prophets in recent times and many longed for their strong leadership, inspiring call to conversion, and brave denunciation of the persecutors of the chosen people. Men like Moses, Elijah, and Jeremiah, and women like Miriam and Deborah didn't come along often. Oh, many of the scribes said they were the successors of the prophets, but generally they were too scholarly and removed from the masses to stir up fervor. Then there were the occasional fanatics who called a group to march to the desert and await the end of the world. These were usually quickly dispatched by the Romans for causing a disturbance among the people.

The only one in recent times that seemed like a prophet was John the Baptizer. He came out of the desert, dressed in animal skins, his eyes burning with passion. John was a scary preacher of hell and brimstone, who denounced the immorality and hypocrisy of the Jewish royalty. He called his people to repent and had a strong following, but was arrested by the Herodians and beheaded.

Clearly Jesus came across to many as a prophet. In Matthew's gospel the crowd describes Jesus as "the prophet, from Nazareth" (Mt 21:11). In Luke the people proclaim: "a great prophet has risen in our midst" (Lk 7:16). And at one point when Jesus asks his disciples how others see him, they tell him that he is thought to be one of the prophets who has returned.

Jesus seems to feel the calling of the prophet within him.

Early on, after doing a reading of Isaiah in the synagogue about the liberation of his people, he identifies himself with the same mission.

On another occasion, when his authority is challenged by his fellow Nazarenes, Jesus remarks: "A prophet is not without honor except in his native place and among his own kin and in his own house" (Mk 6:4).

It might be said that Jesus was a unique prophet, indeed the final prophet, so far as his followers were concerned. He not only spoke for God, but he spoke on his own authority, as though he had experienced an unparalleled intimacy with Abba. Jesus conveyed what he believed to be the central position of the Jewish faith. He reached into his tradition, and though in his teaching there are some references to judgment and punishment, his experience told him that Yahweh is a God of constant and eternal love and mercy toward all, especially toward sinners and those on the margins. This was the good news that Jesus felt compelled to preach.

Jesus knew he would face opposition in his prophetic stance. He was teaching a view of the kingdom that was not acceptable to many in authority. They had found it effective to keep the masses intimidated and helpless with a message of fear. They taught that wealth and power were signs of God's blessing. Those in superior positions were the righteous, while the vast majority, who worked in the grinding heat and struggled with debt, taxes, sickness, and disability, were inferior and unclean. Jesus turned the whole system on its head and cried out that those closest to the kingdom, those who were truly blessed, were the poor, the destitute, and the nobodies. Jesus was a prophet who took aim at the heart of the corruption in the Roman and Jewish systems. His life, his words, and his healing actions revealed that Yahweh was closest to the victims of these systems. In the kingdom of God's love and mercy, the first citizens were the blind, the crippled, the mentally handicapped, those who had fallen into prostitution through abandonment or abuse, and the destitute. This was not good news for those who lived off the domination and oppression of others!

Jesus' prophetic message called for a decision. One either had to accept his message and turn his or her life around or declare Jesus to be a false prophet, an agent of the devil. His person, his words, and his miracles were simply too strong a force to ignore. Jesus was therefore accepted by many, while others, especially those who stood to lose power and wealth if his teachings caught on, rejected him and began to plot his destruction.

An Impassioned Liberator

Like many of the prophets of old, Jesus wanted to bring freedom to his people. He once said: "If a Son frees you, then you will truly be free" (Jn 8:36). He wanted his people to be freed from fearing that God was a punisher, a violent avenger, a sender of disease or handicap. He wanted them to be freed from the leaders who preyed on these fears, many of whom were hypocrites, saying one thing and doing another.

Jesus no doubt rejected the Roman domination of his people and wanted to free his fellow Jews from oppression and violence. He objected to the corruption in some of the Jewish religious leaders, who lived off the wealth and power they received for treacherously going along with the Roman occupation of their land. He had harsh words for these leaders, calling them "blind fools," "sons of hell," "white-washed tombs," and "nests of snakes." He saw many of them as legalistic fanatics, who did little for their people, save intimidate and lay on them the heavy burden of taxes. He chided these leaders for walking around proudly in their long, flowing robes, demanding first place at dinners and in the synagogues.

Game Time

On his last trip to Jerusalem to celebrate Passover, Jesus must have known that his life was in danger. Early in his mission he had heard of plots against his life by some religious leaders who objected to him healing on the Sabbath. Many thought he was possessed and healed by the power of Satan. Others were stung by Jesus' exposure of their hypocrisy. And he knew full well what the Romans did to people they perceived as rabble-rousers—scourged them and subjected them to a slow death, hanging naked, nailed to a cross.

Jesus decided to enter Jerusalem in a manner befitting his mission. Instead of arriving triumphantly on a decorated steed with banners flying, trumpets blaring, and drums beating like the Roman conquerers did, Jesus came quietly and humbly, seated on a donkey.

The disciples, who cherished Jesus and his message, could not hide their enthusiasm and walked alongside him, singing and praising God. Crowds gathered and people began to take off their cloaks and cut palm branches, all to be thrown on the road as gestures of praise and welcome. Jesus' humble entrance had become a magnificent celebration of his mission, and this did not go unnoticed by the Jewish and Roman leaders in the city.

Jesus came quietly and humbly

When Jesus arrived at the Temple, he was angered by all the commerce and commotion there. His Father's House had become a bazaar, where moneychangers were exchanging the Jewish shekels, which were required for offering, for the foreign money brought in by pilgrims. These moneychangers were notorious for taking their cut in the exchange. Then there were those who charged outrageous fees for the doves and lambs required for sacrifice. With a million pilgrims crowding into the city, huge profits from all the buying and selling at the Temple poured into the coffers of the high priests and Roman officials.

In a rare scene for the usually peaceful Jesus, he flew into a rage over how this house of prayer had become a den of greedy thieves. He overturned the money tables, scattering the precious coins in all directions, and knocked the merchants off their chairs. Then he took some rope, fashioned a whip, and drove the merchants and all the animals off the Temple grounds. Quite a scene! And when the high priests and scribes saw what was happening to their wares and their profits and watched all the poor gathering around Jesus looking for healing, they decided that this was the last straw. This young Nazarene had to be destroyed!

The Last Days

Mark's gospel gives us the earliest account of Jesus' last days. He tells of Jesus gathering some of his followers on the Mount of Olives overlooking the city of Jerusalem and warning how all the corruption, greed, and violence will ultimately be the city's downfall. Jesus tells them to be on guard, watchful, and warns them of the persecution they themselves will have to undergo. Mark ominously tells of how the scribes and chief priests were already planning Jesus' death.

At nearby Bethany, where Jesus is waiting for Passover, a woman pours precious ointment over his head to soothe him. Some of the disciples are upset, thinking this to be a waste of precious ointment, but Jesus waves them aside and praises the woman for in fact anointing him before what he senses to be the end of his life. At this point, Judas goes off and agrees to betray his master for money.

The Last Supper

Jesus sent his disciples ahead to secure a room and prepare for what he thought might be his last meal with them. As they sat down, Jesus acknowledged that one among them would betray him. This throws the group into confusion and they begin to ask who the traitor is. Jesus only says that it would have been better if this disciple had not been born.

As the supper progressed, Jesus did something quite unusual.

He took bread, said the blessing, broke it, and gave it to them and said, "Take it; this is my body." Then he took a cup, gave thanks, and gave it to them, and they all drank from it. He said to them, "This is my blood of the covenant, which will be shed for many" (Mk 14:22-25).

The Agony in the Garden

After the supper, Jesus left the dining room and went down into the Kidron Valley to a garden of olive trees where he prayed in seclusion, safe from the hubbub and dangers of the city. He told his disciples that they would scatter if something happened to him, and when Peter insisted that he would never do that, he warned Peter that he would deny him.

Jesus then asked several of his disciples to keep watch while he prayed. Then he went off, fell to the ground, and prayed that this cup of suffering be removed. But as much as he wanted to avoid his death, he knew that Abba wanted him to continue on faithfully with his mission, even if it meant being killed by his enemies. No father would want his son to die, but most would want their sons to be true to their calling and not back away when danger arose. Going back to his disciples, he found them asleep and not watching for dangers. He tried several more times to keep them alert, but eventually gave up, realizing that Judas and the angry mob were coming for him. Judas betrayed Jesus with a kiss, and after a brief scuffle the disciples all ran away.

Jesus was brought before the Jewish leaders, who called forth witnesses, most of whom contradicted each other. Then, according to Mark's gospel, the high priest asked Jesus point-blank if he was the Christ. When Jesus said, "I am," the high priest said that no more witnesses were needed, because Jesus was clearly guilty of blasphemy. Jesus was condemned, spat upon, and beaten. (Everyone there knew full well that blasphemy entailed cursing God and not claiming to be the anointed one of God.)

Meanwhile below in the courtyard, Peter publicly denied any knowledge of Jesus three times over. Then Jesus was brought before the Roman Procurator, Pilate. The Roman leader didn't get very far with Jesus and tried to settle the whole matter by offering to release either Jesus or Barabbas, a convicted murderer. The crowd called for the release of Barabbas, and then shouted to have Jesus crucified.

The Process of Crucifixion

The Romans had mastered the age-old method of crucifixion and used it often to discourage rebellion or even disorder. It was a brutal way to die: hanging in front of the public naked, writhing while wild dogs tore at your feet and legs, and birds of prey tore at your face and eyes. Slowly the victim died from asphyxiation when he could no longer strain and raise himself up to catch a breath.

The ordeal began with the scourging. The naked prisoner was hung by his wrists on a post and muscular soldiers stood on either side with leather whips, studded with sharp pieces of bone and metal.

With a relentless rhythm, they began to whip the victim until the lashes cut through flesh and then muscle to bone. The scourgers were trained to stop short of killing the victim, for the idea was to torture and disable the victim, but allow enough strength in him to carry the hundred-pound crossbeam on his shoulders to the place of execution and enough endurance to last through the actual crucifixion.

Student Reflection

"Last year I saw Mel Gibson's Passion *and it made me realize more than I ever did before that Jesus really did suffer a lot. The movie taught me that Jesus really was human."*

Jesus was thus scourged and then, out of mockery, dressed in a kingly purple robe, crowned with long thorns driven into his skull. Then the heavy crossbeam was put on Jesus' shoulders, and he began the long and painful walk to Golgotha, the Place of the Skull.

At the place of execution, Jesus was thrown down and nailed to the crossbeam. Then the beam, with his body hanging from it, was lifted and fixed to the permanent vertical beam that was lodged in the rocks. There, Jesus hung in severe pain from the raw scourging wounds, the holes in his hands and feet where the nails were, and the many gashes in his skull from the thorns. Slowly and painfully he had to raise himself up to catch a breath and then lean back on the small seat that was provided to prolong the agony. On either side of him, there were two robbers going through the same horrible anguish.

In Mark's drama, Jesus dies amidst the darkness with a line from a psalm on his lips: "My God, my God, why have you forsaken me?" At the end, Mark tells of a Roman centurion acknowledging that Jesus was the Son of God and tells of some women, including Mary Magdalene and another Mary, who stay with Jesus until the end.

The body was then taken down by a Jewish leader named Joseph of Arimathea, then wrapped in linen, and placed in a tomb in the rock.

The young carpenter turned preacher and healer from Galilee was dead and buried. For his disciples it must have meant deep disappointment, for they had left all and followed a leader who had apparently failed in his mission and been put to death as a common criminal. They must have been filled with fear that the hatred directed at their master would soon be directed at them and spell their own deaths. Many were filled with feelings of guilt and cowardice for letting Jesus down, not watching out for him, betraying him, and running away when he was being tortured and killed.

The Resurrection

Just as there are varying accounts of the passion and death of Jesus, so it is with the Resurrection. There is a consistent tradition that early on Sunday morning, some women came to the tomb, found it to be empty, were told that Jesus had been raised from the dead, and were commissioned to spread the word to the other disciples. At the same time, the Gospels give varying accounts of the disciples actually experiencing the risen Jesus: women returning from the tomb, Mary Magdalene and Peter, Thomas, disciples along the road, the eleven on a mountain top, and even the risen Jesus making breakfast for his disciples one morning on the shore of the Sea of Galilee.

The risen Jesus is now clearly the Christ and appears in a new mode of existence, no longer subject to time or space, no longer subject to death. At times he is at first not recognized, at others he comes through locked doors and then later disappears. As Mary Magdalene learned, Jesus could no longer be embraced the way he could before his death. Jesus was not back in town, in that his disciples could show him to others to prove his Resurrection. Jesus' enemies could no longer arrest or kill him. The experience of the risen Jesus was quite real, but it was only experienced through faith. As Jesus said to Thomas: "Blessed are those who have not seen and have believed" (Jn 20:29).

It has been said that Jesus' life was the greatest ever led. It was as though the Creator became a human person to show people how a human life is meant to be led. Jesus' life was a struggle against temptation and a world that can be cruel and dangerous. His life showed that love, compassion, and forgiveness is "the Way" to live one's life and that neither suffering nor death can ultimately prevail against such a life. He called people to a conversion. Jesus taught that those who believe in him and live as he did will have life eternal.

Activities

1. Divide into teams and have each team prepare and offer a presentation on one of the following films on Jesus: *Jesus Christ: Superstar; Godspell; Jesus of Nazareth; The Last Temptation of Christ; Jesus of Montreal;* Mel Gibson's *Passion; The Gospel according to St. Matthew.* Most of these are now on DVD, so it is easy to find clips and comment on them. PowerPoint can be used to highlight key points.

2. Form small groups to discuss miracle stories and parables and then dramatize them before the class.

Sources

Crossan, John Dominic. *The Historical Jesus.* New York: HarperCollins, 1991.

Freyne, Sean. *Galilee, Jesus, and the Gospels.* Philadelphia: Fortress Press, 1988.

Hill, Brennan. *Jesus, the Christ.* 2nd ed. Mystic, CT: Twenty-third Publications, 2004.

Johnson, Elizabeth. *Consider Jesus.* New York: Crossroad, 1990.

Malina, Bruce. *The Social World of Jesus and the Gospels.* London: Routledge, 1996.

Perkins, Pheme. *Jesus as Teacher.* New York: Cambridge University Press, 1990.

———. *Hearing the Parables of Jesus.* New York: Paulist Press, 1981.

Saldarini, Anthony. *Pharisees, Scribes, and Sadducees in Palestinian Society.* Wilmington, DE: Michael Glazier, 1988.

Schackenburg, Rudolph. *Jesus in the Gospels.* Louisville, KY: Westminster John Knox Press, 1995.

2 The Bible

Sometime in the first year of

college, students tour the library and see where the various sections are: here are the reserved books, the history, English, and science books. There are the periodicals, art books, and fiction. And of course today there are computers, electronic books, and databases. It can be a little overwhelming at first, but students know they aren't expected to read or use the entire library, but to find materials according to their needs and tastes.

Well, the Bible is the same in that it is a library of many different kinds of literature. You are not expected to sit down and read it from cover to cover, but to select different "books" according to your taste or needs at a certain time. In this chapter we will tour the biblical library.

The Bible is one of our great literary treasures. After centuries in print, it remains a best seller, with more than thirty million copies a year purchased worldwide. Why so popular after many centuries? The Bible contains wisdom, values, and religious beliefs that have guided people for more than five thousand years, have helped to shape Western culture, and still today provide millions of believers with insight and inspiration. The Church says the Bible should be the primary resource for our faith.

The word *bible* comes from the Greek word *biblia*, which means "books." So, as we said earlier, the Bible is not a single book, but a whole library of different types of ancient literature. In the Catholic Bible there are seventy-three books in all, written over hundreds of years by different authors in Hebrew, Greek, and Aramaic. The books range from plays to poetry, histories to laws, prayers to temple hymns, and miracle stories to great wisdom teachings. The Jewish sections (forty-six books) cover a thousand years of Hebrew faith and tradition, and begin with reference to the time of the first Jewish patriarch, Abraham (ca. 1800 BCE). The central event, which provides perspective to all of these writings, is the great Hebrew exodus from Egypt (ca. 1290), led by Moses. The Christian section (twenty-seven books) covers only seventy to eighty years, and includes the life of Jesus and the forming of his early communities. Here the central illuminating event is the Resurrection of Jesus Christ.

For the person of faith, the Bible is more than a collection of books. Amidst the diverse writing of many inspired authors, the faithful hear the ongoing search of God's people for meaning as they listen to the Word of God spoken to them. They witness the saving presence of Yahweh among God's people, ever calling them to fidelity, always forgiving them for their sins. They hear the memories of Jesus' words and deeds and listen to the testimony of the early Christians' Resurrection faith. Beneath the wide cultural, historical, and literary differences of each text, the faithful are put in touch with the presence of God in human history. They encounter the Kingdom of God amidst the human struggle and in their own lives. In the following we will attempt to give a bird's-eye view of the great library called the Bible. We hope that along the way you will find the opportunity to browse among these literary treasures.

The Old Testament

The Hebrew section of the Bible consists of a canon of texts that, after centuries of discernment and use, were finally fixed in the first century CE. This canon includes the Torah, which is the first five books of the Law (Genesis, Exodus, Leviticus, Numbers, and Deuteronomy). Even today the Torah is held to be the most important part of the Hebrew Bible. The Catholic Bible divides the rest of the Scriptures into the historical books, the wisdom writings, and the books of the major and minor prophets.

The Torah

The first section of the Torah (1 Gn–19 Ex) deals with prehistory, from the "time of creation" to the period when the Hebrews meet God on Mt. Sinai. The Temple hymn 1 Genesis poetically celebrates the one God-Creator as the source of all life and beauty and ends with both woman and man being created in the image of God. The earlier and more primitive 2 Genesis describes the rural God in his garden creating man out of mud and woman from his rib to show that our lives come from God. Then the myth of the forbidden fruit, the serpent, and the downfall of the first couple teach one of the central Hebrew beliefs: that sin comes from breaking God's laws and ultimately brings destruction to those who commit it. The stories of Cain and Abel, and Noah and the flood, further explore the source of evil in the world, the destructive results of sin, and the saving and forgiving nature of God.

Genesis then takes the reader back in history to the first ancestors of the "chosen people." We are introduced to Abraham and Sarah, Isaac and Rebecca, Jacob and Rachel, all of whom lived sometime after 2000 BCE. It tells of their eventual migration to Egypt to escape famine and of their oppressive life in slavery there.

Exodus recalls the enslavement of the Hebrews in Egypt, the birth of Moses, and his call to lead his people. In time Moses emerges as a great prophet who leads his people out of Egypt and gives them the laws of Yahweh, which he receives on Sinai. It falls to Joshua to finally lead his people into the land of Canaan where they settle in, although constantly threatened by the neighboring hostile peoples.

Leviticus goes into great detail listing the many laws that developed among the Hebrew tribes. There were laws to be followed to lead a life of holiness, laws for sacrifice, for ritual cleanness (purification), and for celebrating feasts like the Day of Atonement and Passover.

The book of Numbers is a mixture of narrative and law. There is a historical account of the years of wandering from Sinai to the Promised Land of Canaan. When we say *historical*, we need to remember that this is not "history" in the modern sense. In the Bible, there may be underlying historical events, but history is presented interpretatively and mixed with mythology and symbolism to convey the faith-meaning of an event. Inevitably, the teaching is that humans have a covenant with their Creator that brings blessings and forgiveness to them. Breaking this covenant through sin inevitably brings destruction. Thus with a naïve ancient faith, it was thought that famine, disease, and defeat in battle were punishments from God. Likewise, victories over enemies, however brutal, were attributed to the power of God. Underlying this theology of the punishing warrior God was the revelation that God does indeed protect God's children and that sin inevitably brings destruction upon us.

Deuteronomy, the final book of the Torah, once again states the Ten Commandments and gives detailed lists of primitive tribal laws for many situations such as marriage, war, and the celebration of feasts. The book closes with an account of the death of Moses.

The Historical Books

The book of Joshua gives an account of the conquest of Canaan and the division of the land. This is a good example of mythical history. Although the settling of the Hebrew people of Canaan was a complicated process of migration, integration, and war that lasted several hundred years, here

this is not "history" in the modern sense

it is truncated into a short period to demonstrate God's giving the Promised Land to his people. In reading the Scriptures, we must remember that we are always dealing with a multitude of different cultures where people thought, wrote, and lived much differently from each other and most certainly from us today. Their literature indeed reflects this diversity and the distance from our contemporary mentality.

In Judges, the time before the Hebrew monarchy was established is described through heroic stories of figures like the prophet Deborah, Gideon, and the mighty Samson.

Around the year 1000 BCE, the tribes joined together to become the nation of Israel. First Samuel describes this transition and recalls the leadership of Saul and David. Second Samuel is dedicated to the reign of Israel's greatest king, David. It was David who shaped a tribal people into a united kingdom, making Jerusalem its capital. David was succeeded by his son Solomon, who built Israel into a powerful nation and constructed a magnificent Temple in Jerusalem. Solomon's oppressive taxes and forced labor for his building projects conflicted Israel's people, and upon his death there was a division into the Northern and Southern Kingdoms. First Kings deals with Solomon's reign and the division of the kingdoms, as well as the efforts of the prophet Elijah.

Second Kings describes the next period with its civil wars, bloody purges, the break-off of Samaria, and the great gulf between the rich and the poor. The kings of Judah, the activity of the prophet Elisha, the fall of Jerusalem to the Babylonians, and the Babylonian captivity are described in this book. The books of Chronicles retell the stories of Saul, David, Solomon, and the fall of Jerusalem from another vantage point.

Israel was in fact conquered often throughout its history. From 720 BCE on, there were a series of defeats for Israel. First, the Assyrians conquered the Northern Kingdom and Samaria and deported many of their inhabitants. In 586 the Babylonians conquered the Southern Kingdom, destroyed Jerusalem and the Temple, and exiled many Israelites to Babylon. In 539 the Persians conquered the Babylonians, and the Israelites were permitted to return to their homeland and rebuild the Temple in Jerusalem.

The book of Ezra tells of the return of the Hebrews to Jerusalem from exile in Babylon, the restoration of Jerusalem and the Temple, and the leadership provided by Ezra. Nehemiah's leadership in Jerusalem is described in a book by the same name. First and Second Maccabees tell the story of a much later period (ca. 165) when a family by that name led a successful revolt against the Seleucids, a dynasty empowered by the Greek conqueror, Alexander the Great. The Hebrew monarchy was then reestablished, the Temple in Jerusalem rededicated, and the Jews once again ruled themselves. It is with this period of Jewish history that the Old Testament comes to a close.

These historical books also contain hero stories of women like Ruth, Esther, and Judith, who were saviors of their people.

The Final Conquest

In 63 BCE Palestine was once again conquered, this time by the Romans. From 37 BCE until the birth of Jesus, Judea was governed by a Roman puppet king named Herod, who was a half-breed Jew, largely hated by his people. Herod led with a brutal hand for thirty-three years, during which he built elaborate cities, and fortressed and doubled the size of the Temple. Upon his death, the rule of Palestine was divided among his sons. One of them, Herod Antipas, ruled Jesus' home province of Galilee and would play a role in the gospel accounts of Jesus' passion. In 70 CE, the Jews revolted against the Romans, but they were soon overwhelmed and the Temple was destroyed. There was one final revolt in 132 CE, but once again the Jews were defeated and Jerusalem was made into a Roman city called Aelia Capitolina.

The Wisdom Literature

The wisdom literature is rooted in the early monarchies of David and Solomon, when the successful Hebrew people shifted from focusing on God's role in history to God's presence in everyday life. Wisdom became the process of putting one's life in harmony with creation and following a proper way of living. Following the way of wisdom would bring success and happiness. Failure to do so would result in adversity. The law of retribution, which holds that good will be rewarded and evil punished, prevailed. (Soon we will see how this law was challenged in the book of Job.) Precisely how to carry out the way of wisdom was taught through storytelling, parables, wise sayings, and other literary forms. Much of this was influenced by the wisdom of other cultures in Egypt, Mesopotamia, and Canaan.

The book of Job tells a story that raises the perennial question about why bad things happen to good people (a serious challenge to the retribution theory). Job is a folktale, showing the hand of numerous authors writing after the exile in Babylon. Combining prose and poetry, at times it reads like a play. Toward the end of the tale, Job's challenging questions are met in a magnificent wisdom speech by God, which asks much deeper questions and reveals the limitations of humans in understanding creation and God's purpose.

The book of Psalms is an anthology of some of the most beautiful prayers and hymns ever written. They express the whole range of prayer: great happiness, lamentation in suffering, trust, praise, thanksgiving, repentance, and petitions for assistance. In times of desolation, some (even Jesus) have cried out: "My God, my God, why have you abandoned me?" (22:2). Expressing deep faith, others have declared: "The Lord is my shepherd; there is nothing I lack" (23:1). When thankful, many have prayed: "O Lord, my God, I cried out to you and you healed me" (30:3). And at times when the beauty of nature moved someone, they prayed: "Praise the Lord from the heavens; give praise in the heights. Praise him all you Angels; give praise, all you hosts. Praise him, sun and moon; give praise all shining stars. Praise him, highest heavens, you waters above the heavens" (148:1-4).

Proverbs is an amazing collection of instructions on how to live a good life. Exhortations are given to respect authority, follow a disciplined life, and nurture a good marriage. Proverbs urges the listener to be rooted in an awe (fear) for God, for from there will follow a respect and reverence for all creation. Wisdom is here personified as a Lady who has been with the Creator from the beginning. She is intimately connected to the divine and gathers disciples who are taken with wisdom. Though many of the proverbs may seem naïve and simplistic today, they do reveal the value of learning from human experience.

Ecclesiastes is a unique piece of literature. Here a philosopher, perhaps in the third century BCE, makes rather cynical observations on life and then draws somewhat fatalistic conclusions. He explores the meaning of life, which he largely considers to be "in vain," and acknowledges that seeking wisdom is like "chasing after the wind." He is convinced that there is nothing truly satisfying in life and that all ends in death. The monotony and constancy of nature offers nothing new. Everything is fleeting, so the only alternative is to accept what comes from the hand of God and enjoy.

The Song of Songs is an extraordinary collection of sensuous love poems. Some have seen these as from ancient fertility rites, while others have interpreted them to be ancient wedding songs. Though these songs make no reference to religion, they have been viewed as allegories about Yahweh's relationship with his bride, Israel. Christians have at times viewed them as applicable to the relationship between Christ and his Church.

The Catholic Bible also includes in the wisdom collection the books of Wisdom and Sirach, in which wisdom is personified as Lady Wisdom and the Jews are encouraged to keep their faith in the face of oppression.

The Prophets

The prophets were the conscience of Israel. Chosen by God to give divine messages to their people, the prophets preached against the infidelity of their people and called them back to following the duties of the covenant. From high moral ground, the prophets denounced sin and injustice, threatened punishments from God, and promised deliverance and salvation to the faithful.

Among these prophets was Isaiah, who lived in the eighth century BCE. Isaiah constantly warned the kings of Judah that they needed to be faithful to Yahweh and that only Yahweh could bring salvation to the kingdom. The book of Isaiah also contains earlier prophetic poetry written toward the end of the exile in Babylon, which presents the magnificent messianic oracles that are so precious to Christians.

Jeremiah lived in the seventh century BCE, just prior to the Babylonian captivity. He warned his people about their sinfulness and idolatry and for this was imprisoned, exiled, and eventually murdered by his own people. The Babylonians crushed Judah, destroyed Jerusalem, and took its people into captivity. This book contains some of the most profound Jewish theology in the Bible.

Ezekiel was a prophet who lived with the Hebrews during the Babylonian exile. He often reminded his people of their sins and the coming of the destruction of Jerusalem, which in fact did occur in 587. Ezekiel then promised that they would be saved in a new covenant after they are freed from captivity. This is imaged in the famous depiction of the field of dry bones rising up to new life. His description of the majesty of God and the new Israel is classic religious writing.

Daniel is a prophetic and apocalyptic tale written during a time of oppression. It reveals how God saves his people and overcomes the tyrants who oppress them. The book of Daniel is followed by the twelve Minor Prophets. These are figures like Hosea, whose marriage to an unfaithful woman mirrors Israel's betrayal of Yahweh. At the same time, Hosea's tenderness and forgiveness of his wife, Gomer, parallels the magnificent descriptions of God's love for his people. There is also Jonah, who tried to avoid his prophetic mission, only to be thrown overboard and swallowed by a whale. After being miraculously saved, Jonah ends up warning the Assyrians, the enemies of the Jews. Much to his dismay they are converted and this angers him because he wants God to destroy them. The story is a folktale, teaching the Jews not to be vindictive but to be forgiving and merciful like their Creator. Then there is Micah, with its still-relevant positions on peace and social justice, and the famous line: "Only to do the right and to love goodness, and to walk humbly with your God" (Mi 6:8).

Daniel is a prophetic and apocalyptic tale

Old Testament Themes

This magnificent library of Hebrew writings, which we call the Old Testament, deals with many themes. Central to the Old Testament is the belief that there is but one God, who is the Creator and sustainer of all. This God is active within history and human life. Another theme is the covenant, the eternal bond that God has with all people, within whom God dwells. This covenant holds special meaning for the Hebrew people, who hold the position of being specially chosen by God as a blessing and a sign of salvation to all nations.

The law given by God to his people is another key theme. Obedience to this law purifies God's people and enables them to be holy as their God is holy. Disobedience to this law is sin and can bring destruction. Repentance opens the doors to forgiveness and reconciliation, which is always available from the saving God. And finally, another key theme is the role of the prophets. Prophets point out infidelity and injustice to God's people and call them back to faithfulness.

Thus ends our overview of one of the great libraries of ancient writings, the Old Testament. It holds many treasures for those who know how to search among its volumes with care and diligence. It is hoped that while considering this chapter, you will take the opportunity to browse this library and discover its richness.

The New Testament

The New Testament presents quite a contrast to the Old. Rather than an overview of thousands of years of history and belief, it looks at only a century. The New Testament is a much smaller library of only twenty-seven books that tell of the life and work of Jesus and the spread of the early Church. Here we find the four canonical Gospels, the Acts of the Apostles, early letters written by leaders to communities, and the book of Revelation.

The Gospels

The word *gospel* means "good news" and represents the excited testimony of early Christians that Jesus Christ is their Lord and Savior, the one who taught them how to live a good and holy life that will continue even after death.

The Gospels all come from authors in Hellenized cities and are thus written in Greek. Although they are named after apostles (Matthew and John) or companions of apostles (Mark with Peter and Luke with Paul), we really do not know who the actual authors were. None seems to have known Jesus personally or to have witnessed his ministry. The four Gospels seem to have been written sometime between the years 70 and 90 CE, so they represent the considerable development of Christian thought and living after the time of Jesus.

The central, guiding notion needed to understand the early stories is that of post-Resurrection faith. Several days after Jesus' passion and death, his disciples experienced him as being raised from the dead. This experience, which generated all kinds of emotions at first—awe, fear, doubt—eventually became the rock-solid basis for belief in Jesus' true identity. He was now seen clearly as the Christ, the Messiah, the Son of God, their Lord, worthy of godly faith and worship. A new faith, a new covenant was born, and the faithful couldn't contain themselves before they spread the news "to all nations," even though it might mean losing all: their Jewish religion, their families, or even their lives.

Eventually these stories, which were their memories now seen through the light of post-Resurrection faith, began to be written down. The early eyewitnesses were dying off and their testimony had to be preserved, and there was more need now to have written material for training missionaries and conducting ceremonies. Finally, there was a need to separate the authentic tradition from aberrations. Out of this impetus for written materials the Gospels were born.

The Gospel of Mark

The first gospel to be written was that of Mark. It has been said that the author of this piece invented the gospel literary form. While there were biographies written before by Jewish, Greek, and Roman authors, none of these narratives has the strong call to faith and salvation or theological impact that we find in the Gospel of Mark. It is truly a unique work in the history of literature.

The unknown author neither knew Jesus of Nazareth nor was he familiar with the Palestinian landscape. Many think this gospel was written around 70 CE in Rome, or possibly in Syria, and that it came from a non-Jewish community that suffered persecution.

The author draws from the oral and written stories available to him and masterfully constructs a narrative about Jesus. Bypassing any reference to Jesus' birth, the gospel begins in the Judean desert, where John the Baptizer preaches repentance and baptizes disciples in the Jordan River, including Jesus. Jesus' identity is revealed from the heavens, and then Jesus withdraws into the desert to face extreme temptations.

Next Jesus begins his public ministry in Galilee with his central message: "the Kingdom of God is at hand." He then calls disciples and proceeds to teach and work miracles. From the outset he meets opposition from religious leaders and misunderstanding from his own family. In the background, predictions are made about his passion and death. Eventually Jesus makes his way to Jerusalem, where he is greeted with enthusiasm and praise by followers. Immediately Jesus cleanses the Temple of moneychangers and merchants and enters into controversies with Jewish leaders. After predicting the destruction of Jerusalem and the endtime, Jesus is arrested in a garden after his last meal with his followers. He is tried, condemned, and then publicly crucified. Several days later some women come to his tomb to anoint his body, find the tomb empty, and are told by a young man in white that Jesus has risen. They are asked to tell Peter and the others, but they go off terrified and tell no one. Thus ends the simple yet profound first gospel. Mark is a short piece that can be read in one sitting, and yet what an extraordinary power it has had over people for two thousand years.

The Gospel of Matthew

Matthew's gospel was written in the 80s, probably out of the Antioch community. It is a strongly Jewish gospel, seemingly designed to convince both Jews and Gentiles that Jesus Christ was a Jew who fulfilled all the chosen people's hopes for salvation and extended these hopes to the whole world. The author borrowed about 80 percent of his tale from Mark's gospel and also borrowed from a source called "Q." Q is a collection of parables, sayings of Jesus, and miracle stories without a narrative. Though the document itself has never been found, it has been reconstructed from the dozens of references to it in the gospels of Matthew and Luke.

The Gospel of Matthew is much longer than Mark's and includes a detailed infancy narrative as well as long sermons by Jesus. Many have pointed out that this gospel seems to be a teaching manual for Christian missionaries. Its prominence has resulted in its being placed first among the gospels even though it was written later than, and relied upon, Mark. Indeed it has been the fundamental gospel for the Church, with its ecclesiology, the beatitudes, and the Our Father.

This gospel begins with a magnificent nativity story, complete with Jesus' family tree, an explanation to Joseph of his betrothed's pregnancy, the birth of Jesus, the coming of the Magi, the flight into Egypt to save the baby from the murderous Herod, and the migration to Nazareth to live in anonymity.

Matthew then covers Jesus' public ministry in great detail: his teachings, miracles, and conflicts with the Jewish leadership. Just before Jesus moves on to Jerusalem, he describes his church as a community of childlike, humble people who avoid scandal, seek out lost sheep, provide correction, forgiveness, and mercy to each other, and live in union with him. "For where two or three are gathered together in my name, there am I in the midst of them" (18:20).

Journeying to Jerusalem, Jesus has much to teach, and once in the city he cleanses the Temple and clashes with the Jewish leaders. After he speaks of the endtime and has his final meal, he is arrested, tried, and executed. Women coming to the tomb are told by an angel that Jesus has risen, and when they joyfully run to tell the others, they meet the risen Lord, worship him, and are told to tell the brethren that he will meet them in Galilee. The eleven meet him on a mountain there and are commissioned to spread his message and baptism to all nations. They are promised: "And behold, I am with you always, until the end of the age" (28:20).

The Gospel of Luke

The author of Luke wrote his gospel sometime in the 80s, somewhere near either Syria or Greece. He was a master theologian, and his inspiring theology is demonstrated in his magnificent birth story with the Annunciation to Mary, her Magnificat when she visits Elizabeth, and the birth in Bethlehem with the coming of the shepherds. Mature Christian theology is also reflected in Luke's portrayal of Jesus' teachings, especially to the multitude on the plain, in Jesus' eschatological discourse, in the many parables, and in the unique and moving account of the passion and death, which focuses on forgiveness. Luke's account of the Resurrection is well developed, especially in the story where two of Jesus' disciples meet him on the road to Emmaus and in the appearance and last words of Jesus to the eleven in Jerusalem.

The Gospel of John

This gospel is in a class by itself. It was probably written in its first form in Ephesus (modern-day Turkey) around the year 90 CE and, after some editing and additions, was finished in 100 CE. This amazing gospel came out of the community of the beloved apostle described in the gospel. It was a community that felt it lived in the glow of Jesus' love.

John begins with a magnificent hymn on how "the Word" (the creative aspect of God) became flesh in Jesus the Christ. Here Jesus is portrayed as the majestic and divine savior, who through many signs (e.g., the wedding at Cana, the healing of the royal official's son, the multiplication of the loaves) replaced the feasts and rituals of Judaism. This gospel is noted for its profound images: light, bread, the vine and branches, washing of feet. All of these images serve to reveal the sacramental principle through which the faithful can attain intimate contact with Jesus' presence.

Jesus' discourses at the last supper are extraordinary expressions of his love and glory, and how he communicates these to his followers through his Spirit. In the passion, Jesus reigns over all his enemies, even causing his arresters to fall to the ground. He intimidates Pilate and dies with power. The many stories of miracles in John reveal the life-giving power of God, and how it is uniquely expressed in Jesus the Christ.

The Acts of the Apostles

The author of Luke's gospel wrote a second volume called the Acts of the Apostles. It is a theological-historical creation that gives an account of the spread of Jesus' good news to "all nations." In a stylized interpretation of God's plan for the Jesus' movement, it begins with stories of the risen Lord appearing to his disciples and promising them they will be empowered to be his witnesses to the world. The end of such appearances is symbolized in an ascension scene, and then the actual empowerment of the community for this mission is told in the famous Pentecostal scene. Stories of sermons, miracles, persecution, martyrdom, internal conflicts, and the sharing of goods are used to characterize the early communities as they begin their challenging mission.

The conversion of a Pharisee named Saul (given in three differing accounts) by the risen Christ leads to the new and controversial mission to Gentiles. As Paul (Saul was his given name), the new apostle, undertakes many arduous journeys, the Jesus movement begins to spread rapidly beyond its Jewish beginnings. Paul is ultimately arrested, sent to Rome for trial, and presumably dies a martyr's death there.

The Letters of Paul

Second only to Jesus, Paul was a major player in the establishment of Christianity. Jesus was a Jewish reformer, who set down the new gospel and covenant. It was Paul who spread this movement beyond Palestine and Judaism to the Gentile world.

Student Reflection

"Why are these letters of Paul read so often in church? Why did Paul write them and what significance do they have?"

Paul wrote his letters to fledgling Christian communities, some of which he himself had established. He intended his letters to bolster their faith and settle some of the controversies they were experiencing. Curiously, Paul does not use the oral or written traditions about Jesus, but rather develops theology about Christ, faith, and salvation. All of his letters were in fact written before the four canonical gospels.

Background on Paul

Paul was born around 10 CE, when Jesus was but a teenager. Although he was a contemporary of Jesus and spent some time in Jerusalem, he doesn't seem to have met Jesus in person.

Paul was raised a Jew in a Hellenized (Greek-influenced) culture. He was well educated and quite familiar with Gentiles (non-Jews). He was trained as a Pharisee, and to support himself, worked as a skilled tent-maker. (Given the popularity of pilgrimages to Jerusalem, there was a good market for well-made tents among the Jews.)

As a young Jew, Paul vigorously persecuted Christians because he considered them to be heretics. On one trip pursuing Christians, Paul was literally knocked on his rear end and blinded by an experience of the risen Jesus, about seven years after the crucifixion.

Paul converted to Christianity and for the rest of his life was a devoted missionary for Jesus Christ. For twenty years he journeyed through what is now Syria, Greece, Turkey, possibly even Spain, preaching the gospel of Jesus Christ and establishing communities of disciples. In 58 CE, he was arrested and imprisoned in Jerusalem, then sent off to Rome, where he was imprisoned, tried, and executed.

The Letters

Only seven of Paul's letters are thought to be personally authored by him: these are the First Letter to the Thessalonians, Galatians, Philippians, Philemon, 1 and 2 Corinthians, and Romans. The other six Pauline letters seem to have been written by his disciples. We will provide a sketch of a few of these letters. Along the way we would like you to read one or two of them yourself, imagining that you are an early Christian listening to the teachings of Paul, the apostle.

The First Letter to the Thessalonians

This is the earliest of Paul's letters, written in 50 CE, less than two decades after Jesus' death and Resurrection. Paul wrote to the Christian community he had established in Thessalonica, Greece, a church composed of both Jew and Gentile converts. Paul begins by thanking them for giving such an enthusiastic reception to Jesus' gospel, and he insists on the authenticity of his ministry over false teachers who are confusing them. He then gives them some encouraging advice: work hard even though the endtime (which for Paul includes the expectation of the Second Coming of Christ) is soon approaching, and in the meantime live lives of virtue. He urges them to have respect and care for the genuine ministers who serve their community. His blessing is touching: "May the Lord make you increase and abound in love for one another and for all, just as we have for you" (3:12). Such love is still the basis of discipleship!

Letter to the Galatians

Paul wrote this letter in 55 CE to the community of Celtic converts in the Galatia area (modern Turkey). Here too he is upset with missionaries who are undoing his work there. Paul strongly defends his teaching that Gentile converts are not bound to the Jewish laws of circumcision and diet, a major conflict in the early days. He insists that Christ and his cross are the way to salvation and holiness. Paul stresses the importance of a deep faith and freedom for Christians, proclaiming: "For freedom Christ set us free; so stand firm and do not submit again to the yoke of slavery" (5:1). Paul also lists the so-called fruits of the Spirit, signs of authentic Christian living: love, joy, peace, patience, kindness, goodness, faithfulness, humility, and self-control (5:22-23).

Paul lists the fruits of the Spirit

Letter to the Philippians

Paul wrote this letter in 56 CE to a Christian community he had established in Philippi, a bustling commercial city in Greece. The community was noted for its women leaders, people like Lydia, a successful businesswoman who dealt in purple dye. Paul wrote from prison, probably in Ephesus, where his life was in danger. He encourages them to have the Christian characteristic of joy, and to remain close to one another. In the letter, Paul is tender and loving toward these converts and reminds them that they may have to suffer for their faith, just as he is now languishing in prison. He passes on to them a magnificent hymn to Jesus showing that through Jesus' emptying of himself for others he achieved glory (2:6-11). This is their calling also!

First Letter to the Corinthians

This letter contains some of the best of Paul's theology of the Christian life. Paul shares the earliest formula for Eucharist: "This is my body that is for you" (11:24), which teaches that Christians are all one body in Christ. He reveals the earliest forms of ministry (apostles, prophets, and teachers), writes his classic statement on the primacy of love (13), preaches the centrality of the Resurrection (15:17), and proclaims the resurrection of the spiritual body.

Letter to the Romans

The Christian community in Rome seems to have arisen from Jewish converts in the 40s. Around 49 CE, some of these Christians were driven out of Rome, including Priscilla, a woman who was a major leader there as well as in Corinth. In 58 Paul writes to the community, telling them of his dangerous plan to go to Jerusalem, and then to visit Rome on his way to Spain.

This is one of Paul's most significant letters, in which he carefully develops his theology of faith and salvation through Jesus Christ and explains how this faith is related to the Judaic religion. It is universal in its outlook, revealing how "creation awaits with eager expectation the revelation of the children of God" (8:19). He exhorts the community to live in humility and love, recognizing the differing gifts possessed by each person. Peace, mercy, and patience are essential for Christian living!

There are many other marvelous letters in this library, as well as the amazing apocalyptic book of Revelation. Taste them and get in touch with Christian roots—how your church began—and discover Christianity's most central teachings. Let the Bible be *your* primary resource!

Reading the Bible

The Scriptures can be read in different ways. The reader can explore the culture, history, and literary expressions of other eras. Or one can use the Bible to examine its positions on beliefs about such topics as God, morality, suffering, or prayer. Others read the Scriptures prayerfully, meditating on its inspiring messages. Some gather in groups to study the Scriptures and connect it to their lives. In Central and South America, many groups have been formed to see what the Scriptures can say to them in their struggle against violence and oppression.

Scripture can be interpreted in different ways. Literalists (fundamentalists) see the Scriptures as the words of God, dictated by God to the human authors. From this point of view, the Bible contains factual history, biography, and dialogue. The creation of the world and the Fall in the garden happened as described in Genesis. (For these reasons, creationism rejects the scientific theories of evolution and astrophysics.) This perspective holds that the Gospels provide an inspired account of what Jesus said and did, told by apostles who were there and who were inspired to record events accurately.

Others study Scriptures as literature. This is a more academic study of Scripture, often using the original language of Hebrew for the Jewish Scriptures, and Greek for the Christian Scriptures. Here the cultural, political, geographical, social, and religious background behind each text is studied so that its original meaning can be best ascertained. The various literary forms used are explored; the editing of earlier sources is studied to better understand the meaning of the author. Here the parables, nativity stories, differing dramatizations of Jesus' passion and death and accounts of Resurrection experiences are studied in depth, not to discover what happened but to understand what these accounts mean to faith.

The academic approach has had a checkered history. It goes back to the seventeenth century with the studies of Fr. Richard Simon (d. 1712). Simon is sometimes referred to as the father of biblical criticism. In the nineteenth century, Pope Leo XIII encouraged biblical criticism. But at the opening of the twentieth century, the Vatican shut down scientific study of the Scriptures. Then in 1942, the scholarly approach was once again approved by Pius XII, and it again received confirmation in 1965 by Vatican II. Since then there has been an explosion of interest in biblical studies in the Catholic Church, with exciting archaeological findings, fresh interpretations, and new literary analyses of the texts. Dozens of institutions of higher learning have been founded for the study of Scripture throughout the world, and many professional biblical journals and associations have been established. The academic study of the Bible has become a priority in both Catholic seminaries and universities.

Scripture as a Primary Resource

Catholics on the whole have been rather shy toward the Bible. Ever since the Reformation, when Catholics were warned against private interpretation of the Bible, many have been quite unfamiliar with Scripture. The Second Vatican Council gave great impetus to the study and use of Scripture by Catholics. The Scriptures are now proclaimed in a systematic fashion throughout the liturgical year. Biblical studies are emphasized through the Catholic educational system; Scripture has become the very heart of theological study; and Scripture has become crucial in the prayer of individuals and communities, as well as in the pastoral and sacramental practices of Catholic parishes.

Exercises in Biblical Interpretation

We have been discussing the contemporary approach to Scripture. Now let's see how it works. We will consider three sets of passages: the two creation stories in Genesis, the two nativity stories in the Gospels, and the four passion stories.

The Creation Stories

The first creation story (Gn 1-2:4) seems to have been written during the Babylonian exile around the sixth century, five hundred years before the birth of Jesus. It is a highly developed myth, probably originally a hymn sung at Temple. Influenced by the Babylonian creation myth, *Enuma Elish*, it begins in primordial chaos. Suddenly and majestically, a transcendent cosmic God (from the priestly tradition of writing) creates light with a mere word. God then on each following day separates day from night, the waters above the dome of the sky from the waters below, the waters from the land, and then creates vegetation. All the while, the Creator proclaims that it is all good! The Creator proceeds to create the light in the sky and the creatures in the sea and on land. The chorus continues to chant: "God saw how good it was." Last, God decides to make creatures in the divine image, male and female. He tells them to increase and multiply and gives them dominion over creation. On the seventh day (Sabbath), God rests, and blesses that day as holy.

This highly sophisticated myth has much to teach about Hebrew beliefs: God is one and is the powerful Creator of all that exists. All of creation is good. Human life, both male and female, comes from the hand of God and shares in the divine mission to love and care for creation. Sabbath is to be a time of prayer and rest—a sacred time and space in which to appreciate the great blessings of creation and life, as well as the meaning and purpose of life.

From this perspective, this creation story is prescientific and is intended to teach *who* created, not *how* creation came about. It stands as a wonderful profession of faith in God as Creator and sustainer of all good things.

The Second Creation Story

The creation story in 2 Genesis is a primitive myth written nine hundred years before the birth of Jesus. Its sacred trees, snakes, search for immortality, and concern with divine punishment show the influence of other Mesopotamian myths. (Most notable is the influence of the Babylonian myth *Gilgamesh*.) In this story we have more of an earthy, rural God, who takes mud and breathes life into it to form a human. God then plants a garden and trees, including the tree of life and the tree of the knowledge of good and evil. Then God places man in the garden to tend it, but warns him not to eat of the tree of good and evil.

Moved by the loneliness of the man, God struggles to find him a companion, first creating animals and birds, only to find that these fall short as companions for man. God then puts the man to sleep, takes a rib, and creates woman. Success at last!

Then follows the account of the Fall: the woman, Eve, is deceived by the serpent, eats the forbidden fruit, and persuades Adam to do the same. God seeks them out, and now having lost their innocence and needing clothes, each passes the buck for breaking God's law: Adam to Eve, and Eve to the serpent. God is angry: he curses the serpent, and curses Eve and Adam, punishing them with birth pain, sweaty toil, death, and banishment from the garden.

Many mysteries of life are explored in this ancient myth. From where does life come? Why are men and women attracted to each other? Why do we wear clothes? Why is there pain and so much hard work in life? What is the source of sin? Here the fundamental Jewish beliefs are revealed: the one God is the source of all life, and pain, toil, and evil come from rejecting God's sovereignty.

The Nativity Stories

The ancient Jewish question about history was not "What happened?" That tends to be our modern, factual question. Their question was "What does this event mean to our faith?" So when the gospel writers look at

Jesus' birth, they are not concerned with the details, but rather with what the birth means to their faith.

Mark's community in the earliest gospel does not seem concerned about the meaning of Jesus' birth—they are preoccupied with making sense of his horrible crucifixion. Ten years later, Matthew's community takes on Jesus' birth and creates a myth that explores the faith dimensions of the birth.

Matthew's Nativity Story

The author of Matthew begins by creating a family tree for Jesus that connects him with Abraham, the father of the Jewish faith, and David, the greatest king of Israel. Jesus has good genes! Then focusing on Jesus' father, Joseph, who has a house in Bethlehem, he tells the story of Joseph's predicament. His fiancée is pregnant with someone else's child! Joseph knows that he must have Mary put away, but is told in a dream by an angel (a messenger for God) that this child is begotten of the Spirit. A man of incredible faith, Joseph agrees to marry Mary and the baby is born, presumably in Joseph's house, and named Jesus.

Next follows an exotic story of Magi from the East, star-readers, perhaps Zoroastrian priests, who have come to worship the new King. They encounter Herod, who sends them looking for the King and lies about wanting to worship him when in fact he wants to kill him. The Magi proceed after their star, enter Jesus' house in Bethlehem, proceed to worship him, and offer him gifts of gold, frankincense, and myrrh. They are warned in a dream of Herod's murderous intentions and choose a different way back home.

Joseph dreams of the danger to his son and plans to take the family to Egypt. Herod proceeds to slaughter all the boys in Bethlehem under age two, hoping to dispose of Jesus. When Herod dies and the coast is clear, the family travels to the northern village of Nazareth where they can live safely.

This myth teaches us much about what Jesus' birth meant to the early Christians. It is the birth of the most prominent Jew, a descendent of

Abraham, and the new King David, the new Moses. His birth is uniquely from God and to accept this requires deep faith, similar to that of Joseph. Though the Jews had the Scriptures to prepare them for the messiah, they have rejected him, and the Gentiles (Magi) have been much more responsive. The three gifts represent royalty (gold), the worship now due Christ (incense), and his saving death (myrrh is used to anoint the dead).

The Herod scenes suggest that danger, even death, will stalk this baby throughout his life, which will end with his execution. But he will be brought out of Egypt, saved, and proclaimed as the new Moses to save God's people.

As the renowned biblical scholar Raymond Brown has written, we have the "gospel in miniature" in these birth stories, professions of the central Christian beliefs.

Luke's Nativity Story

Luke begins with the announcement of the miraculous birth of John the Baptizer. Imbedded in this story is the Annunciation to Mary by an angel that she will give birth to the Son of the Most High, who will rule over a kingdom forever. Mary lives in Nazareth and is engaged to Joseph. When Mary asks how she can be pregnant without having had sex, she is told that the baby comes from the power of the Spirit. She then is told about Elizabeth's pregnancy and travels to help her.

Before Mary and Joseph even have a chance to marry, the emperor issues a decree to put Joseph on the tax rolls in Bethlehem. They have to set out on a long and expensive caravan trip, and when they arrive in Bethlehem, Mary gives birth to Jesus. They have to use a barn because there are no rooms available. An angel tells the local shepherds that the Savior, the Lord, and Messiah has been born. They immediately find the infant and then spread the good news abroad. After the circumcision and presentation of their baby, Mary and Joseph return to their home in Nazareth.

Quite a different story from Matthew's! Here the couple hails from Nazareth instead of Bethlehem. At the birth of their child, they are engaged, rather than married, as in Matthew. The baby is born in a manger, rather than in Joseph's home. And shepherds come rather than Magi. Obviously, the concern here is not what happened, but what does the birth of Jesus mean.

The story is rich in import. Resurrection faith has taught the Lucan community that this was the birth of the Son of the Most High, who rules over the Kingdom of God (as the announcement to Mary professes). This birth is uniquely from the Spirit of God. The decree from the emperor for enrollment doesn't match up with history, but does show that Jesus is born into a people during a time of oppression and that he is the true Son of God and not the emperor, as the Romans fear. The manger seems to symbolize the rural poverty of Jesus' background and the fact that he dies an outcast. The shepherd symbolism is particularly rich in meaning. David, Jesus' forbear, was a shepherd. Jesus is the good shepherd who seeks lost sheep. Moreover, Jesus comes for outcasts, and shepherds are in that category. Once again the angels' announcements and chorus in heaven reveal that this birth is from the power of the Spirit of God and has global significance.

The Passion Stories

All four gospels have passion stories, revealing that all the communities had to struggle with the rather embarrassing fact that their savior died naked among criminals. Each gospel takes the event and develops it into a play that wrestles with the faith-meaning of this calamitous event. Again, they are not concerned about what happened as is Mel Gibson in his movie. Rather they are exploring what this passion might mean to their faith many years after the event.

Mark's Passion

The passion play of Mark is the earliest and starkest. In the garden Jesus is deeply grieved and struggles with his fate. He is deserted by his careless sleeping disciples and is betrayed by one of his own—with a kiss!

When his disciples cut off the ear of a soldier who has come to arrest Jesus, Jesus questions why they come for him in this way. At the trial, Mark shows Jesus' innocence. The witnesses are false, and when Jesus admits to being the Messiah, he is charged with blasphemy, which only entails cursing God, not claiming to be the Messiah. He is spit upon, beaten, and his prime apostle, Peter, denies knowing him three times. When Jesus is taken to Pilate, the charges are changed—he claimed to be king of the Jews. A murdering terrorist is chosen to be released rather than the innocent Jesus. Jesus is crowned with thorns, beaten, spat upon, mocked, and is so weak he has to have help with his cross. Jesus dies between two bandits, crying out: "My God, my God, why have you forsaken me?" A Roman centurion proclaims that Jesus is the Son of God and the Temple veil is torn.

The play is filled with symbolism and dramatic effect to show that Jesus was indeed an innocent victim and died at the hands of his Jewish and Roman enemies. Even in the early church, there would be those who would reject Jesus as Savior, and even disciples would abandon him and betray his followers. Ironically, Gentiles, even Romans (symbolized by the centurion), are being converted to the faith rather than his own people. But Jesus was raised on the third day. He is their King and his followers will stand by their faith in him even when death threatens them. In their own fear, terror, and abandonment, they will know that their innocent Lord went through the same and never gave in.

Matthew's Passion

The author of this play repeats Mark's version, with just a few changes. When the arresting soldier's ear is cut off, Matthew uses the incident to reflect on Jesus' commitment to nonviolence. Jesus tells his disciples to put away the sword, because he who lives by the sword dies by the sword. His innocence at the trial is again stressed, but now Jesus is

at the trial, Mark shows Jesus' innocence

falsely accused of blasphemy for saying that the Son of Man will come in judgment. This gospel tends to exonerate the Romans (Pilate washes his hands) and has the Jewish leaders take Jesus' trial and execution upon themselves. Tragically this has been falsely interpreted as the "blood-curse" passed down upon all Jews and has been used to persecute them, even attempt to exterminate them in the Holocaust. The Catholic Church, in modern times, has strongly rejected such prejudice toward God's chosen people.

In this play Judas returns the money and seems at least partially re-pentant for betraying the innocent Jesus, but he isn't able to fully repent and hangs himself. Peter, on the other hand, weeps bitterly for his own betrayal and is able to receive forgiveness. The early Christians here are exploring the nature of true repentance, needed for forgiveness. At Jesus' death, Matthew adds an earthquake and the dead rising from their graves. Nature itself enters into the event and points to the last days.

Luke's Passion

Luke changes the tone in his play and accents themes of compas-sion and forgiveness. In the garden an angel comes to minister to Jesus, and the disciples sleep out of grief rather than abandonment. Jesus heals the ear of the arresting soldier! At the hearing, Jesus is quite noncom-mittal, but is charged nonetheless. Jesus' innocence is further demon-strated when Pilate fabricates new charges of perverting the nation and encouraging tax resistance. When that doesn't work, Jesus is accused of saying he is Messiah and King, and when Jesus still resists, he is charged with stirring up the people. The scene with Herod is vintage Luke and provides a stark contrast between the corrupt Herodians and the noble Jesus. Then the power of Jesus' forgiveness is dramatized by the rather extreme friendship that is struck between Herod and Pilate! The theme of compassion is dramatized by the women who weep for him along the way of the cross. From the cross, Jesus forgives all and then promises the "good thief" a place in the Kingdom. The crowds leave the scene beating their breasts in repentance over this travesty.

The Passion of John

This play stands out for its originality. Here Jesus is majestic and truly the Son of God. There is no falling in the garden, no prayers for reprieve, and no sleeping on the part of the disciples. Jesus asks who his arresters are looking for and when they say, "Jesus," he answers, "I am he," and they all fall to the ground. Here again is the cutting off of the ear (likely a historical event), and Peter is named and told to put away his sword for Jesus must drink this cup. Jesus overwhelms the old high priest Annas, confronts the soldier who strikes him, and Caiphas is able to get nowhere with him. He is sent to Pilate under vague charges (once again innocent) and intimidates the Roman procurator. Along the way to Calvary, there are no mocking crowds and Jesus needs no help with the cross. From the cross, Jesus forms his community, giving his mother and the beloved disciple to each other. Crying out with thirst, Jesus himself declares the whole ordeal finished. Sacramental symbols of blood and water come from his side after he dies. It is a majestic death of the divine savior!

Conclusion

Our tour of the library in the Bible and our exercises in contemporary scriptural interpretation are complete. Consult the Bible library and do your own interpretations. In so doing you will join countless generations of Jesus' disciples who have had their spirits nourished by the Word of God.

Activities

1. Schedule a visit to a Jewish synagogue for a service. Ask the rabbi ahead of time if he will show your group the Torah after the service and give some background and explanation.

2. Individuals can memorize the two creation accounts and present them as they once were: oral stories. Comparison and commentary by the class can follow.

3. A group can rewrite the Job play in a modern setting and perform it for the class.

4. A group can review the film *The Nativity Story* and report on the value of its historical approach and whether or not the film is compatible with biblical criticism.

5. Compare the accounts of the passion of Jesus in *The Greatest Story Ever Told*, *The Last Temptation of Christ*, *Jesus of Nazareth*, and Gibson's *The Passion of the Christ*.

Sources

General
Saint Mary's Press College Study Bible. Winona, MN: Saint Mary's Press, 2007.

Old Testament
Carvalho, Corrine L. *Encountering Ancient Voices*. Winona, MN: St. Mary's Press, 2006.

Barton, John. *Reading the Old Testament*. Louisville, KY: Westminster John Knox Press, 1996.

King, Philip, and Lawrence Stager. *Life in Biblical Israel*. Louisville, KY: Westminster John Knox Press, 2001.

Murphy, Roland E. *Wisdom Literature*. Grand Rapids: Eerdmans, 1981.

New Testament
Branick, Vincent. *Understanding the New Testament and Its Message*. New York: Paulist Press, 1998.

Brown, Raymond. *An Introduction to the New Testament*. New York: Doubleday, 1997.

———. *The Birth of the Messiah*. New York: Doubleday, 1997.

———. *The Death of the Messiah*. New York: Doubleday, 1997.

———. *A Risen Christ in Eastertime*. Collegeville, MN: The Liturgical Press, 1991.

Harrington, Wilfrid. *Jesus and Paul*. Wilmington, DE: M. Glazier, 1987.

Ralph, Margaret N. *Discovering the Gospels*. New York: Paulist Press, 1990.

3 The Christian Church

The church as we know it

began after Jesus was raised from the dead and began to appear to his disciples. As his followers experienced Jesus present among them in an altered state of existence, a new faith was born. Now they came to believe that Jesus was more than a gifted young preacher and healer through whom God seemed to work uniquely. They now were coming to believe that Jesus was the Christ, the anointed one of God, the Messiah and Savior. Now they not only followed him, they worshipped him as their God in human form. They felt his presence among them, in each other, in the memories and stories they exchanged, and in a special way in the "breaking of the bread," the memorial meal he left for them to share.

The early disciples were Jews who still attended synagogue as well as the Temple for the great feasts. These disciples formed small communities, called each other brother and sister, and viewed themselves as following the way of Jesus. (The word *church* only appears twice in the Gospels—Mt 16:18 and 18:17.) The early disciples met regularly in "house churches," where they shared an agape, a "love meal," followed by the breaking of the bread. The gatherings were presided over by the host of the home, female or male. (There were no priests yet in the community.)

We have the early witness of a Roman named Pliny, who spied on the followers of Jesus. Pliny wrote to the Emperor Trajan that these "Christians" seem to practice a "perverse superstition," that they gather on a fixed day before daylight and recite words to a Christ as a God. He pointed out that they take an oath to live virtuous lives and then meet to take food together. In what might be considered "famous last words," Trajan says that it seems possible to stop the group and set it right! The emperor decides that anyone accused of such a practice should be punished, but if they denounce their faith, sacrifice to the gods, and curse this "Christ," they can be set free. The application of this policy seems to have been left up to individual governors. As emperors changed, some were quite tolerant of Christians, while others saw them as a threat and tried to kill them off. The emperors Nero, Marcus Aurelius, and Decian were among the most brutal to Christians. Punishments ranged from death to fines, slave labor, exile, or confiscation of property. Being a Christian was a risky business!

Although Jewish, these early communities held unique beliefs. They viewed Jesus as the Messiah, the Son of God. They had their own initiation rite—baptism—and they shared the Eucharistic meal that Jesus had left them. They were conscious that a new covenant and a new Israel had been born, and now they had to figure out how all this fit into their identity as Jews.

Two major developments challenged the movement's Jewish identity. First, the Jewish community rejected the disciples, casting them out of the Temple and even seeking them out for punishment. This division became final when Jerusalem and the Temple were destroyed in 70 CE. Second, the Christian movement spread to non-Jews. This led to a major controversy over whether Gentile converts had to be circumcised and follow the

Torah. Paul, a leading missionary to the non-Jews, took a strong negative stand on this point and ultimately prevailed.

Leadership

Primary among the early leaders were the twelve, who came to symbolize the heads of the "new tribes." Peter was first among these because, even though he had denied the Master, he had been chosen to be the first apostle. The earliest leaders in the Jerusalem community seemed to have been members of Jesus' family, the main one being James, Jesus' brother. The original disciples who followed Jesus on his mission were no doubt key figures because of their firsthand experience with Jesus and his message. They had known him well, had walked with him. They had sat around campfires at night listening to his reflections. They had shared meals with him, at times serious, at times uproariously funny. They had seen him rise before sunrise to pray, had witnessed the extraordinary powers that came from him when they encountered crowds of poor and handicapped people seeking out his blessing. They had prayed with him. They had seen Jesus joyful and they had seen him in tears.

 Student Reflection

"Did they have priests in those days? Were any of them women?"

Jesus himself was not a Jewish priest, nor were any of his disciples. Jesus had key women disciples—Mary Magdalene, Joanna, and Susanna—which was unprecedented for a Jewish teacher. Paul refers to a number of women leaders, notably Priscilla, who led in Rome and Corinth; Lydia, Euodia, and Syntyche, leaders in the church at Philippi; Phoebe, who took Paul's letter to Rome, and Junia, Mary, Tryphaena, Tryphosa, Persis, and Olympas, whom Paul describes as coworkers. Paul speaks of apostles, prophets, and teachers as being very early roles of leadership and these seemed to be open to women and men. By the second century, offices such as deacon, presbyter, and overseer began to form in some areas. By the third century, the patriarchal model of leadership began to emerge and ultimately prevailed. In spite of Jesus' efforts to include women, patriarchy soon began to dominate the early communities.

The Communities Spread

The small community of disciples in Jerusalem began to hear of the spread of their movement. A strong community developed in Antioch and spread through Asia Minor (Turkey) to Lystra, Iconium, Antioch of Pisidia, Ephesus, Smyrna, Perganum, and other cities. In Greece, communities developed in Athens, Corinth, Philippi, and Thessalonica. A strong community even began to develop in Rome. By the second century, Christians were found in Gaul and North Africa. The poor and outcast were especially attracted to Jesus and his message that they were blessed and could have eternal life. But even Roman officials, aristocrats, and learned teachers were attracted to the movement. The Christian message and way of life gave them hope and joy, a sense of fellowship with Jesus and with truly good people who had a mission in this life and looked forward to the next.

Controversy

Early on there was controversy in the Christian movement. We have already seen the first significant argument over whether non-Jewish converts (Gentiles) had to follow the Jewish laws and practices. Some communities, now labeled Gnostics, denied the Incarnation and held that salvation comes through secret knowledge. They believed the created material world is evil and that women could preside over liturgy. These communities developed their own gospels, many of which were discovered in Egypt in 1945, millennia after they were rejected by what are now seen as the traditional communities. Some of these gospels have

Gnosticism

The term *gnostic* is a slippery one, and scholars have diverse interpretations of its meaning. Fundamentally, it refers to one who claims to have special knowledge that others do not have. Gnostics have been known to be dualistic and thus to have negative views toward the material world. They have also traditionally valued the activity of the feminine principle. The term has been applied to pagan, Jewish, and Christian thought.

Some Christian communities were labeled Gnostic in the early centuries and rejected by the mainstream. Their writings were excluded from the canon of gospel writings when the canon was set to include only Matthew, Mark, Luke, and John. Fragments and gospel texts from these communities were discovered at Nag Hammadi in Egypt in 1945, and since then have been studied in great detail by scholars. Biblical scholars are divided with regard to the value that these texts have within the Christian tradition. Some scholars give the so-called Gnostic gospels significant weight and maintain they were rejected for reasons more political than doctrinal. Others hold that these writings were legitimately discarded by the early church and have little doctrinal value.

come into popular notoriety with the appearance of the *DaVinci Code* and the recent publicity given to the *Gospel of Judas*.

Marcion, in the second century, was another teacher who is now viewed as nontraditional. He rejected the Jewish God of law in the Old Testament (as opposed to the God of love in the New Testament) and caused a great deal of stir over the canon of the Scriptures. Another teacher, Montanus, claimed to be the New Prophet and gained a following around his message that the Second Coming was imminent and that all should prepare with severe penance and even martyrdom. These controversies sparked strong theological schools, and by the third century there were centers in Antioch (Syria) and Alexandria (Egypt).

Christians also faced enemies from outside. As we have seen, the Romans often viewed Christians as a superstitious cult who refused to accept that the emperor was a god and merited worship. Many Jews held that Christians followed a false messiah who was nothing other than a sorcerer; there is a second-century prayer that cursed Christians as "heretics and Nazarenes." In return many Christians felt that Jews were responsible for Jesus' death and were wrongly rejecting him as Messiah. One strong Christian opponent, Celsus, said his research proved that Christian doctrine was false. Christians, he pointed out, were the dregs of society who followed a charlatan who practiced witchcraft. A story even spread that Jesus was the bastard child of a Roman soldier who had relations with Mary. Apologists such as Justin, Origen, Irenaeus, and Tertullian rose up to defend Christians against such attacks.

Concern for the Kingdom

As the Gospels indicate, the early Christian movement was not so much concerned about the church as it was about the kingdom or reign of God. The synoptic Gospels refer to the kingdom of God more than one hundred times, indicating that it is the central teaching of Jesus. Even Paul and other early Christian writers were more concerned about proclaiming Jesus and his message than they were about the church.

Student Reflection

"I have trouble with the term *kingdom of God* and think it is too archaic. After all, it is a notion about a society where some are superior to others. In the past, I think this kind of thinking led popes to see themselves as kings and bishops to live like princes. In my opinion it is too much a male-centered term and not appropriate in this day of democracy and gender equality."

Kingdom is a term from the past and is difficult to salvage as the centerpiece of Christianity. Nevertheless, it was the key notion in Jesus' plan to reform religion. For the Jews, God was the Creator and sustainer of reality. For all, God was like a king, but they differed on how this was interpreted. Some believed that God ruled as a warrior God, defeating the enemies of his people. Others saw God as a judge, punishing sin with calamities and even disabilities.

For Jesus, God as Abba ruled through love, compassion, and forgiveness. This was a God who wanted people to be whole and healed, a God who held special care for sinners and outcasts. For Jesus, wherever love and goodness reigned, it was from the power of God. And even in the midst of evil and violence, somehow the God of love ultimately prevailed.

 ## Student Reflection

"Last summer I visited Auschwitz, where nearly four million people were murdered. I experienced the horrors of the place and yet heard stories where people offered their lives to save others, or shared their bread with the starving children, or stayed up late in the barracks to hold prayer services. Even amid the atrocities of Auschwitz, love, service, compassion, and forgiveness were able to prevail through the power of God. I've read stories about Corrie ten Boom and her sister, who were beacons of love and compassion among the prisoners at the infamous camp at Ravensbruck. After Corrie got out, she spent many years traveling the globe preaching that love always reigns more supreme than hate."

So the early disciples believed that they existed, lived, and moved in the presence of a loving, caring God. This was a God who so loved the world that he gave his only Son so that those who believed in him might be saved. It was their mission to continue Jesus' work of spreading the good news of this kingdom of love and justice and to have it rule their lives. For them, the kingdom was the loving, saving presence of God among them. They would continue to promote Jesus' mission, living and preaching this kingdom and challenging oppression, violence, hypocrisy, and those who ruled through fear. In Jesus' footsteps they would expose the kingdom of evil, where corruption, abuse, and greed reigned supreme; and in their lives and their treatment of others, they would offer a godly alternative of simplicity, forgiveness, humility, love, and freedom.

A Community of Equals

The community that would promote such a kingdom of God would be, according to Jesus' wish, a community of equals. Jesus had rebelled against the oppressive hierarchy that had developed in his own religion and in imperial Rome and that dominated his people. Among his followers, the first would be last. Anyone who wanted to be first would have to be the servant of all. Jesus demonstrated this in a shocking manner at the last supper when he washed the feet of his disciples. Paul stressed this equality when he wrote: "For all of you who were baptized into Christ have clothed yourself in Christ. There is neither Jew nor Greek, there is neither slave nor free person, there is not male and female; for you are all one in Christ Jesus" (Gal 3:27-29). Every person belonged to the chosen race. "You are 'a chosen race, a royal priesthood, a holy nation, a people of his own'" (1 Pt 2:9). The distinction between clergy and laity did not appear until the third century, hundreds of years after the original community. Ministry was based on need and the gifts of the Spirit given to individuals, rather than on offices.

But the essentials of "church" had been established for all time: Jesus Christ, the Gospels, the community of disciples, the rituals, and the life of service to others.

Constantine's Era

Constantine's rule of the Roman Empire is one of the most important periods in the history of the Church. It is said that a vision of the cross helped Constantine win a key victory in his run to rule the empire, an event which brought about his conversion. In 313 CE, Constantine legalized Christianity, in part as a means to stabilize the empire, and later in that century Christianity became the official religion of the empire.

Conversions abounded and numbers grew, unfortunately, often more to build résumés and obtain positions than to follow Jesus and his gospel. Constantine moved the center of his empire to Constantinople and, in 325, held the Council of Nicea to settle the Arian heresy about the divinity of Jesus, a dispute that was hindering his goal to unite the empire.

All this had a tremendous impact on the Christian church. Temples became churches, Roman offices and laws shaped the authority of the Church, and imperial power served as a model for its popes and bishops. Christians, who had been persecuted, now at times became persecutors of non-Christians. Those who had been called to poverty, now often aspired to power and wealth. Those who had been shown the power of nonviolence and urged to reject the sword and avoid military service, now took up the sword as soldiers in the imperial army.

Christianity Spreads

As the Roman Empire slipped into decline, Christianity spread to the European tribes. Converts appeared in the British Isles as early as the fourth century, and that area had its first martyr, Alban, who saved a priest on the run, took on the priest's identity, and was killed in his place. Ireland was Christianized by the great St. Patrick, and Northern England, by Columba. A strong Celtic Christianity developed with its own spirituality in these areas.

In the fifth century the faith spread to Scotland, with Ninian, the son of a Briton chieftain who had studied in Rome. In the same century, Clovis, the head of the Franks, was baptized. Clovis set up his capital in Paris under the patronage of St. Denis, who gave his life to strengthening a fledgling church there. In the sixth century, Pope Gregory the Great sent Augustine to England to reinforce the Roman version of Christianity.

As mentioned earlier, in the first century there were house churches in Rome. Because both Peter and Paul had been martyred in that city,

a strong Celtic Christianity developed

the center of the empire, the Church grew and the papacy was gradually established there. The Church also got a boost there in the fifth century when Benedict wrote his famous monastic rule and established a monastery at Monte Cassino, which still exists there today. To spread loyalty to the papacy, the pope in Rome sent Boniface to Germany in the eighth century.

Central Europe

Tensions increased between the two centers of Christianity, Rome and Constantinople. In the ninth century, Constantinople sent Cyril and Methodius, two brothers from Greece, to the Slavs in Russia and Moravia. Christianity was already there but not in the Slavic language. The faith spread further to the Poles and Bohemians. Today, the Poles begin their history with the baptism of their king in 967 CE.

The Orient

In 1542, one of the original Jesuits, Francis Xavier, arrived in India and spent the next ten years learning the language and culture as he traveled to remote islands and villages teaching the gospel and tending the sick. Xavier received much criticism from religious leaders in Western Europe, but was successful in establishing a mission mentality that honored indigenous cultures. His mission was continued by another Jesuit, Robert de' Nobili, who adapted the Christian religion to the Hindu culture and language.

The Christian mission was significantly extended in China by Matteo Ricci and his fellow Jesuits in the sixteenth century. Ricci, like Xavier before him in India, thoroughly learned the Chinese language and customs and even dressed and cut his beard in the Chinese style. He gained great respect among the Chinese nobility for his vast knowledge of Western mathematics and science, which he shared with them. Ricci also drew some of the original maps of China in relation to the rest of the world. All of this helped many Chinese gain respect for and interest in the Christian religion. Previously, the Chinese had thought that everything Western was barbaric. Ricci referred to God in Chinese terms and in the Christian rites saw no problem with continuing the Chinese tradition of honoring ancestors and revering Confucius.

Eventually other Western missionaries who did not understand these rites reported them to Rome, and ultimately the rites concerning ancestors and Confucius were banned from Christian services. This angered Chinese leaders, who expelled the missionaries, and the Christian mission in China was severely damaged.

 Student Reflection

"This same lack of being sensitive to other cultures still hurts the Church today. In my country (Nicaragua), many Catholics are joining the charismatic Bible churches because they are allowed to sing and dance at the services and in the sermons there is talk about their social needs."

Francis Xavier also helped establish Christian missions in Japan in the sixteenth century. The success of these missions was also hindered by the subsequent persecution of Christians and the expulsion of their missionaries. Many Christian converts and missionaries were martyred in Japan at the end of the sixteenth century and in the seventeenth century. But there was still a large Catholic community in Nagasaki when the United States dropped the atomic bomb in 1945.

The New World

Christianity arrived in the New World with the Spanish explorers and conquerors. When the navigator, mystic, and entrepreneur Christopher Columbus accidentally encountered the New World while searching for a trade route to India, he was baffled by the peaceful, fine-looking natives he met. "How could these be descendents of Adam and Eve?" he wondered. He thought they would make good slaves. On his return home he brought back several natives to be examined, as well as some souvenirs: gold, tobacco, pineapples, a turkey, and a hammock.

On his second journey, Columbus brought many ships and more than a thousand men to conquer the area. Disobeying the monarchs' order to treat the natives well and convert them to Christianity, Columbus rounded up many of them for slaves. Because he had hoped to keep half of the wealth that he found, he forced natives to find gold under penalty of death. Columbus made two more voyages. After being imprisoned briefly for mismanagement, he lived a comfortable life in Spain.

The Conquistadores and South America

The natives of the New World were considered pagans without human rights. Their lands, largely in South America, were annexed and given to Spain and Portugal by the infamous Pope Alexander VI. From the time of Columbus' second voyage, Spain and Portugal's goal was to conquer these people and acquire their gold. Those on the original ships took over modern-day Haiti and the Dominican Republic. Ponce de León then took over Puerto Rico and Cuba. Balboa took Panama in 1512. Still no treasures of spices or gold! Then Cortez conquered the Aztec empire in Mexico, and Pizarro, the Incan empire in South America. The natives were no match for the Spanish warhorses, armor, and steel blades, nor were their "divine" leaders, who had anticipated conquest early on. Hundreds of Spanish soldiers defeated tens of thousands of natives. Aztec and Incan altars were torn down and replaced with Christian altars, where the bloodied conquerors could attend Mass. Gold and silver flowed. Most of these explorers brought missionaries with them, who hoped to convert these pagans and save their souls.

A meeting was held in Spain to address the brutal slaughter, rape, and enslavement of the native people, many of whom had also died from diseases brought by the West. A Spanish priest, Bartolomé de las Casas, defended the natives, arguing that they were children of God. But he lost the debate. The natives were declared to be subhuman and, though there were some official efforts to sustain their rights, their severe oppression continued. Their land and wealth were confiscated, and if they did not convert to Christianity and submit to slavery, they often were killed.

European Settlers and North America

The first European settlers brought Christianity to North America. The Puritans, escaping religious oppression in Europe, settled in modern-day New England in the 1630s. Also in this period, Catholics settled in Maryland. Heroic Catholic missionaries left the comforts of Europe and faced hardship and the risk of death to convert American Indians. One extraordinary priest, Eusebio Kino, brought the gospel to what is now Arizona. Another, Junipero Serra, erected Catholic missions in California, which still stand today. The Jesuits and Franciscans built missions in Florida. Budding cities in the New World began to take on names like St. Augustine, Santa Fe (holy faith), Los Angeles (the angels), and San Francisco (St. Francis).

French and British explorers also brought missionaries with them, who spread the gospel to what is now Canada. Many set out thinking this was the beginning of a new age and they would see the Church flower among the native converts as it had in the early church. There were inspiring examples, but many of the missionaries found lasting conversions difficult to achieve. Others, like the Jesuits Isaac Jogues and John de Brebeuf, despite efforts to learn and adapt to local beliefs, had native people turn on and kill them.

A number of women missionaries also came to the colonies to spread Catholicism and bring good health care to colonists and American Indians alike. By the nineteenth century, a large number of Sisters had established houses of prayer and also served as teachers and nurses. I remember visiting the cemetery of one of these orders and was amazed at how young these Sisters were; when they died, some were only in their twenties. I was told they had come over here as Sisters in their teens and endured severe hardship for the Lord, only to die young from cholera and other frontier diseases. Ultimately, the Sisters' orders would provide the backbone for the many Catholic hospitals and schools in America. St. Elizabeth Seton, the first American saint and founder of the Sisters of Charity, is an icon of these Sisters.

Catholicism Grows

Surprising as it may seem, there were only thirty thousand Catholics in this country in 1789. Largely uneducated, they were dispersed in rural areas. A native of Maryland, John Carroll, was the first Catholic bishop in America. Then in 1840 a potato famine hit Ireland and immigration began on a large scale. One and a half million Irish died and an equal number came to America. By 1852, when the American bishops held their first Plenary Council in Baltimore, there were 1.6 million Catholics here. Many of them fought in the Civil War, declaring their loyalty and patriotism to their new country. Between 1852 and the beginning of the twentieth century, many millions more came: first, Germans suffering from crop failure and persecution or simply looking for new opportunities; later, people from Italy and Central and Eastern Europe. (As has been said in the current debate about what to do with all the illegal immigrants in this country, we were all immigrants at one time!)

Catholics gradually became a major force in the industrial cities of the Midwest and New England. They established parishes, schools, and colleges: Georgetown was the first in 1789, Spring Hill College in 1830, Xavier in 1831, Notre Dame in 1842, and Holy Cross in 1843. Today there are more than 230 Catholic campuses in America. And Orders of Sisters have established many schools, hospitals, and service centers.

Catholics fought in the revolution, the Civil War, the two world wars, and subsequent wars. With the election of John F. Kennedy, the United States had its first Catholic president and put to rest the fear that Rome would try to run the White House. The bishops' conference in America reached its most influential period in the 1980s with two powerful documents: one on the economy and the other on peace.

At the time of this writing in 2007, there are about 65 million Catholics in the United States, or about 23 percent of the population, up from 45 million in 1965. But there are sixteen thousand fewer priests than in 1965, and their average age is sixty-eight. Fifty percent fewer candidates are now studying for the priesthood. There are 110,000 fewer Sisters, and their average age is seventy. There are more than 1 billion Catholics worldwide.

Christianity in Africa

Christianity came to Africa from Jerusalem to Egypt and then to Ethiopia in the first and second centuries. Though nearly wiped out in northern Africa by Islam in the seventh century, the Church remained strong in Ethiopia. In the fourteenth century, the Portuguese brought Christianity to sub-Saharan Africa and in the seventeenth century, the Dutch brought it to South Africa. The rest of Africa came into contact with Christianity through nineteenth-century European colonialism. The West has always had a strong missionary commitment to Africa. Today Catholicism is growing rapidly in many parts of Africa.

Great Divisions

It is understandable that Jesus would pray for unity in his community, as division dogged it from the start. There were disputes among the apostles over who would be first, arguments concerning non-Jewish converts to the faith, stress between so-called Gnostic and traditional communities. Major controversies also arose about the person and nature of Jesus in the early centuries, and the councils of Nicea and Chalcedon were called to settle these matters.

Catholicism is growing rapidly in Africa

The Eastern and Western churches split in the eleventh century, and the Reformation of the sixteenth century further split Western Christianity. We will be discussing these divisions in detail in chapter 4.

Vatican I

The first modern attempt at church reform came three hundred years after the Council of Trent tried to answer the attacks of the Protestant Reformation. Pope Pius IX called the First Vatican Council in 1869. The Church and papacy at that time were under serious attack. The pope was in danger of losing his Papal States and his temporal power to the Italian nationalists. At one point gangs forced him to slip out of the Vatican in disguise. Many European nations were persecuting Catholics, rationalists were denying the tenets of faith, and communists were denying the existence of God.

Pius IX called the council to officially back his denunciation of what he considered to be modern errors: rationalism, the separation of Church and State, freedom of religion, the myth approach to Scripture, resistance to Church authority, and modern progress were all condemned. Protestants were informed about the council and, though not invited, were asked to think about returning to the true Church.

The agenda included dealing with rationalism, defining the true Church of Christ, marriage as a sacrament, and many issues calling for Church discipline. Infallibility was not on the original agenda but it was widely known that the pope wanted it to be defined. The council continued until 1870, when it was disrupted by the Italian nationalists, who captured the last of the Papal States and invaded Rome. By that time half of the bishops, including most of the Americans, had left.

Before disbanding, those remaining cast the final vote on the infallibility of the pope. Much debate had focused on the issue of infallibility, and many opposed its being defined, believing that it would turn away converts and anger many national leaders. When infallibility was defined, the boundaries of papal authority were narrowed. The doctrine of papal infallibility states: "The Roman pontiff [...] when he by virtue of his supreme Apostolic authority, decides that a doctrine concerning faith or morals is to be held by the entire Church, he possesses [...] that infallibility with which the Divine Savior wished to have His Church furnished for the definition concerning faith or morals."

Other issues the council dealt with were the "errors" of rationalism, materialism, and atheism; the use of reason in dealing with revelation and the supernatural; and, perhaps most important, the primacy of power of the pope over all other churches. Although now relieved of his temporal power over the Papal States and viewing himself as a "prisoner in the Vatican," Pius had been successful in placing an infallible papacy at the center of the Catholic Church.

The Church after Vatican I

Vatican I was held at a time when the world was going through great changes and the Church's fortress mentality could only deal with modern progress as "erroneous" and look to the pope for definitive truth. In the next hundred years, progress continued at a dizzying pace. Science made tremendous advances with the theories and discoveries of Darwin (evolution), Curie (radioactivity), Hubble (the big bang), Einstein (relativity), Freud and Jung (psychology), Morgan (genetics), Planc and Heisenberg (quantum physics), Crick and Watson (DNA), Hawking (black holes), and with the development of nuclear power, space exploration, computers, as well as many other advances.

The official Church remained aloof from scientific development and was antagonistic. It resisted the fact of evolution and silenced the Jesuit Teilhard de Chardin, who connected the Christian faith with evolution. Pope Pius XII forbade the teaching of evolution in Catholic education. Freud's atheism gave the Church a deep prejudice against modern psychoanalysis. Major social and political movements arose that were hostile toward the Church. Marxism and communism took root in Russia as well as China, Vietnam, Korea, and Cuba, and National Socialism or fascism dominated Germany. Two world wars erupted in which millions of people were killed. The Second World War was fought in Europe and in the Pacific (1941–45), with forty million deaths in the European arena and twenty million in the Pacific arena. More than twelve million people were killed in German Nazi concentration camps, and millions more were killed by the Soviet Union's Stalin in gulags (labor camps). This war saw the only use of the atomic bomb when the United States bombed Hiroshima and Nagasaki, killing more than two hundred thousand people, mostly Japanese.

The Church was hostile toward communism, largely due to the movement's atheism and persecution of religion. After the Russian Revolution, Church property was confiscated, monasteries and convents were closed, and many priests, nuns, and lay people were sent off to gulags or were executed. By the 1960s, there were few outward signs of Catholicism left in Russia, and yet the faith was still very much alive in the people.

At first the Church in Germany strongly resisted National Socialism or fascism, but a concordat between Rome and Hitler blunted this resistance and gave the German Nazis a free hand. Still a number of German bishops and theologians remained hostile toward Hitler and often paid a severe price for their resistance. Dachau was the concentration camp where resisting priests and nuns were sent. Many priests, Sisters, and lay people were executed by the Nazis for assisting Jews. Some of the heroes of this era were Maximilian Kolbe, Titus Brandsma, Edith Stein, Corrie ten Boom, Franz Jägerstätter, and Gertrude Luckner. Many Christians also strongly opposed Stalin and as a result disappeared or were imprisoned or executed.

Vatican II

The period after World War II was a time for regrouping and healing. The war had brought much suffering and persecution to Christians and peacetime was a time for renewal. We have seen the many factors that caused the Church to withdraw over the centuries. The Reformation had put the official Catholic Church in a defensive posture, and the Church viewed modern movements—the Enlightenment, nationalism, scientific discovery, communism, National Socialism, and secularism—as adversaries. The sense of the official Church was often that of an embattled hierarchy preserving the institution it held to be the sole vehicle for truth and salvation.

Pope John XXIII

"Good Pope John," as many called him, came to the papacy in 1958. He was quite a contrast from the ascetic aristocrat Pius XII, who had reigned since 1939. John was a plump, jolly fellow, the son of Italian sharecroppers. A man of broad experience, he served as a sergeant in World War I and held a wide range of jobs for the Vatican in Bulgaria, Turkey, Greece, France, and Venice. During World War II, John heroically helped Jewish refugees to escape the Nazis. His extensive experience helped him keep his feet on the ground and gave him a deep respect for other churches and religions. He was a loving and outgoing man who was highly regarded everywhere he worked. He extended his warm friendship equally to simple people and celebrities.

From the beginning it was clear that John was going to be a unique pope. He went out in the streets, visited the prisons, and asked people to share meals with him in his residence. Then, in January 1959, he stunned the world by announcing that he wanted to convene a worldwide council. Many of the cardinals reacted negatively to the idea and said it would take too long to prepare such a meeting. John persisted and told them they had three years to get the council up and running: it opened in October 1962!

Preparations for the Council

Pope John entrusted preparation for the council to Cardinal Ottaviani, who headed the Roman Curia, an office that had led the Church for centuries. Ottaviani was used to the Italians leading the Church in its preservation of doctrine and was reluctant to allow Church leaders from other parts of the world help in the preparation. As Ottaviani saw it, all that was needed was to collect Church doctrines as the Curia understood them and call in the bishops for an affirming vote. He was not keen on opening a council to discuss new European theology, nor was he comfortable with the pastoral approach proposed by the pope.

Pope John put his own personal stamp on the Second Vatican Council, or Vatican II. His travels and work had taught him that the Church had become like a museum: a stuffy, dusty institution that needed to open its windows and let in fresh air. He wanted to renew the Church to how it was when it was begun by Jesus. He wanted leaders to be seen as people who know the signs of the times and are prepared to bring the gospel to the needs of their world. Not wanting to be a dominant figure, John stayed in the background and invited thousands of cardinals, bishops, theologians, and observers to come to Rome to renew the Catholic Church.

For the first time in history, with the advent of air travel, these representatives could easily fly to Rome for a number of sessions until the council's work was done. As it happened, John died after the first session, but the work of the council was courageously carried forth to the end by John's successor, Paul VI.

The Council Opens

In his opening address to the twenty-five hundred bishops attending the council, John pointed out that Catholic tradition needs to be preserved but at the same time has to be restudied with modern tools and presented in new ways that are predominantly pastoral. (He liked to say that the gospel has not changed, we have grown to understand it better.) There was urgency in John's voice. The people of the world were threatened by so many dangers, not the least of which was nuclear destruction. The world needed the Gospel of Jesus. He stressed that in dealing with those who seem to be in error, the Church must use "the medicine of mercy rather than that of severity." He clearly wanted to depart from the "anathema" or condemnation approach that the Vatican had taken toward "adversaries," including many of its own theologians. He wanted Church leaders to have a respectful dialogue with the world, rather than form a fortress opposed to the world. He deeply desired that the Church be seen as a loving mother, not only loving its own but also those separated from the Church and all the people of the world. John wanted the Church to be much more than a centralized Roman institution. He wanted it to be a community of people reaching out to the world, especially to the many poor and outcast. John's words were filled with joy and hope, and he believed that this was the dawn of a new day for the Church!

Given the attitude of the Curia during preparations for the council, it was not surprising that when the council opened, the delegates found before them very conservative documents out of the old fortress days. With the exception of an excellent document on the liturgy, the other documents had to be sent back to the drawing board.

At the outset, one cardinal put his finger on areas that the Church needed to improve. He said the Church was just too clerical, triumphant, and legalistic. In other words, too often it is identified with the pope and the hierarchy. This was a Church that thought of itself as the only true way to salvation, one that placed obedience to doctrine and law above the central gospel virtue of love.

A Tug of War

As the council progressed, a struggle quickly emerged between the traditionalists who did not want to see much change and the progressives who did. Gradually, progressive theologians, scholars such as Karl Rahner, Henri de Lubac, and Yves Congar who had been silenced since the 1950s, were brought on board and given a hearing in what one cardinal described as "the most important adult education program in history." The prelates learned about biblical criticism, the role of the laity, and the value of other churches and religions. They received a short course in all the changes in the Catholic Church throughout history and came to see how doctrine and practice had always developed.

As documents were debated and voted on, a new vision of the Church emerged. Perhaps one the most significant shifts was from seeing the Church as a hierarchy to seeing it first and foremost as a "people," the people of God. That meant that every single person in the community could now say: "I am Church!" And, as Jesus said, every time two or three gather in his name, he is in their midst. Each small community, each parish, and each family was indeed truly "Church."

Calling the Church "people" did not mean that the priests and hierarchy were not also Church. They too are "people," and their role is to serve the people in a loving and caring fashion. Loving, pastoral care was to replace leading through fear and demanding obedience. As the great moral theologian Bernard Haring said: "The highest law is the law of Christ—the law of love."

The council described the people of the Church as a pilgrim people ever journeying through history, always standing for the teaching and the presence of Jesus in the world, and always in need of reform to keep the mission on track. The council used a startling new image: the Church as a sacrament, a living symbol of the presence of Jesus Christ in the world. As a sacrament, the community should be an active reminder that the Savior is present in the world: loving, forgiving, sharing, and struggling for justice.

Student Reflection

"My father's generation was really affected by Vatican II, and when he and the others show up with some furniture and food for a poor family they believe that they are doing the work of Jesus. My father has been a regular demonstrator against war of any kind. Now I think I better understand what he is up to. I think we had the same feeling last summer when a group of us went to work on houses near New Orleans after the flood, but we didn't use 'church' to describe ourselves."

During the council, John wrote two blockbuster papal letters that were read worldwide: one on social justice and one on peace. These letters made it more evident that John's focus in the council was on world problems, poverty, and the danger of nuclear war. These writings underlined the "signs of the times" the council should address.

The Council Documents

The Second Vatican Council produced sixteen documents, which purported to renew the Catholic Church so that it could better reflect its origins and more effectively address the needs of the modern world. Let's look at some of the key documents now and deal with these issues in more detail in later chapters.

Liturgy

From the outset, the material on liturgy had been well prepared and caused little debate. *Liturgy* was described as "the summit toward which the activity of the Church is directed and the fountain from which all her power flows." Significant here were the decisions to turn the altar around to face the people, to celebrate liturgy in the language of the people attending, and the call for active participation. Contemporary music was to be encouraged and the customs of all cultures, respected. Scripture was given "paramount importance" and Christ's presence in the Word was to be emphasized along with his presence in Eucharist. Sermons were to be integral to Mass to connect the Scriptures with everyday life. The cup along with the host were now to be freely offered to the faithful, not restricted to special occasions. The "priesthood of the faithful" was emphasized for the first time in centuries.

The Church

The document on the Church is a fundamental statement of its new understanding of itself; all the other notions of the council flow from this historically unique perspective. Some have called this document the "magna carta" on the nature and mission of the Church.

The shift here is from institutional language to seeing the Church as Mystery, or in Paul VI's words: "the reality imbued with the hidden presence of God." Jesus Christ is placed at the center and those related to Christ stand as a symbol (sacrament) of the unity of all people with God and with each other. The Church is fundamentally "the people of God," chosen to prophetically witness to the world that all are God's chosen ones. As a people, the Church is subject to faults and failings and must therefore always be open to self-criticism and reform. As a "pilgrim people," the Church must continually march through time, renewing itself and searching for ways to better carry out its mission in the world.

At the same time it was reiterated that the Church is also hierarchical, with a structured leadership and authority. This structure was declared to be collegial, in that the pope must work with councils, as well as bishops, in their local conferences.

The priesthood of all believers was underlined, as well as the fact that all of the faithful are called to holiness, not just those called to priesthood or religious life. Mary was recognized as the "mother of the Church."

The Church in the Modern World

This document is at the very heart of what Pope John wanted to accomplish in calling this council: to renew the Church to better respond to the "signs of the times" and better serve the pastoral needs of the world in which we live. Cardinal Suenens had advised the pope that the council should not only consider internal issues but also external concerns. This document effectively addresses the latter issue.

The council taught that the Church as a people should be positive toward the world and its social, political, and scientific development and in solidarity with all people. Gone were the past triumphalism and condemnatory attitudes toward human progress and scientific development. The Church now took a strong stand for human dignity, human rights, equality, and freedom.

Much emphasis was given to the role of the laity in the mission of the Church; this role was further developed in the decree on the laity. The dignity of marriage was emphasized, and marriage was described in personalistic terms as a covenant that nurtures marital love. The Church also firmly stated its intention to be active in efforts for peace and justice.

Revelation

For Catholics, this document was a long overdue "back-to-the-Bible" declaration. Rather than seeing Scripture and tradition as two sources of revelation, the Church now recognized that they are closely connected and that Scripture and tradition "form one sacred deposit of the Word of God." Both serve as the "rule of faith." Affirming the authorship of God in Scripture, human authorship was also recognized. After much debate, the scientific study and interpretation of Scripture was at last officially approved. The faithful were to be given easy access to Scripture, and the Bible should have an exceptional place in preaching, theology, catechetics, liturgy, and prayer.

Ecumenism

Pope John called the council for two reasons: Church renewal and Church unity. The Church in this document acknowledges its own blame for the divisions of the past and calls those separated from the Church separated "brothers and sisters," "churches," and "ecclesial communities." Both Orthodox and Protestant were given prominent positions as observers at the council, and the pope put the Secretariat for Christian Unity in the hands of the able and influential Cardinal Bea. The document acknowledges that Christ's work goes on in other churches and ecclesial communities, and that baptism establishes a communion among all believers. It calls for dialogue among the churches and a common joining in prayer and social action. Special attention is given to the need for unity with the Eastern churches.

Non-Christian Religions

This document really broke new ground. It explicitly condemns anti-Semitism and admits that there are elements of truth and goodness in other religions. It expresses gratitude for the nourishment that Christianity draws from Judaism and shows high regard for Islam. Hinduism and Buddhism are mentioned with respect, but more descriptively than with any kind of evaluation. The council again calls for future cooperation and dialogue among religions.

Religious Freedom

This turned out to be one of the most controversial issues of the council because it involved a distinct reversal in teaching and a change in policy. The Church had taught that it was the one true religion and that other faiths were in error. Thus in any country where the Catholics were the majority, they were intolerant of other religions. But when Catholics were a minority, they demanded freedom to worship. Now the Church taught that religious freedom was a universal human right.

This document recognizes the right of conscience and the free exercise of religion. Within due limits, everyone has the right to act in accordance with his or her beliefs. No one is to be forced to act contrary to conscience, especially in matters of religion. Thus faith cannot be forced on people, as it had been in so many instances in the past. The council states: "The act of faith is of its nature a free act."

This position was not only given to the Church to follow; it was also addressed to world governments. In Nazi Germany and communist countries, there had been widespread religious suppression and even extensive extermination of people for religious reasons. Today such repression still exists in Pakistan, India, Sudan, China, Turkey, and many other countries. Here the council clearly states that governments have no right to repress people for their religious beliefs and must protect the right to religious freedom for all of their citizens.

The Council Ends

After four sessions of intense debate, study, and voting over a three-year period, the council was over. The bishops went home prepared to participate in the most extensive renewal of the Church since the Reformation. They had made statements of repentance for faults of the past that caused division and oppression. They had shown that the Catholic Church had a new self-awareness as a people who follow Jesus and his gospel of love and forgiveness. The people of the Church were now called to a more active participation in their liturgy and sacraments, all of which were about to be renewed. Catholics were to be a people open to and respectful of other churches and religions, recognizing their truth and power to save while working for unity. Catholics were a community of disciples in solidarity with the world and addressing its problems of poverty,

violence, and injustice. Religious freedom and honoring the human conscience were now values to be preserved. The bishops had their work cut
out for them!

Fast-Forward Forty Years

It has been more than forty years since the Second Vatican Council ended,
and there have been many gatherings and efforts to take stock of how
renewal is going. Because you are in a Catholic college or university, we
might focus on how things are going where you are.

Things were certainly different in college life before the council. For the
most part, at that time men and women went to separate Catholic colleges.
As women began to enter men's campuses, there were separate dorms for
men and women. Often there were prayers before meals, in classes, and at
night. Sunday Masses, confession, and yearly retreats were widely attended
by students. Often there were dress codes, strict moral codes (especially
with regard to sexuality), and many of the professors were priests and
nuns. A considerable number of graduates entered a seminary or convent.
The United States' participation in the Second World War, even its dropping of two atomic bombs, were for the most part accepted. In fact, most
Catholic colleges had benefited greatly by enrolling the returning veterans
with their GI Bill of Rights money. There was little discussion about other
religions. Issues such as homosexuality, abortion, divorce, premarital sex,
and birth control were settled with no further discussion. Theology departments consisted mostly of priests, and their job as teachers was to pass on
the official doctrinal and moral teachings of the Catholic Church and help
students understand these teachings.

My, How Things Have Changed!

In the last fifty years, there have been amazing changes at Catholic institutions of higher learning. Changes in culture as well as in Catholicism
have given these colleges a new face. Men and women attend together,

share dorms, are free to come and go as they please, and live their own lives. Diversity is prominent: students are from different races, nationalities, states, and countries. Students belong to different churches and religions; many have no religious affiliation at all. Students are also free to have their own sexual preference, and gays and lesbians generally have an organization on campus and are respected and protected by the university like all students. The professors, even in the theology departments, are usually lay people, hired more for their academic expertise than their religious affiliation.

There is still a strong Catholic identity on most of these campuses. Weekly Masses are spirited and youthful experiences. There are regular student retreats. Many students are engaged in service activities for the needy and in efforts for social justice, freedom, and environmental conservation. Priests often live in the dorms and make themselves available as mentors. Campus ministry is usually quite active in such colleges, and there are opportunities for "alternative breaks," where students travel to serve others, and service-learning semesters, where students can travel to another country and spend a semester working with and learning from those in need.

Theology has changed a great deal since the Second Vatican Council gave its support to biblical study and modern theological interpretation. Now students are taught to think critically about the Catholic tradition and learn new interpretations. In addition, there are courses on the theology of other churches and religions. More than fifty percent of Catholic students marry someone of another faith. Few move on to a seminary or convent, and yet many look forward to being active serving others.

Not Everyone Is Satisfied

There have been serious challenges in recent years to Catholic higher education in the United States. In 1990 the Vatican issued a challenge to these institutions to consider whether they truly merit the title "Catholic" and required that Catholic theologians be issued mandates from their

many students are engaged in service

local bishops, certifying their orthodoxy. Catholic colleges and universities embarked on a soul-searching process of self-examination, and the bishops debated the mandate issue for ten years. Ultimately, each bishop issued mandates to the Catholic theologians in his diocese. Not every teacher chose to accept his or her mandate.

A recent survey by the Cardinal Newman Society, an organization that promotes conservative values on Catholic campuses, reports that Catholic colleges do a poor job of imparting official Catholic teachings and that many students in these institutions gradually come to approve of abortion, casual sex, and homosexual unions. Some parents, who pay dearly to send their young adults to such institutions, feel betrayed when they hear such reports.

Conservative Catholic Colleges

In a backlash to the perceived excessive liberalism on Catholic campuses, other more conservative institutions are appearing. The most prominent of these is the Franciscan University of Steubenville, Ohio. Since the 1970s, this university has offered a quality liberal arts education. It is somewhat charismatic in its spirituality and dedicated to orthodoxy, in line with the magisterium of the Church. Most of the theology courses offered concern Catholic theology. Also since the 1970s, at least four other purposefully conservative Catholic colleges were founded, including Christendom College in Virginia, which uses the magisterium as its guide. They hold that Catholic universities have largely lost their Catholic identity. There are more such Catholic colleges appearing. Ave Maria University has been established in Naples, Florida, funded by Thomas Monaghan, the founder of Domino's Pizza. Here, Mass is celebrated throughout the day, Latin is a required subject, and divorced Catholics are not welcome on faculty. The university is solidly committed to following the magisterium on all issues. Premarital sex is strictly forbidden and gay support groups are not allowed. In addition to Ave Maria, there are five other such conservative Catholic colleges now being established in the United States.

Conclusion

The Catholic Church has entered a new millennium. Globally, it faces challenges including environmental degradation, terrorism, the spread of AIDS, and deepening problems of hunger and poverty. Internally, the official Church has faced many challenges to its authority: the scandal of sexual abuse by members of the clergy, a growing shortage of nuns and priests, and division among its own people on doctrinal and moral issues. In response, the Vatican has made a controversial return to centralized authority.

The agenda for discussion grows longer and longer, and many think that it is time for another council to address these issues openly and with the same willingness to change that characterized Vatican II. The signs of the times do not remain static, but are ever changing. The Church is constantly challenged to read these signs carefully and find the wisdom and courage to renew itself so that it can effectively carry the gospel to the contemporary world.

Activities

1. Teams can visit parishes along the spectrum of traditional to progressive and compare liturgies, religious education, and staff perspectives.

2. Students can write some of the more traditional colleges (University of Steubenville, Ave Maria College) to get in touch with some of the students and faculty for e-mail interviews concerning their perspectives on the Catholic Church.

3. Investigate the Legionnaires of Christ and Opus Dei and report their positions on Church issues.

4. Interview your local bishop about his thoughts on the future of the Catholic Church.

5. Brainstorm possible agendas for the next Vatican Council.

Sources

Alexander, Faivre. *The Emergence of the Laity in the Early Church*. New York: Paulist Press, 1990.

Bokenkotter, Thomas. *A Concise History of the Catholic Church*. Rev. ed. New York: Doubleday, 2005.

Brown, Raymond. *The Churches the Apostles Left Behind*. New York: Paulist Press, 1984.

———. *The Community of the Beloved Disciple*. New York: Paulist Press, 1979.

Doyle, Dennis. *The Church Emerging from Vatican II*. Mystic, CT: Twenty-Third Publications, 1992.

Froehle, B., and M. Gautier. *Global Catholicism*. New York: Orbis Press, 2003.

Lakeland, Paul. *The Liberation of the Laity*. New York: Continuum, 2003.

Madges, William and Michael Daley, eds. *Vatican II: Forty Personal Stories*. Mystic, CT: Twenty-Third Publications, 2003.

Osborne, Kenan. *Ministry*. New York: Paulist Press, 1993.

Schillebeeckx, Edward. *Church: The Human Story of God*. New York: Crossroad, 1985.

Schüssler Fiorenza, Elizabeth. *In Memory of Her*. New York: Crossroad, 1984.

4 Christian Divisions and Efforts for Unity

At the last supper Jesus prayed:

"That they may be one." He must have anticipated divisions, and so there have been from the very beginning. The following is a tale of many divisions. It is a history lesson and history can be boring. But I believe that educated Christians need to know their story, so hang on!

The original community of Jewish converts wanted the new non-Jewish converts (Gentiles) to be circumcised and follow the Torah like good Jews. Paul opposed that and his position prevailed. There were those who did not believe Jesus Christ to be truly human, and those who did not believe that he was truly divine. In the third century, Arianism, which taught that Jesus was higher than human but not divine, swept Christianity. A council was called in Nicea in 325 CE to try to settle that dispute. There were Nestorians who did not believe that Mary could be called the mother of God. Some communities believed that Christ had two natures, others that he had only one. There were Gnostic communities that believed they held secret revelations. Other communities did not believe that Jesus truly suffered and died. In the second century, Marcion and his followers rejected the Old Testament because of its distortion of God. Soon after, the Montanists expected the Second Coming imminently, developed extreme fasting to prepare, and sought to be martyred. The two major schools of theology, Alexandria in Egypt and Antioch in Syria, also differed on many points of belief.

Once Christianity was accepted in the Roman Empire, councils could be called, doctrines defined, and mainline Christianity established. Those who disagreed with these councils were simply cast out as heretics, and though these communities remained active, they eventually were pushed to the edges and their Scriptures burned. Still, there are Christian communities today that embrace Nestorian and Arian beliefs.

Tensions between Eastern and Western Christianity go back to the early centuries of the Church. Soon after the Roman emperor Constantine accepted Christianity, he moved the center of the empire to Constantinople (modern-day Istanbul) and called councils to be held in Turkey. This set up two competing centers of Christianity, one in Rome where the pope resided, and one in Constantinople where the emperor resided.

In the fourth and fifth centuries, new problems arose with the Donatists, who believed that because the Church must remain holy, the validity of the sacraments depends on the worthiness of the minister. Another important division came in the fifth century with the teachings of Pelagius, who seems to have been a holy monk from the British Isles and a popular preacher. Pelagius had a positive view of human nature and did not believe that humans were corrupted by original sin. Humans can do good deeds on their own and win salvation through their own goodness. Divine grace can help but is not necessary. From this perspective, Jesus Christ has saved us by good example, not by restoring us to grace.

Augustine, the great theologian from North Africa, took on both the Donatists and the Pelagians, and shaped the future of Christian thinking. To the Donatists, he argued that the sacraments work through their own power and do not depend on the goodness of the minister. To the Pelagians, he taught that original sin corrupts human nature and no one can be saved without the divine grace of God, won for us by Jesus. As we will see, these disputes return again in the Protestant Reformation.

In the fifth century, the Roman Empire collapsed under the attacks of northern tribes. The last Western emperor, Romulus, was deposed in 476. The bishop of Rome (the pope) then became more prominent and now stood as an important leader of the West. Struggles over authority and Christological issues continued between East and West. Clovis, the great leader of the Franks, asked for baptism, established strong leadership in the West, and allied with the Western bishops. At the end of the sixth century, Pope Gregory the Great established a strong papacy in Rome and also began to lead in matters of State. In the eighth century, Pepin, the ruler of the West, gave the papacy imperial authority and a vast territory called the Papal States. Pepin's son, Charlemagne, then ruled for forty-three years, working closely with the pope. In 800, Charles was crowned in Rome as Holy Roman Emperor by Pope Leo III. Two great powers stood side by side in Rome: the emperor and the pope. But power struggles were soon to reemerge. One pope, Nicholas I (858–67), declared that he was to be described as "Lord of all the World." Others lost power to the Roman aristocracy. Pope John VIII was murdered; another, Formosus (891–96), was dug up after burial, tried, condemned of high crimes, and his body thrown in the Tiber River!

East and West Drift Apart

Imperial authority in the East was weakened by massive internal problems, one of which was the serious debate over whether religious icons could be venerated. The East also stood helpless to stem the growth of the West and papal authority. In 858, a serious breach occurred when the pope interfered in the controversy over who was the rightful patriarch of Constantinople. Several years later the same pope upstaged the East and organized the Church in Bulgaria, considered to be Eastern territory. Then in 876, Photius, the patriarch of Constantinople, summoned a council that excommunicated and deposed the pope. The rift lasted about ten years before relations between East and West were restored. The doctrinal dispute over whether or not the Spirit proceeded from "the Father" (East) or from "the Father and the Son" (West) continued, but there were no further clashes until the middle of the eleventh century. The East and West were now two churches. The pope no longer participated in the election of the patriarch of Constantinople, and he was removed from Eastern prayers.

In 1040 things heated up again. The pope imposed the Latin rite on Eastern churches in Italy, and the East imposed its rites on Latin churches in Constantinople. Michael Cerularius, the feisty patriarch of Constantinople, refused to help Rome fight the Normans and condemned the Latin practices of using unleavened bread, teaching "and from the Son," and enforcing celibacy on the clergy.

The big year for the final separation between East and West was 1054: the pope sent a delegation to Constantinople to ease tensions. But Cerularius was so put off by the discourtesy of the papal delegates that he refused to meet with them. Outraged, the delegates left a bull of excommunication on the altar of Santa Sophia, charging the patriarch with many heresies. The patriarch in return proclaimed the West anathema for its heresy,

The Filioque Controversy

The Western and Eastern churches have long feuded over the Trinitarian question surrounding the origin of the Holy Spirit. The Eastern Church goes back to the Council of Constantinople (381 CE), which declared that the Holy Spirit "proceeds from the Father." The Eastern Church recognizes that the Spirit comes "through" the Son, but holds that the Father is the source and origin of the whole divinity. The Western, or Latin, tradition maintains that the Holy Spirit "proceeds from the Father and from the Son" (filioque). Contemporary efforts to restore unity to the Western and Eastern churches have led theologians to reexamine the meaning and significance of this controversy.

burned the Roman bull, and declared that Rome and Constantinople would now go their separate ways. The split deepened when Western Crusaders installed a Latin patriarch in Antioch in 1098 and then sacked Constantinople in 1203 and declared that the pope now had authority there. Though attempts to reconcile were made at various councils, the two churches remained separated. In 1453, Constantinople fell into the hands of the Ottoman Turks.

Then in 1964, Pope Paul, in the spirit of Vatican II renewal, met with the much-loved Patriarch Athenagoras in Jerusalem. Mutual regrets for offense were expressed, excommunications were lifted, and hopes for full communion were restored. One of John Paul II's major goals was to reunite the two churches, and Benedict XVI recently visited Turkey to continue this effort.

The Pre-Reformation

The most tragic and momentous division in the Church was caused by the Protestant Reformation, which began in the sixteenth century. There were many factors in the period before the Reformation that led to this historic upheaval and division in Christianity. First, the papacy had become extremely controversial. Innocent III (1198–1216) saw himself as the "Lord of the World," a semidivine figure "below God but above man." Likewise, Boniface VIII (1294–1303) declared, "it is altogether necessary for salvation for every human creature to be subject to the Roman Pontiff." At the same time, the papacy was unstable. In the eleventh century, three men claimed to be pope. In the fourteenth century, the pope resided in Avignon, France, for nearly seventy years. In the fifteenth century, two and then three men claimed the papacy. In addition, some popes became so powerful both spiritually and politically that they were a major threat to local princes as well as to leaders

some popes were a threat to local princes

of the growing national movements. Not only did the pope have access to financial and military power, he could devastate a leader with excommunication, an embarrassing liability for anyone wanting prestige and power. With the rise of nations and local governments, many rulers wanted to get out from under the papal thumb.

The absolute power and wealth of the papacy often attracted individuals with ambitions other than serving the Church. The papacy was often characterized by corruption. During Martin Luther's youth, the pope was Alexander VI, of the corrupt Borgia family. Alexander was infamous for his political intrigues, mistresses, and children. He often used his children's marriages to make political alliances and held lavish orgies in the papal palace after their weddings. Two of his children were known for their maliciousness: the much-married Lucrezia and the brutal Cesare. Alexander raised enormous sums to fund his lavish lifestyle and military campaigns by selling indulgences.

The notion of indulgences was developed in the Middle Ages in regard to confession. To be forgiven, the penitent needing absolution had to do certain penances for the "temporal punishment" attached to sin. These penances, which were often extreme, could be taken care of by buying an indulgence and thereby sparing a family member or oneself from the fires of purgatory. From rich and poor vast sums of money poured into the coffers of the Church and were used by bishops to purchase their positions, to fund crusades and the royal life of the hierarchy, and to build churches, including the magnificent St. Peter's Basilica in Rome. Alexander used this system of selling indulgences extensively and imprisoned or executed nobles or preachers who got in his way. Savonarola, the great Dominican Florentine preacher, attacked these papal abuses and was ordered burned at the stake by Alexander.

Early Protesters

There were early revolts against the wealth and power of the popes, the Church hierarchy, and even some of the clergy. These came from people who wanted to return to the example of Jesus and the Gospels. For instance, in 1173 Peter Waldo, a wealthy French merchant, decided to follow Jesus' admonition and gave away all his money. Waldo became a beggar and a preacher of the gospel. He was allowed to preach only if he had the permission of the clergy, but he and his followers decided to ignore that rule. They were then excommunicated for disobedience and also for translating the Bible to read and interpret on their own. The Waldensians believed they were imitating the early church by meeting in small communities and allowing women equality in their ministry of preaching. Their excommunication pushed them outside the periphery of the Church, where they opposed purgatory and the use of relics. Later they condemned the violence of the Inquisition and the Crusades, declaring that they were opposed to war. The Waldensians, as well as other reform movements like the Cathars and the Albigensians, were early Protestant groups that gained the sympathy of many for their positions and because of the way they were repressed and even slaughtered. These movements were absorbed into the Protestant Reformation, but remnants of them exist today.

Another early protester was John Wycliffe (d. 1384), who strongly criticized the wealth of the Church, the papacy, the selling of indulgences, and the traditional notion of the "real presence" in Eucharist, and who translated the Bible into English and maintained that the Scriptures should be the only norm for Christian faith. After his death, Wycliffe was declared a heretic, his body dug up and burned, and his ashes thrown into a river.

A devoted follower of John Wycliffe was Jon Hus (d. 1415), who taught at the University of Prague and is still honored in the Czech Republic with a prominent statue in Prague. Hus' sermons and Bible translation in the Czech language made his people proud of their heritage. He took up many of Wycliffe's positions including the primacy of the Bible and criticizing the corruption of the Church and its clergy, including the selling of indulgences. Hus was summoned to the Council of Constance and was guaranteed protection. He went in good faith, hoping to have an opportunity to present his views for consideration and debate. Instead, he was imprisoned and abused. When he refused to recant, he was sentenced to be burned at the stake. Hus faced death with courage and faith, and his execution aroused much antipathy toward the Church among his Bohemian people.

The Black Death

Another major factor leading up to the Reformation was the spread of the Black Death, a quickly fatal disease that killed off one-third of Europe's population, beginning in 1348 and flaring up again every ten years after that. Many in the convents and monasteries died, leaving those places open to marauders, who attacked the monks, raped the nuns, and laid these institutions to waste. Many of the clergy who served the sick and dying were themselves killed by the disease and to replace them, the Church had to lower its standards. The plague also produced a preoccupation with death in the European culture, a fear of hell and purgatory, and an interest in superstition. Many, especially those selling indulgences, preyed on these fears.

A Church Disrupted

The Church was desperate for funds to sustain the extravagant lifestyle of the popes now in residence in Avignon, France. In order to raise money, they instituted a severe system of taxation on bishops and pastors. Many Church leaders who could not pay were excommunicated, causing a further lack of ministers and much hostility toward the papacy. The seventy-year absence of the papacy from Rome was then followed by the Great Schism when two and then three popes struggled against each other for control of the Church. This struggle further contributed to the instability of Church leadership. In 1417 the Great Schism ended and one pope alone ruled from Rome.

For a while Church authority shifted from the papacy to councils, but this shift stirred much controversy and popes were reluctant to call the councils so needed for reform, lest they lose authority or have the spotlight shone on their corruption. The papacy remained degraded after the long period in which two of three popes condemned each other. Many bishops and clergy were absentee landlords, merely using their dioceses for fundraising. The nobility, who were sometimes mere children, would "buy" a Church office and use it as a source of income and influence, never having to appear on the scene to serve the people. The state of the clergy was decadent; many were uneducated and their personal lifestyles were scandalous. In the cities there were many "Mass priests," whose function was to say many Masses each day to collect the stipends. The monasteries were in a state of decline and even the friars, who had been held in such high esteem in the early Middle Ages, by the fifteenth century were held in low esteem. Simony, especially the selling of positions in the Church, was widespread. It was said that a cardinal's hat went to the highest bidder! The selling of dispensations and indulgences was rampant and had become a cancer growing in the papacy and Roman Curia.

Several pre-Reformation popes made attempts at reform, as did many bishops and pastors in Germany, some lay leaders in Italy, and some religious leaders in Spain. Erasmus (d. 1536), the great Christian humanist from Holland, hoped to bring about reform through his careful work in biblical criticism and the writings of the fathers. His writings on how to live the Christian life and how to be the ideal Christian leader, as well as his parodies on the dysfunction and superstition in the Church, were immensely popular. Many of these efforts at reform were well conceived and powerful, but it seems that none of them came to maturity; they were simply too little, too late.

Education and Reading

Other changes during the pre-Reformation period were in education and the development of reading. The establishment of the medieval universities gave many people the opportunity to develop critical thinking and to become scholars. The theologians produced an "alternative magisterium," which became a challenge to the pope and his Curia. The invention of the printing press in the mid-fifteenth century shifted the center of learning from the monasteries (where for centuries manuscripts had been hand copied) to the streets, where books fresh off the press could be purchased. The need for literacy spread quickly across Europe. In particular, the Bible now became accessible to all and each person could make up his or her mind about what it meant. The Renaissance, with its focus on classical resources, turned scholars to earlier Greek texts and alternate versions of the Scriptures. Comparable to the introduction of today's Internet, the invention of printing revolutionized education and communication in the Western world.

Ground Zero for Reform

The stage had been set for a major conflagration in the Church, and it was an unlikely person who ignited it and precipitated major divisions in Christianity. The Catholic Church, which had such power over both private and public life, was shaken to its foundations, its authority and influence cracked, and it came crashing down. And the person who started it all was a scholarly Augustinian monk by the name of Martin Luther.

Martin was born in 1483 to a mining family in Eisleben, Germany. He studied the classics and then enrolled at the University of Erfurt, received his master's degree in 1505, and planned to be a lawyer. Suddenly, the young Luther decided to enter an Augustinian monastery, possibly to get away from the cruelty of his parents and also to keep a vow he had made after being struck by lightning that if he survived he would join up. The life in the monastery was quite strict and austere and perhaps gave Martin, who was given to introspection and even scrupulosity, too much time to brood. He was a very conscientious monk in a respectable monastery, and after nineteen months he was ordained a priest and sent on to study theology. He became more and more aware of sinfulness and guilt and fell into depression and fear of damnation. He prayed, fasted, and confessed, but his agonizing fear of condemnation only increased. He believed himself unable to love a God who punished sinners like himself, yet too unworthy to do the good works necessary to be saved.

Amidst all this personal turmoil, Martin was assigned to teach, first philosophy at the University of Wittenberg and then theology at Erfurt. Meanwhile he began reading Augustine, whose negative view of humanity affected Martin's spirituality even more. In 1511, Martin returned to Wittenberg, received his doctorate in theology, and began teaching Scripture there. Two years later, Martin had a mystical experience reading Paul's letter to the Romans. He woke up to the awareness that the "justice of God" did not mean the punishment of God, but the saving power of God. Suddenly the lines "the one who is righteous by faith shall live" (Rm 1:17) exploded in front of him and he knew that only through faith alone could he be saved by a just God. He realized that he could not be saved by his own unworthy merits, but only by the mercy of God. As Martin continued his commentaries on the Psalms and Paul over the next few years, his theology of personal salvation deepened. He had come to the two foundational blocks of the "Lutheran" position: "faith alone saves" and the truth is discovered through "Scripture alone."

Martin's conviction that salvation comes from Christ's saving grace put him in direct opposition to much of the Catholic religious practice, which emphasized salvation from pilgrimages, relics, having Masses said, and the buying of indulgences. So when he heard about the Dominican John Tetzel selling indulgences nearby to rebuild St. Peter's in Rome with the promise that "As soon as the coin in the coffer rings, the soul from purgatory springs," Martin thought something needed to be done. He decided to compose a number of theses on indulgences, which he hoped would be debated, and he had these sent to several bishops. When they didn't answer, he sent them to his colleagues. (The story that he nailed them to the cathedral door seems to have been developed after his death).

Well, these became the theses heard around the world. Martin's assertion of the saving power of Christ and challenge to indulgences and the pope's authority over the souls in purgatory were printed up, circulated throughout Germany, and sent to Rome. Martin suddenly became the poster child for all the nobles who wanted out from under Rome's authority and for the countless numbers who were aching to attack the

Church. They all had their champion in this young, scholarly Bible teacher. The pope at the time, Leo X, paid little attention to what appeared to be just another "monk's squabble," but as he realized all the controversy Martin was stirring up, he summoned him to Rome to answer for heresy. The papal summons was not friendly: it gave no mention of the abuses of the indulgences, and called Luther "a leper and loathsome fellow [. . .] a dog and the son of a bitch, born to bite and snap at the sky with his doggish mouth," and also said that Luther had "a brain of brass and a nose of iron." So there, Martin! Being a bombastic man himself, Luther reacted angrily and now moved to a more hostile and extreme position. War was under way.

Rome, needing a favor from Martin's protector, Frederick of Saxony, softened its position and sent Cardinal Cajetan to get him to recant. The meeting ended in a deadlock, and Martin left questioning papal authority. Other matters preoccupied Rome, and so for several years Martin was free to take center stage with his sermons, pamphlets, and debates, now radically challenging the whole Church and sacramental system. Luther developed his notion of "Scripture alone" and could not see in Scripture any basis for a divinely founded Church, a papacy, bishops, or ordained priests.

The pope eventually saw Luther as a danger and issued the papal bull condemning forty-one of Luther's propositions, but was vague on which were heretical and did not excommunicate Martin. Martin's attacks on the pope became more crude and vehement; he called the pontiff "the anti-Christ." Martin was now in high gear as a reformer, and his pamphlets and manifestos against the Church and on Christian freedom could be read in every German city and hamlet. Luther at first called for limiting the papacy to spiritual leadership, ending the rule of celibacy, forbidding Masses for the dead, and allowing the election by each Christian community of its own ministers and bishops. He proposed a common priesthood of all believers, with the ordination of those who could preach and lead services as a means for providing order. Luther recognized only two sacraments, baptism and Eucharist, both of which were only efficacious through the faith of the recipient. Luther simplified the liturgy to its bare essentials, making it understandable in the vernacular and calling for participation, especially in exciting new hymns that he wrote, insisting that a stirring sermon be the centerpiece. Eucharist could be taken in the recipient's own hands, both with the bread and the cup. Luther allowed for confession, but not as a sacrament, and with the elimination of the "power" of the priest to forgive and other "abuses" that had become attached to confession. In 1520 Luther gathered with his students and followers and burned the papal bull against him and a copy of Canon Law. The Reformation was fully under way and Catholicism would never be the same.

Luther was called before the emperor and all the dignitaries of Germany at the Diet of Worms in 1521. When asked to recant, he refused. His life was now in danger, so his protector hid Luther in a castle. There he spent his time gathering with colleagues and translating the Bible into German, so that it would be accessible to his people.

The reform movement spread quickly. Many left or were driven out of their monasteries and convents. Changes occurred in beliefs and practice. But there was much confusion, a great deal of debate about priorities, and much experimentation. The reform was especially popular in the cities, where many wanted to end the Church's civil authority as well as remove the wealth and authority of the bishops, whose influence could reach all the way to Rome. A conference was called at Augsburg in 1530, and many hoped for reconciliation, if only the clergy could marry and the cup could be restored at liturgy. Rome was adamant against change, and so Protestant and traditional parishes began to compete with each other.

There was also civil unrest. Many peasants felt that with Luther, freedom was in the air, and so they began to revolt against their princes, sack the wealthy monasteries, convents, and castles, and spread violence. The princes' armies began to slaughter the poorly armed peasants, and when they called to Luther for support, he told the leaders that they were right in slaying the revolting peasants. This disillusioned many of the common folk, who turned against Luther. Now married to a former nun, Luther took up residence in his old monastery, where he often held council and continued to write and lead his movement.

The emperor Charles V worked diligently for decades to save the Roman Church from the reformers, sometimes using violence and at other times calling for theological conferences. In 1541 Catholics and Protestants came close to an agreement. Protestants asked for four concessions: marriage for the clergy, communion with both bread and cup, the dropping of transubstantiation as the explanation of the real presence, and freedom from papal jurisdiction while recognizing papal primacy. Again, Rome would not yield. Soon after Luther's death in 1546, armies on both sides marched against each other and brutal wars broke out, with reformed states battling Roman states. In 1555 the schism became final and legal, the decision of whether an area would be Catholic or Protestant resting with its government.

Other Reformers

While the Lutheran reforms were sweeping Germany, other reformers were at work elsewhere. England's King Henry VIII (d. 1547) wanted his country to remain Catholic, but broke with the Church because the pope refused to annul his marriage to Catherine of Aragon so that he could marry his new love, Anne Boleyn. Henry overruled the pope, declared himself to be head of the English Church, and married Anne. Under Henry's son, Edward VI, England became more Protestant, then moved nearly back to Catholicism under Mary Tudor, and finally under Elizabeth I settled into a moderate Protestantism.

Ulrich Zwingli (d. 1531) brought the reform movement to Switzerland. Originally, Zwingli was a Catholic priest, a Roman loyalist, and a dedicated humanist. Appointed as a preacher in Munster, he had an affair with a woman of the streets. Reading Erasmus about the need for Church reform inspired Zwingli, wanted no and he began preaching against indulgences and insisting that the Bible was the only source of faith. Zwingli wanted no distractions from the Scriptures in the Church, so as both a political and religious force in Zurich, he began to abolish statues, altars, relics, and

Rome would not yield

organs. He even began to abolish the Mass itself. He also challenged the legitimacy of some of the sacraments. Zurich began to seize Church property, rejected celibacy, and the convents and monasteries were suppressed.

Zwingli had gone beyond Luther in his reform. His most radical position was his teaching that Jesus was not really present in the Eucharist. The communion service for him was just a meal held in memory of Jesus' last supper. Luther once debated Zwingli on the real presence, and their lack of common ground revealed that the reform was itself now divided. Zwingli's radical doctrines drew criticism from the Catholic cantons and even from some in his own ranks. The peasants surprised Zwingli, who was a loyalist to the government, by pointing out that the Bible (the only source of faith) does not say that they should contribute to their Lord's taxes and thus they refused to pay. The Anabaptists confronted Zwingli with doctrine more radical than his, denying infant baptism and rejecting the authority of the State. Zwingli mercilessly persecuted the Anabaptists, using prison, torture, and execution. He had their founder, Felix Manz, taken out on Lake Zurich and drowned. When war broke out between the Protestant and Catholic cantons, Zwingli was murdered by the "old church" people, who quartered his body and burned him as a heretic. Still, his influence continued to spread through the cantons of Switzerland.

John Calvin (d. 1564) was another key reformer and instrumental in making Protestantism an international phenomenon. Born in France, Calvin began studying theology for the Catholic priesthood, but then switched to law and the classics. Later in life he wrote about his conversion to the Protestant cause in 1533. It seems that the Catholic experience had filled him with fear of God and prevented him from having peace of conscience. The reform offered the comfort of having faith in Christ's power to save. So Calvin decided to become a reformer of the Church and joined in the efforts to expose the papacy as a tyranny without a basis in the Scriptures. He soon joined the reformers in France, but when he saw his Protestant colleagues being executed, he decided to move to safer ground in Basel. There he began writing the first installment of his *Institutes of the Christian Religion,* a brilliant handbook of Protestant doctrine, which would later be added to and would become one of the most influential religious books in modern history. Calvin hoped to lead a quiet life as a scholar and reformer, but that all changed for him when he stopped in Geneva and was persuaded to work in the reform movement there. Calvin came on so strong with his teaching and rules that the local authorities banished him and his associates. He then settled in Strassburg, where he designed public worship for Protestants and continued to work on his *Institutes* and biblical commentaries.

When things began to go the way of the Protestants in Geneva, Calvin was asked to return and went there believing he had a divine calling to found the ideal reform community. He used the New Testament and began to draw up the code, creed, and cult for a Christian community. To enforce strict discipline, a consistory was established that could supervise the behavior of all the members, who if necessary could be excommunicated by the civil authorities. The laws were strict: no laughing during a sermon, no singing songs against Calvin, no dancing, and no going to the theater. Prostitution was stamped out and adultery could be punished with death. Calvin ruled with an iron hand, and those who opposed him paid dearly. Jacques Gruet, who protested the strict lifestyle that Calvin imposed, was arrested, convicted of blasphemy, and beheaded. And there was the celebrated case of Michael Servetus, who while running for his life from the Catholic Inquisition, had stopped in Geneva and was burned at the stake there for heresy.

In many ways Calvin went beyond Luther, whom he admired greatly. Like Zwingli, Calvin opposed the real presence and the belief that the divine gift was not given "in or under" bread and wine. But Calvin had his own view that the divine gift came "with" the bread and wine. Calvin also pushed the gratuitousness of God's saving grace to a doctrine of predestination, where eternal decree decides that some are saved and others damned.

It was Calvin's version of Protestantism that would spread through much of Europe, moving to Germany, Poland, Bohemia, Hungary, and Moravia. Calvinism also spread to France as the Huguenots fought a series of bloody wars with Catholics. It spread to the Netherlands, Belgium, and Luxembourg. John Knox, who had learned his Calvinism from Calvin himself in Geneva, brought these teachings to Scotland, where they established deep roots. The Calvinists even surfaced in England as "Puritans," who were bent on purifying the English Church of anything popish. Their influence moved the English Church closer to radical Protestantism. Under Charles I, the Puritans came under so much persecution that in the 1630s, twenty thousand left England and established the Massachusetts Bay Colony in New England, where they became a major force in shaping a new nation. Today they are known in the United States as Presbyterians.

The Catholic Response

As mentioned earlier, Catholic reform movements were already under way when the "protesters" appeared. These efforts intensified as it became clear that Protestantism posed a real threat to the Church. Seminary reform intensified and new groups were founded to revitalize the Church and carry out its educational and missionary work. The Society of Jesus, founded by Ignatius Loyola in 1534, made major contributions in carrying out the much-needed reforms of the Church. Starting with just a small company of men, the society grew quickly and spread through Europe, Asia, and the New World, owing to effective preachers, teachers, theologians, and pastors. Peter Canisius, a Jesuit, was a major Catholic reformer in Germany, where he established colleges and published the popular *Catechism*. The Capuchins were established to reform the Franciscans, and the great mystical writers John of the Cross and Teresa of Avila reformed the Carmelites. New orders of Sisters were established that contributed mightily to the reform of Catholicism, providing hospitals, schools, and many other services for the people of the Church.

From the beginning of the reform movements, there was a call for a council to resolve the many urgent issues. Unfortunately, the popes at the time were reluctant to call such a council, because they viewed it as a threat to their authority. This, along with political unrest and conservative forces in the Curia, prevented the opening of the Council of Trent until 1545. Even then, the council met only sporadically for three sessions, and it wasn't until 1563, almost three decades after Luther laid down his challenges, that Trent was prepared to publish its decrees. At first, Protestants were invited but they did not come because they were not permitted to vote. Unfortunately, the council proceeded without them and the church divisions became permanent.

The Trent decrees were clear and definitive statements in defense of Catholicism over and against Luther and the Protestant teachings. Both the Bible *and* tradition were necessary to determine the faith, and only the Church can interpret Scripture. Justification was not only by faith, but also by hope and charity, the latter expressed in good works. The council taught that original sin did not totally corrupt human nature. It also affirmed the divine institution of all seven sacraments and was definitive on the real presence in Eucharist. The Mass, which had often degenerated into a circus spectacle, was completely reformed and unified. The seminaries were reformed through strict recruiting and sound training. A papacy was defined as "divinely instituted," bishops were required to live in their dioceses, and the purchase of these offices was forbidden. Priestly ordination and celibacy were affirmed, and the sacrament of marriage was defined as indissoluble-divorce was forbidden. Indulgences and pilgrimages were still approved but the monetary abuses were firmly addressed. In 1542 the Inquisition was established, which sought out and punished heretics, and in 1571 the Index was established to list condemned books.

 Student Reflection

"I am Lutheran and I just don't see how Catholics can say that the papacy is divinely instituted. There is nothing in the Scriptures about the papacy and it seems to have developed later in the Church into a political office."

Trent, though belated, soundly reformed the Catholic Church, with modified traditions and structures that would prevail for the next four hundred years. Great hostility existed between the Catholic Church and the radical reform movements, as evidenced in the Thirty Years' War (1618–48) in Germany, but Catholicism regained some of the ground it had lost during the Reformation: Poland, large parts of Germany, France, and the Netherlands returned to Catholicism. In addition, the missions overseas made many converts, and Rome flourished as the center of Catholicism. The papacy would remain strong and free of scandal; a well-established structure of dioceses would be established in Europe and later throughout the rest of the world. Catholic universities and theology flourished. Trent was a successful endeavor at reform, though it was largely in a defensive mode, limiting itself to the agenda voiced by Protestantism and reacting with an absolute finality that was not open to negotiation or diversity.

Trent insured that the Roman Catholic position was preserved. But the Church had moved into a fortress mentality that was not only hostile toward Protestantism but also defensive toward the modern and secular developments that would appear in the following centuries, including the new cosmology of Galileo, rationalism, Deism, biblical criticism, evolution, and nationalism. The democratic movement, which arose out of the French Revolution wherein the Church was brutally persecuted, became anathema, and it was often insisted that "the Church is not a democracy." In 1864 Pius IX condemned liberal Catholic thinkers in his *Syllabus of Errors*. In 1870 the Church lost the Papal States but rebounded with a definition of papal infallibility, and by the turn of the century, Pius X made a sweeping condemnation of modernism. Change would be an unacceptable concept for the Catholic Church until the Second Vatican Council in the early 1960s.

The Ecumenical Movement

Up until the Second Vatican Council, efforts for Christian unity were largely made by Protestants. The official Catholic position was to avoid all participation in ecumenical councils because that would be participating in "false Christianity." The Vatican position was clear: if Protestants want unity, they should return to the "true fold." In the twentieth century, there was a growing awareness that the Church itself was missing something in all this division and that it should be more open to communication.

It was John XXIII who achieved major breakthroughs in ecumenism by making it one of the focuses of Vatican II and allowing Protestants and Orthodox to participate in the council as observers. He also established the Secretariat for Christian Unity in the Vatican, appointed the highly influential and progressive Cardinal Bea as its head, and urged reconciliation without trying to focus on who was right and who was wrong. In 1961 Pope John granted permission for Catholic participation in the World Council of Churches (WCC) that met in New Delhi, India. Pope Paul VI officially asked forgiveness of non-Catholics for any wrongs the Catholic Church had done to cause the separation. He also visited the World Council's headquarters in Geneva in 1971 and prayed with its leaders.

The Protestant efforts at unity began with conferences in Scotland in 1910 and 1937 and with the organization of the World Council of Churches in 1948. Today the WCC brings together more than 340 denominations and fellowships from more than 100 countries. It represents more than 550 million Christians. The Roman Catholic Church, though still not a member, has a strong working relationship with the council. Besides supporting study and dialogue, the WCC is strongly committed to acting for peace, justice, and human rights throughout the world and to defending against environmental abuses. In this country the National Council of Churches has done much to promote Christian unity.

Vatican II on Ecumenism

As discussed in chapter 3, the Second Vatican Council made major break-throughs on ecumenism. It shifted the focus to the common ground shared by Catholics and their "separated brethren": belief in Jesus Christ; the Scriptures; the life of grace; the virtues of faith, hope, and charity; and the gifts of the Spirit. It acknowledged that all baptized people are members of Christ's body, all brothers and sisters in the Lord, and that truth and salvation can be found in these separated communities (also now referred to as *churches*). It also declared that the liturgical actions of these communities can engender grace and give access to salvation. The council acknowledged that not all truths of the faith exist on the same level, but rather there is a hierarchy of beliefs. This left some of the traditions more open to debate and reinterpretation. The Church now committed itself to an active role in ecumenism and encouraged respectful dialogue, as well as mutual worship, prayer, and cooperation. No longer was the phrase "outside the Church there is no salvation" to be found, nor any reference to "heretics" or "schismatics."

Ecumenism Since Vatican II

Following the Vatican Council there were many high-level ecumenical dialogues, including a series between Lutherans and Catholics (1964–2005) dealing with ten major topics and producing major breakthroughs in clarification and agreement. Much common ground was established on the topic of the real presence and the link between Eucharist and sacrifice. In 1999 the two churches published a groundbreaking joint statement on the doctrine of justification, a major source of division since the time of Luther. Here, from their joint exploration of the Scriptures, both churches articulate a common understanding of justification by God's grace through faith in Jesus Christ. Both agree that justification is the work of God through Jesus Christ and that God's mercy can never be "merited." Even the human consent necessary for this justification is a work of grace. Forgiveness can be sought by believers but is ultimately the work of God. As for good works, the sticking point in the Reformation, both churches agree that good works follow justification as its fruits. Both see good works as integral to justification, but only made possible by God's grace. But they still seem to have different perspectives on the role of good works for salvation. The perspectives presented set aside forever the mutual condemnations that were hurled during the Reformation. From now on, Lutheran-Catholic dialogue will begin here and not in the Reformation. In 2006 this document was also accepted by the World Methodist Council.

In this country the Anglicans and Roman Catholics have had more than sixty high-level dialogues on numerous topics. Largely this has resulted in the churches having a much better understanding of each other's beliefs and agreeing to disagree. Recent decisions by some Anglicans to sanction gay bishops, women priests, and same-sex marriages have become serious obstacles to unity. There has also been a strong desire on the part of the Vatican to have closer bonds between the Orthodox and Catholic churches, but the papacy, celibacy, and other issues make it appear that any real unity between the two could be a long way off.

John Paul II and Ecumenism

Pope John Paul was tireless in his efforts to promote both Christian and interfaith unity.

He visited and preached from the pulpits in Lutheran churches in Germany and Sweden. He walked down the aisle of Canterbury Cathedral, shoulder to shoulder and on an equal basis with the Archbishop of Canterbury. John Paul also made many efforts to mend the break with the Orthodox churches. He stood with Patriarch Athanasius, the Anglican Archbishop Carey, and many other Christian leaders and opened the holy doors at St. Paul Outside-the-Walls to begin the new millennium. In 2004 he prayerfully returned treasured relics to the patriarch in Constantinople. Unity was one of his key goals. He even called for a serious study on the nature of the papacy after one of the Eastern patriarchs said: "The one problem standing between us, Holy Father, is you!" In a moving homily on the steps of St. Peter's in 2003, he said: "I renew today [. . .] my full willingness to put myself at the service of communion among all the Disciples of Christ." And on the fortieth anniversary of the decree on ecumenism, shortly before he died, he said that Christian unity had always been one of his top priorities.

Many Protestant leaders have praised John Paul's heroic efforts toward Christian unity.

Bishop Lazareth of the Lutheran Church recalls how this pope moved ecumenism from being a Church appendage to being a vital part of its life and work. He cites the outstanding biblical, patristic, and liturgical studies conducted by Catholics and Lutherans during John Paul's papacy, which replaced the old contradictory formulations with new complementary ones. Such collaboration moves the two churches ever closer to unity. For Bishop Lazareth, the Joint Declaration on the Doctrine of Justification represents a historic breakthrough in Christian ecumenism. When the pope died, the General Secretary of the World Council of Churches praised John Paul for his vision of unity and many efforts toward bridge-building among churches and religions. The general secretary said, "No one has contributed more to the ecumenical movement from the Catholic side since the Vatican Council than Pope John Paul II."

That All May Be One

In 1995 John Paul published a historic document on ecumenism. In it, he begins by remembering the Christian martyrs of all faiths in the twentieth century who gave up their lives for their faiths. He notes that they were our brothers and sisters and are proof that we can rise above our divisions and unite in self-sacrifice. He sadly notes the misunderstandings and prejudices of the past on both sides and calls all Christians to a conversion of heart and a desire for forgiveness and reconciliation. In a rare admission, the pope acknowledges and confesses that the weaknesses and sins in the Catholic Church had betrayed God's plan for unity. At the same time he notes that the power of the Lord can fill the Church with holiness and dedication to live the gospel. John Paul says that the Church should not close in on itself but should be open to the world, and its mission should be a beacon of unity. This unity with God is announced in the Old Testament when God speaks: "I will be their God and they shall be my people," and is the prayer of Jesus before he died: "That they may be one." The pope notes that unity is the will of God and that many Christians long for one visible Church of God. To accomplish

unity is the will of God

this there is a "duty of conscience" for every Christian, and this is the very essence of the Christian community. Church renewal and ecumenical openness are of a piece.

 Student Reflection

"During a trip to Austria several years ago, we were on a train passing through Graz and there was a lovely old lady across from us. She was ninety-two years old and said she was on her way to an international ecumenical conference. She said that she was an 'ecumenist' and had been one since she was a teenager. The main mission of her life had always been to work for unity among Christians. I was amazed because I never knew there was such a thing as an 'ecumenist.' It really opened my eyes to how important this work is."

The pope said that all Christians share a communion with Jesus and share his life. He reiterated that truth and salvation exist in the separated churches and communities. Many have in common their baptism, Eucharist, and devotion to prayer. They are called to the same conversion of heart and can be united in love and prayer. The pope recalled the many times he prayed with Christian leaders in their churches and in his. He called for continued dialogue and renewed effort for unity, not just on the part of experts or ministers but by all Christians. Dialogue is the way to discover that we are all brothers and sisters and that we stand in solidarity in the struggle for freedom, justice, and peace. He called all Christians to be aware of the wonders that God can work in us if we are but open to it.

Interchurch Marriages

Although high-level dialogues have contributed much to Christian unity, interchurch marriages have perhaps made more progress toward mutual understanding and acceptance. From what used to be called "mixed marriages" that were frowned upon by the Catholic Church and held privately, interchurch marriages are now accepted and can be celebrated at Mass or in a Protestant church with both minister and priest officiating. In the past the spouse from another faith had to promise to raise their children as Catholics. Now, out of respect for the other churches, only the Catholic has to promise "to do all in one's power" to raise the children as Catholics, leaving room for each couple to decide how they are to deal with this issue.

Interchurch or ecumenical marriages are no longer looked upon as a problem or risk so much as a challenge, a special commitment to respect and understand the faiths of both spouses. And such marriages have increasingly become more common. Exact figures are hard to determine, because such marriages are lower in the Latino communities and higher in the South where there are fewer Catholics. But it seems safe to say that more than 50 percent of Catholics marry someone outside their church, and that number seems to be growing.

There are numerous reasons why interchurch marriages are becoming more common. First of all, since Vatican II there has been much more regard among Catholics for Protestant churches, because they have been recognized as having religious truth and the means for salvation. In addition, few Catholics grow up in religious "ghettos" as they did in the past. Young Catholics often live in diverse communities, their families are more mobile, and they have more access to travel.

I have found that among students in my marriage course, religion is usually not high on their list when seeking someone to marry. Personality, compatibility, and appearance are often higher priorities. In part this might be because many college-age students are at a time in life when religion might seem unimportant. Or they may have taken a "leave of absence" from religion at this time in their life. I always remind them that after they get married, and especially after having children, religion might take on more importance in their lives. Religion can be an important and vital bonding force in marriage. But the fact remains that at the time of marriage, many young people have things other than religion on their mind, and indeed their faith-life might be quite dim.

Challenges with Families

Spouses in interchurch marriages, through no fault of their own, inherit divisions and disputes that have continued for centuries. The problem is not with their marriage so much as the tension between churches and their lack of finding ways to be one again. And each spouse can bring more than one religion into the marriage. There are often misconceptions, myths, and prejudices within family systems that the couple bring with them into the marriage. Parents of a young Catholic woman were perhaps hopeful that their daughter would marry a "good Catholic boy," rather than one of those Presbyterians. They wanted their grandchildren to be good Catholics who went to Catholic schools. Now they hear that the child is going to Bible class in the Presbyterian Sunday school! Like it or not, such tensions can overflow into the marriage and need to be dealt with carefully.

Marriage counselors tell us that young people in interchurch marriages certainly can listen to their parents' fears and concerns. At the same time the couple has to be clear that it is their marriage and their family and that they have to work it out on their own, just as their parents did. It is important to help the parents of both spouses become familiar with the church that is new to them. A visit to the church that is new to them and a talk with the priest or minister can do a great deal to dispel old Reformation ghosts.

Special attention has been given to the marriage ceremony. Protestants are sometimes sensitive to the devotion to or even the presence of statues or an altar. Catholics, on the other hand, often like "smells and bells," elaborate rituals, and much-decorated churches. So care has to be taken with the setting, the ritual, the songs, and what is said at the homily. Careful planning and consultation about sensitivities are certainly called for here. It might be quite offensive, for instance, to be celebrating marriage as a sacrament with a family that does not believe it is a sacrament, or joining a couple in a sacred union at a Mass where one partner cannot receive the Eucharist. In other words, the ceremony should celebrate the reality here before us, and if the reality is diverse, the ritual should respect the richness of both communities. And, of course, during the years of the marriage, there also has to be sensitivity toward the in-laws with respect to the celebration of feasts such as Christmas, Good Friday, and Easter. Churches often have different interpretations of what these feasts symbolize.

Challenges for the Couple

Some studies have shown that having different faiths puts no more pressure on a marriage than sharing the same faith. Keeping a marriage strong takes enormous effort in many areas besides religion, as we can see from the fact that 50 percent of marriages fail. Being in the same church is no guarantee of success in marriage.

Student Reflection

"My parents are both Catholics and that has always been a source of tension. My mother is a very strict, conservative Catholic, who still goes by the book. She insisted that we all go to Catholic schools and made us go to Mass every Sunday. Dad is casual about it all. He goes to Mass once in a while and wants us to be able to decide for ourselves. The two of them have had some real battles over this."

Experts in interchurch marriages tell us that each couple has to deal with religious issues the way they see them. One university center reports that "the more religion was seen as a strength in marriage, the greater was the likelihood of marital satisfaction." Interchurch couples are advised to make serious efforts to understand each other's religious traditions. It also seems beneficial to attend each other's church services. Many couples in such marriages tell me that praying together is a good way for them to feel religiously united. Somehow prayer seems to transcend doctrinal differences and can be a good way for a couple to feel close. Some couples say that going to each other's educational programs and Bible classes helps them not only understand each other's faith but also gives them interesting things to talk about. Family rituals and prayers can also be an effective way to deepen the faith of the parents and children. Another way to strengthen marriage and family bonds is to do acts of service for the needy, whether it be tutoring, visiting the elderly, or conducting clothes drives. Charity gets to the heart of it all and transcends doctrinal differences.

The children's religious upbringing is usually a serious matter for all couples, but especially for those in interchurch marriages. A lot depends on how seriously each spouse takes his or her faith. A Methodist with little religious background and commitment might not mind that the children be raised Catholic. But a devout Lutheran might be just as concerned about the children knowing the Lutheran tradition as the Catholic is about sharing his or her faith with the children. Each couple has to work within their own context, respecting each other's traditions, seriously communicating, and carefully planning. As the children get older, they too have to be brought into the discussion. Most experts agree that if the children are given no religious background, they will probably end up with no religious identity. As one put it, "Those parents who don't lay a religious foundation for their children are making it easy on themselves, not their children."

Some Red Flags

There are some circumstances where differing views toward religion can be a red flag in selecting a mate. A Catholic who believes that marriage is a sacred relationship where one promises before God to be faithful in a permanent relationship, enters an extremely risky marriage if his or her partner has no faith and does not believe in the values of fidelity and permanence. Moreover, the Catholic partner is entering a sacramental marriage, which if it does not work out, will make it difficult to get a divorce and be free to

charity gets to the heart of it all

marry again. By the same token, to marry someone whose morality allows for drug addiction or spousal or child abuse is to enter into a dead-end situation that is ill-fated from the start.

Finally, what are we to say when both partners in a couple are baptized, want a church wedding (often for the sake of the parent), and one or both do not have the Christian faith? Are they really entering into a sacrament (Catholic view) or a covenant (Protestant view)? Well, according to the Church, once two baptized persons marry and consummate the marriage, they are in a sacramental marriage. Many theologians and also ordinary Christians see a problem with this, for it seems to come out of an older "automatic" Catholic view of sacraments. Some suggest that there be a simple blessing for such a union and that only later, if and when they both have faith, should there be talk of a sacrament or covenant.

Conclusion

As we have seen, in spite of Jesus' prayer for unity before he died, Christians have always been divided. Early separations over Torah obligations, controversies over the nature of Jesus, the tragic split between Western and Eastern churches in the eleventh century, and the horrendous splintering after the Reformation have left Jesus' simple movement divided. And yet, the language of "heresy," "schism," and "excommunication" are gone. We no longer fight wars and kill each other as we did in the post-Reformation period. The Catholic Church recognizes that truth and salvation exist in other churches. The Vatican Council no longer identifies the Church exclusively with Catholicism, but instead says that the Church "subsists" in Catholicism, leaving it open that it subsists in other churches and communities also. For decades now there have been major breakthroughs toward agreement in dialogue, and many Christian leaders have met and befriended each other. In the ever-increasing interchurch marriages, our families are worshipping together, praying together, and experiencing the power of God together. Perhaps never before in history have we been better prepared to return to the center, Jesus Christ, and to live the gospel life as sisters and brothers.

Activities

1. Develop a panel of students in your class from different churches. Compare notes on your beliefs and views about each other's churches.
2. Prepare a discussion on the influence of the "religious right" on politics in the United States.
3. Conduct a survey of ecumenical activities that are happening in your area and in your college or university. Make a presentation in class on these activities and the issues they address.
4. Review the movie *Luther* (2005) and discuss it in class.

Sources

Bagshi, David, and David C. Steinmetz. *The Cambridge Companion to Reformation Theology.* New York: Cambridge University Press, 2004.

Bokenkotter, Thomas. *A Concise History of the Catholic Church.* Rev. ed. New York: Doubleday, 2002.

Holmes, Derek, and B.W. Bickers. *A Short History of the Catholic Church.* London: Burns and Oates, 2002.

Noll, Mark. *Turning Points: Decisive Moments in the History of Christianity.* Grand Rapids: Baker Books, 1997.

Owen, Chadwick. *The Early Reformation on the Continent.* New York: Oxford University Press, 2001.

Spitz, Lewis. *The Protestant Reformation.* New York: Harper Torchbooks, 1987.

5 Interfaith Dialogue

In our global society, one of the greatest challenges for Catholics will be to learn about other religions and to grow closer to the followers of these faiths. In this chapter we offer a brief introduction to the great world religions, discuss the dialogue we have been sharing, and consider the all-important area of religious freedom.

The great religions of the world are quite complex and diverse, and yet they share a simplicity about them, and much that can serve as common ground. They all arise from the human heart's search to understand and for union with the Mystery we call God. The five great world religions have their roots in just two divine revelations: Judaism and Hinduism.

Several thousand years before the birth of Jesus, these two religions had their beginnings in the East: Judaism in the deserts of modern-day Iraq and Hinduism at the source of the Ganges River in the misty Himalayan Mountains of present-day India.

From Judaism arose Christianity two thousand years ago with a young Jewish preacher and healer, who set out to reform his religion. Then Islam began nearly seven hundred years later with a manager of caravans, Muhammad, who received revelations to support the Jewish and Christian revelations and bring them to completion. And there we have one major religious tree, the so-called Abrahamic religions: Judaism, Christianity, and Islam. To understand one without the others is to have only partial knowledge of this major tradition.

The other foundational religion is Hinduism. It began in the lovely mountain passes of the Hindu Kush, with holy men and women singing the praises of Brahman, the God above Gods, the source of all beauty and life. This magnificent religion with all its gods and goddesses, its chants and rituals, its dedication to the sacred circle of life, developed into an extremely diverse panorama of traditions. Then, in the sixth century BCE, a young prince by the name of Siddhartha Gautama set out to discover ultimate truth and had an "enlightenment" that would radically simplify Hinduism. He became known as the Buddha, the Enlightened One, and spent the rest of his life preaching his message of detachment and contemplation as he gathered followers. This is the second great tree of religion: the Hindu religion developing into the Buddhist tradition. We will now look at four of the major religions and discuss the Church's interfaith dialogue with them. We will not give an overview of Christianity here as that is the focus of this book.

Judaism

The Jewish tree of religion begins with a revelation and a call to Abraham nearly four thousand years ago to leave his homeland in Mesopotamia and seek a new and Promised Land known as Canaan. There he would found a new people, a people chosen to be in a special relation or covenant with the Creator of heaven and earth, whose oneness, justice, and mercy they would reveal to the world. Abraham and Sarah had a son, Isaac, who in turn married Rebecca and fathered Jacob and Esau. Jacob tricked his father and stole the blessing of the birthright by impersonating his twin brother, who had been born first (Gn 27). His name was changed to Israel and his twelve sons became the twelve tribes of Israel. Jacob's favorite son, Joseph, was sold by his jealous brothers into slavery in Egypt, where he became a prominent figure in pharaoh's court. Joseph eventually brought his family to Egypt, where they also fell into slavery.

Moses, the most prominent figure in Judaism, was born in Egypt in the thirteenth century BCE. He was saved by his mother from slaughter by the pharaoh, then found by the pharaoh's daughter and raised in the palace. After killing an Egyptian for beating a Hebrew slave, Moses fled to the desert and settled in with the Midianites as a shepherd. In a startling revelation from a burning bush, Moses was called to free his people from bondage. Moses returned to Egypt and led his people to freedom in the Exodus, the central event in Jewish history. Wandering in the desert with his people, Moses then had another revelation, on Mt. Sinai, of the Torah, the commandments to be followed by the chosen people in their covenant with the one God, Yahweh. Moses died as the liberator, lawgiver, and prophet of the Jewish people, but it was given to his brother, Aaron, to lead the Jews into the Promised Land.

By the 800s the Jewish people had established a kingdom in Israel, and there a series of notable kings, Saul, David, and Solomon, built the first Temple, in Jerusalem, in 825 BCE.

Soon after the Temple was completed, Israel was divided into two kingdoms, the north and the south. A series of disastrous conquests followed. In 555 the Assyrians conquered the northern kingdom, and in the next century the Babylonians overran the Assyrians, conquered Israel, destroyed the Temple, and dragged the Hebrews into exile. Around 370 the Persians conquered the Babylonians and allowed the Hebrews to return to their homeland, where they reconstructed the Temple. Then in 312 the Greeks conquered Israel. The Torah was translated into Greek, and in 167 the Maccabees rebelled against their oppressors. In 63 the Romans invaded Israel and during Jesus' life, dominated Palestine. After several rebellions, the Romans leveled Jerusalem, destroyed the Temple, and drove the Jews out of Israel. They would not return until after the Second World War in 1948.

Judaism Today

Like Christianity, Judaism is divided and there are numerous ways to observe Judaism. The three main groups are: Orthodox, Reform, and Conservative. The Orthodox are traditional and do not like to see change in their beliefs or practices. They believe that the Torah and the laws derived from it should not be changed to fit cultures or lifestyle trends. There are different interpretations of the traditions within the Orthodox communities.

Reform Jews

After the many political and social shifts in the eighteenth century, many Jews began to modernize their beliefs and practices. They no longer saw the Torah as divinely dictated and came to believe that their rituals and practices could be adapted to changing cultures. Religious services could be in the vernacular, men and women could sit together, and women could be ordained as rabbis. Sabbath and diet practices were relaxed and traditional prayer garb became optional. These reforms began in the nineteenth century in Germany and then spread to the United States with Jewish immigrants.

Conservative Jews

Among the growing Jewish population in the United States in the late nineteenth century, there were those who were not happy with the Reform movement. Many broke away and formed the Conservative movement, which is a mixture of modern and traditional Jewish traditions. Here, the decision of when to adapt does not rest on the individual conscience as it does with Reform Jews, but on accepted practice as decided by the community. For instance, the community has decided that it is all right to drive to Temple on Sabbath because of modern logistical circumstances.

Religious Practices

Jews gather in synagogues, which have become places for prayer, study, worship, and sharing the Jewish heritage. Members generally call themselves a congregation and are led in Sabbath services by an ordained rabbi and a cantor. The centerpiece in the service is the Torah scroll, a hand-written copy of the first five books of the Hebrew Bible. Other texts studied in the synagogue are the commentaries on the Torah contained in the Mishnah and the Gemara, which together compose the Talmud.

When young Jews turn thirteen, their reaching adulthood is celebrated with bar mitzvah for boys and bat mitzvah for girls. At this time there is a religious celebration followed by a reception.

Shabbat or Sabbath is a special day for Jews, a sacred time and space. From sundown Friday to sundown Saturday, Sabbath is a time to share special meals and prayers with family, friends, and God. Orthodox Jews observe Sabbath strictly, whereas other Jews vary in the ways they observe the day.

The high holidays are important for most Jews. Rosh Hashanah is a ten-day period to repent for one's sins and ask for God's forgiveness. It usually falls in September and closes with Yom Kippur, the Day of Atonement. This is a day of prayer and fasting, the most solemn day of the Jewish year. During this time Jews attend services in their synagogues. These high holidays are marked by the blowing of the shofar, a wind instrument made from the horn of a ram. This period is also considered to be the Jewish New Year.

Another holiday, which falls on the fifth day after Yom Kippur and lasts for seven or eight days, is Sukkoth. Sukkoth commemorates the Jews wandering in the desert for forty years. During this time Jews build sukkahs, or small huts, that represent how their ancestors lived in the desert. Many Jews use this time of prayer to gain a better understanding of their environment and their responsibilities toward it. And there is Hanukkah, a holiday that falls close to Christmas. It is an eight-day celebration of the Maccabees' victory over the oppressive Syrian Greek empire, the restoration of the Temple, and the lighting of the seven-branched candelabra or menorah. During this celebration, candles are lit and special prayers are recited before eating the special holiday foods.

Passover is one of the most important Jewish holidays. It commemorates the Jews' enslavement in Egypt and their deliverance in the Exodus. In the midst of recounting these stories, Jews eat a highly symbolic meal called the Seder. The celebration of Passover occurs in the spring for seven or eight days and involves eating special foods.

Circumcision of Jewish male babies is one of the oldest Jewish rituals. It commemorates the practice of Abraham on himself and the males of his family and represents the covenant between God and his chosen people. Special prayers are said at the event and the child is given his Hebrew name, which he will use at his bar mitzvah, his wedding, and on other religious occasions.

As we have seen, the Jews were driven out of Palestine by the Roman army, and Jerusalem and the Temple were destroyed in the first century. In the centuries following, the Jewish people suffered many brutal persecutions by Christians and were exiled from a number of countries. Their plight culminated in the German Nazi Holocaust during World War II, when more than six million Jews were killed in the infamous concentration camps. Anti-Semitism is still prevalent in many parts of the world today.

 Student Reflection

"This summer I visited Auschwitz and was really shaken up by what I saw. The 'stables' where they kept the people were burned down but you could see their old chimneys for miles around. As you stared at the rubble, it was hard to imagine how human beings could haul a million people out of trains, gas them to death, and then put their bodies on assembly lines to be burned. My whole family was speechless and had to sit apart on benches for a long period before we could even talk to each other."

After the war, the State of Israel was established in 1948 and for the first time in nearly two thousand years, the Jewish people had their own nation.

In 1967 the Jews acquired control of Jerusalem and access was gained to worship at the Wailing Wall, the only remaining wall from the ancient Temple. The State of Israel has been highly controversial since its inception and continues to struggle with the Palestinians, who were displaced when Israel was founded, as well as with its neighboring Arab states.

Islam

Islam began almost two thousand years after the start of Judaism and more than six hundred years after Christianity. In fact, Islam, which goes back to the seventh century, began in support of the monotheism of these two religions, and its revelations are believed to bring the earlier revelations to completion. Islam looks to the Prophet Muhammad for its foundation. Muhammad was born in Mecca, possibly around 570 CE, and stories say his birth was accompanied by signs and portents indicating the birth of a great prophet. Muhammad was orphaned as a child and taken in by an uncle who eventually gave him a job in the caravan business. Other stories tell of the nine-year-old Muhammad being recognized as a prophet by a Christian monk during one caravan trip.

Muhammad was raised in Mecca, which was a bustling place of pilgrimage to the Kaaba, a cube-shaped building that housed the gods and goddesses of pre-Islamic Arab tribes. The Quraysh was the tribe that controlled Mecca and the Kaaba, a lucrative endeavor indeed in view of the custom of all the peoples of the Arabian Peninsula to make pilgrimages there. The concentration of wealth among a few families had broken down traditional tribal morality and led to growing numbers of poor and dispossessed persons in the tribes. The ruling families controlled the money and lent it out to the poor at high interest rates, which led to many being crushed by debt and falling into slavery.

Muhammad's position with his uncle's caravan business protected him from debt and slavery but did not give him enough financial security

Muhammad was born in Mecca

to marry well. He was known to be a handsome man, who was reliable and honest. As a broad-shouldered twenty-five-year-old camel driver, Muhammad caught the eye of a successful merchant, a widow fifteen years his senior, by the name of Khadija. She hired Muhammad to lead one of her caravans, and he did so well that she offered him a proposal of marriage, which he accepted.

Muhammad's wealthy wife gave him financial security and new status in the community, but he felt conflicted over his complicity in the corrupt economic system in Mecca and the dominance of pagan beliefs. He generously gave food and money to the poor and spent time in solitary retreat. On one of these retreats, Muhammad, who was now about forty years old, was meditating in a cave on Mt. Hira when an invisible presence crushed him in an embrace so strong he could not breathe. Almost dead, he heard a terrifying voice say, "Recite!" When he asked what he should recite, the command was repeated, and he was again held in the crushing grip. As the pressure released, he felt the words of a divine revelation stamped in his heart. Muhammad was frightened and went home and asked his wife to wrap him up and help him overcome his trembling. Khadija threw a cloak over him, embraced him, and tried to convince him that he had not gone mad. She stroked his hair and argued that God would not deceive him because he was a truthful and kind man. But Muhammad was not to be consoled, so Khadija sought the advice of a cousin, Waraqu, who had been converted to Christianity and knew the Scriptures well. Waraqu assured Khadija that her husband was indeed a prophet and told her to tell him to be of good heart.

Muhammad was still unsure, and after a long period of silence from God, both he and his wife began to disbelieve. Muhammad was in a deep depression when the presence once again returned in the same violent manner and assured him that he was not a madman, but a messenger from God. Muhammad arose and for the next twenty-three years recited the revelation that would become the Qur'an. He now became the "Messenger from God."

The movement was slow in beginning. In his earliest verses of magnificent poetry, Muhammad revealed that God was not the distant and powerful God that those in Mecca believed in, but a good, merciful, and generous God who loved Creation. Early on Muhammad did not focus on there being one God, but urgently condemned the oppression of poor and told the rich that they had a duty to care for the weak and unprotected. He warned the rich that God would cast them into the fire for their greed and wickedness.

The ruling class in Mecca ignored Muhammad's radical call for social reform, and Muhammad focused on converting his family and close friends. His closest allies were his cousin, Ali, who married Muhammad's daughter, Fatima, and his two legendary grandsons by them, Hasan and Husayn. One of Muhammad's most ardent followers was his dear friend Abu Bakr, who after his conversion nearly went broke buying and freeing slaves and spreading Muhammad's message throughout the city. The prophet soon began to attract followers among young men from influential families in Mecca and also among young women, who had to risk their lives rejecting the traditions of their patriarchal families. Muhammad and his companions now actively preached in Mecca and met little resistance, because they were not yet seen as a threat by the ruling powers.

Three years after the original inspiration, Muhammad's revelation became more radical: "There is no god but God, and Muhammad is God's Messenger." He was now commissioned to preach monotheism and tell his people to turn away from polytheism. Islam, which means "submission to the will of God," was under way.

The oneness of God was not news to the town leaders, for they had heard this from the Jews and Christians. What was different here was that Muhammad was claiming to be a divinely inspired prophet, preaching about the one God with an authority beyond that even of Abraham and Jesus. He was declaring that the Kaaba, where the gods and goddesses were worshipped, was useless. If this were true, then Mecca would no longer be a religious or economic center. Profits would shrink! Now Muhammad had the city leaders' attention, and when Muhammad refused all offers to silence him and began preaching to the pilgrims at the Kaaba, they had to stop him. The leaders began by intercepting the pilgrims and telling them that Muhammad was a sorcerer and a maniac poet who should be ignored. Instead the pilgrims gave Muhammad an ear, and when they went home, discussed this new prophet.

The city leaders now decided to shun Muhammad and his companions by cutting them off with a boycott that barred citizens from trading goods or food with the prophet and his followers. This lasted several months, and Muhammad nonetheless continued their mission when tragedy struck: his beloved wife Khadija and influential protector Abu Talib both died. The prophet was now vulnerable and was publicly abused and not allowed to preach or pray in public. Eventually, after threats to his life, and with a price on his head, Muhammad and his seventy or so followers ended up in Yathrib, a foreign city 250 miles from Mecca populated by Arabs and Jews. The city leaders invited him to stay and to lead them in settling their religious and political disputes.

Muhammad and his companions established an oasis at Yathrib, built the first mosque, and began shaping a new society based on his revelation. This is viewed as year "1" by the Muslims, and the city would be called Medina, the City of the Prophet. Here he was free to preach his revelation, and gradually he formed a new society that went beyond tribal identity. Each member would be protected and though justice would be imposed by retribution, forgiveness and reconciliation were stressed. The community was egalitarian, high-interest loans were forbidden, and instead of heavy taxes, a tithe was collected according to each one's means and then redistributed to the needy. Although the society remained patriarchal, many new rights were given to women, who were seen as equals in the eyes of God. They were to be cared and provided for by men, who were thought to have greater strength. Muhammad also amended the patriarchal marriage and inheritance laws to give women more rights. He allowed polygamy and himself had nine wives, although a number of these marriages seem to have been for political reasons.

Muhammad held that the Torah, the Gospels, and the Qur'an were to be seen in continuity with each other. For him, the Jews, Christians, and Muslims shared a single revelation from God, with the Qur'an being the final revelation. Surprising to many Christians, Muhammad revered Jesus as the greatest of God's messengers and included many of the gospel stories in the Qur'an, including the virginal conception, the miracles, Jesus' messiahship, and his coming in judgment at the end of time.

Later Muslim scholars, however, rejected the connection between Judaism, Christianity, and Islam and called non-Muslims unbelievers or even infidels. They also took the position that the Qur'an was the only true Scripture.

This was the Islamic community that, in the future, would provide varying interpretations of how Islamic society should exist. Extremists, traditionalists, and radicals all have different ideas of what life in Medina was like.

Muhammad and his followers fought a number of battles with armies from Mecca and after executing many Jewish leaders, they were able to retain control of their land in Medina. Muhammad now turned his attention to Mecca and, gathering a thousand of his followers, marched on the city as pilgrims. Caught by surprise and overwhelmed by Muhammad's audacity, the city leaders agreed to make certain concessions if Muhammad agreed to visit Mecca as a tribal leader but not as the Messenger from God. Several years later, Muhammad overwhelmed Mecca with ten thousand men and the city was his. He proceeded to clean out the Kaaba of its idols, which he smashed to the ground. It was now sanctified and declared the House of the One God. But then Muhammad surprised all and returned to Medina, where he established the pillars of the Muslim faith and the foundations of Muslim government. Several years after his return to Medina, Muhammad died.

The time after his death was tumultuous. In less than half a century, a Muslim split occurred that remains today. The governor of Syria usurped power from Ali, the son-in-law of Muhammad, and moved the capital from Medina to Damascus. When Ali tried to found a rival capital, he was murdered. When Ali's son Husayn tried to regain leadership, he was killed, and his head was brought back on a lance and presented on a golden tray to the caliph in Damascus. The followers of Ali, the Shiah, were devastated by this and broke away from the Sunni (the majority of Muslims who follow a leading apostle of Muhammad) and still mourn the martyrdom of Muhammad's grandson Husayn. The country of Iraq is currently beleaguered by conflict between Sunnis and Shia.

The tiny community that began in Medina soon grew into the hundreds of thousands and began to expand militarily. Although Muhammad had led raids on caravans and had easily taken Mecca, he was not known as a warrior. He supposedly allowed war only in self-defense, but lines in the Qur'an about slaying unbelievers and gaining heaven if you are slain in the way of Allah were soon interpreted as grounds for invasion. The Muslims swallowed up the Sasanian Empire (Iran) and then India, North Africa, and the Byzantine Empire. Then they moved deep into Europe through Spain and southern France. Conquest was by revelation and by sword. The wandering tribes with their caravans eventually gained an empire spanning three continents. Arab fleets made the Mediterranean a Muslim sea. By the ninth century, the caliph in Baghdad was the most powerful man in the world.

Jihad

After 9/11 in 2001 came much discussion about the meaning of jihad in the Muslim tradition. The terrorists who flew into the World Trade Center projected one frightening interpretation: a Muslim willing to commit suicide for Allah in order to destroy the infidel enemy and receive an eternal reward. Most Muslims see this as a fanatical interpretation of jihad, one that promotes the stereotype of Islam as a warrior religion, a religion of the sword. They point out that this stereotype was produced by Christian Crusaders and more recently by Arabs struggling against colonialism. And now this fanaticism is embodied in the terrorist strapped with explosives, preparing to become a martyr for Allah.

Islamic scholars tell us that *jihad* does not mean "war." The word *jihad* literally means a struggle or a great effort, the challenge involved in overcoming sinful obstacles to union with God. Primarily, this is the struggle for the welfare of others, and only secondarily, the struggle against oppression and tyranny. The notion of holy war is in fact not Islamic, but comes from the Crusaders. For Muhammad, war was never holy, but could be just to defend oneself and one's loved ones or to fight oppression. The Islamic scholar Reza Aslan points out that when jihad refers to war it presents a primitive "just war" theory. As it developed in Islam, the just war theory forbade the killing of noncombatants and torture of prisoners of war, and included many other restrictions that are now part of international law. War was to be strictly defensive and there was to be no compulsion in the area of religion. This contradicts those who have said that Islam advocates forced conversions or the killing of nonbelievers. It certainly rules out the killing of thousands of innocent people on 9/11.

During the Dark Ages in Europe, Islam shifted from conquest to intellectual enlightenment. Arabs developed mathematics, medicine, astronomy, and philosophy. Averroes' commentaries on Aristotle provided the framework for Thomas Aquinas' monumental *Summa*. The medieval Crusaders learned from Arabs about warfare, chivalry, and magnificent weaving. The pointed arches of Arabia significantly influenced the designs of the medieval cathedrals.

The Qur'an

As the Muslim Empire spread, it became more diverse and open to interpretations of the Qur'an that were more opportunistic than authentic. Thousands of beliefs and practices were attributed to Muhammad that were mere fabrications. For instance, the Qur'an tells believers not to pass on their wealth to the feebleminded. Later commentators changed "feebleminded" to "women and children." One close follower of Muhammad is known to have simply made up the teaching of the prophet that if you entrust your affairs to women you will never get rich.

During Muhammad's lifetime, the Qur'an was not collected into a book. As the prophet poured out his revelation, it was memorized by followers and only the legal issues were written down. After the prophet's death, the message began to appear in diverse versions in Iraq, Syria, and Basra. The followers in Mecca became concerned, and in 650 the caliph authorized a single, binding text, but followers of other Qur'anic texts still claimed legitimacy. Traditionalists do not allow the Qur'an to be translated from Arabic, claiming that these are the words of God and cannot be changed. They also closely monitor interpretations. Traditionalists believe that the Qur'an is direct revelation from God, the actual words of God handed down through Muhammad. It reveals God's self and therefore is not only the speech of God, but actually God. Most Sunnis are traditionalists. Here there is little room for seeing the evolution of Qur'an through culture or free interpretation. At best, the traditionalists allow for the literal meaning and for a hidden meaning that can only be carefully discerned by appointed experts. From this perspective, Islamic tradition is static and absolute. Many see parallels to Christianity's evangelical fundamentalists and with churches that profess doctrines that they see as unchangeable.

More liberal Muslims view the Qur'an as eternal but also the result of human authorship and changing cultures and situations. Here the revelation evolves to meet modern questions. They argue that Muhammad himself amended the revelation as he went along and never authorized a codified book. Rather, he saw the Qur'an as a living Scripture that adapts itself to new situations.

Even today the dispute goes on and some traditionalists have become rigid, often fanatical, about the meaning of the revelation and want to silence those who disagree. In 1990 a professor at Cairo University who said that the Qur'an is both divinely revealed and a cultural product of early Arabia was branded a heretic and forced to leave the country. In 1985 a Sudanese scholar who claimed that the Qur'ans from Mecca and Medina have different historical origins was executed.

More liberal Muslims allow translations and recognize private and diverse interpretations, even those over the Internet! Many Muslim women today are reading and interpreting the Qur'an through feminine eyes. They are able to sift out the liberating aspects of the Qur'an from those that come from the patriarchal norms of the past. Influenced by

most Sunnis are traditionalists

such interpretations, Shirin Ebadi in 2003 won the Nobel Peace Prize for her effort to defend women's rights in Iran. Besides the Qur'an, there is a collection of Muhammad's sayings and deeds in the much-revered Hadith. Many new and fresh interpretations of these are appearing also.

Islam's Five Pillars of Faith

The five pillars of faith are the solemn obligations of Muslims. The first pillar is the confession of faith: that God is one and Muhammad is his prophet. The second is prayer: Muslims are called to prayer five times a day (dawn, noon, late afternoon, sunset, and nightfall). They are called to prayer by a muezzin, who in times past would call from atop a tower. Today the call is usually made electronically. The third pillar is almsgiving to the poor. The fourth is fasting during the month of Ramadan. And the final pillar is a pilgrimage, or *hajj*, to Mecca during one's lifetime.

Current Extremism in Islam

Unfortunately, at the present time those at the radical and often fanatical extremes of Islam have gained center stage. Their interpretations of Islam first formed in post–World War II Egypt, when Britain occupied that country much as it had ruthlessly occupied India in the nineteenth century. In the late 1920s, Hasan al-Banna organized the Society of Muslim Brothers to protest the colonial oppression of Muslims, the rise of Zionism in Palestine, and the wealthy Arab monarchies that were oppressing people in the Arab world. In 1949 al-Banna was assassinated, but his movement grew stronger and his cause was taken up by Sayyid Qutb in Egypt. Qutb and his Muslim brothers were tortured and imprisoned, but from his cell, Qutb wrote of revolution and the founding of an Islamic state that would restore power to God. In 1965 Qutb was hanged for treason, but his followers escaped to Saudi Arabia, then as now a largely radical Wahhabi fundamentalist Islamic state that controls the pilgrim sites of Mecca and

Medina. Here with the wealth of oil, they would become some of the richest men in the world. Soon the Islamic fundamentalists grew hostile to the wealth and influence of the foreign nationals (Britain and America) that were drawn to the oil. In 1991 a small group of Saudi dissidents, led by the now-infamous Osama bin Laden, founded al-Qaeda. The group turned against the Saudi family and wanted to expel Saddam Hussein from Kuwait. They were infuriated when the United States was allowed to intervene in the Persian Gulf War and became a terrorist group that divided the world into "the people of Heaven" (themselves) and the "people of Hell" (everyone else).

Another extremist Muslim group in the news is the Taliban. They first came on the scene as the Mujahidin in the late 1970s and were trained and financed in part by the Saudis and the CIA to oust the Russians then attempting to occupy Afghanistan. In the 1980s the United States supported bin Laden as a "freedom fighter" in Afghanistan. But by 1996 the Taliban came into Kabul, murdered the president of Afghanistan, took over the government, and provided training for the terrorist group al-Qaeda.

Another extreme version of Islam was promoted by Ayatollah Khomeini in his takeover of Iran in 1979. His vision of jihad as a weapon of war spawned the militant Hezbollah and the terrorist suicide bombers now so common. The Hezbollah are now active in Lebanon and have been a destabilizing factor in this war-torn, fragile country. Another group, Hamas, which is now ascendant in Palestine, derived its warlike doctrine from Assam, a professor in Saudi Arabia, who also strongly influenced bin Laden.

It is important to realize that though these radical groups are in the headlines, they represent only a small fraction of Muslims. The majority of Muslims are just as distressed by the violence and destruction coming from Islamic fundamentalists as are non-Muslims. I have friends in the local Muslim community and from time to time have worshipped with them in their mosque. They are devout people, dedicated to their families, and thoroughly opposed to terrorism and violence. They rightly maintain that they represent the majority of followers of Islam.

Hinduism

We have looked at the Abrahamic religions, Judaism, Christianity, and Islam. Now let us examine the other major root of organized religion, Hinduism, and then Buddhism, which grew from it.

The origins of Hinduism go back thousands of years before the birth of Jesus to the area of the Indus River. This religion, the third largest after Christianity and Islam, began with the Aryans bringing the beautiful Veda poems that celebrated the beauties of nature. These poems influenced the religions that were already established in the Indus Valley.

Hinduism centers on one Supreme Being, Brahman, who is manifested in millions of other gods and goddesses. There are three major reflections of Brahman, which represent the three dynamic life forces. They are Brahma, the Creator; Vishnu, the Preserver; and Shiva, the Destroyer. Shiva is a well-known god image, a dancing figure with four arms. He stands on one foot, crushing sin, while one arm bears the drum of creation and another holds the flame of destruction. A figure of compassion, Shiva holds up a hand saying, "Fear not," while with another, he points to his foot lifted in blissful joy. This image of a god, filled with so much symbolism, typifies how Hinduism captures the various aspects of human experience and ties them into divine power. Vishnu is the god of love and has come to earth in human form a number of times. Two of Vishnu's favorite incarnations are Rama and Krishna. Krishna is a loveable hero, and there are many stories about him in Hindu lore. There are marvelous symbolic stories about Krishna defeating demons as a child and becoming a heroic warrior as a young man. These stories, thrilling and sometimes violent, are meant to teach Hindus how to live virtuously. There is Agni, the god of fire, who gives one appreciation for the power of the divine in the sun, fire, and lightning, and Ushas, the dawn goddess, who drives seven cows, symbolizing the sanctity of the days of the week. And there is Chandra, the moon goddess. One of the most intriguing is Ganesha, an elephant-headed, potbellied figure with four arms, attended by a rat and a serpent. This god, whose symbolism points to the many forms of life from the godly to the rat, is the god of success, education, and wealth. Ganesha's bearing, in spite of his fearsome appearance, represents the importance of modesty, and his riding the rat can reveal the power of the mind over desires. The many stories of how Ganesha got his elephant head teach many lessons about life, and children love these stories.

Hinduism is filled with ritual songs and dances for worshipping their many gods and goddesses, who guide them in their search for truth. The Vedas contain ancient hymns and rituals, whereas the Upanishads deal with the philosophy of life and describe how the soul (atman) can be united with ultimate truth (Brahman). The main sacred text of Hinduism is the Bhagavad Gita, which Gandhi once described as "the book par excellence for the knowledge of Truth." The book most certainly had a profound influence on his own search for truth and mission.

Hindus believe that all creatures undergo a process of spiritual evolution that extends over vast cycles of time. A person's lifetime is but one bead in a necklace of past and future lifetimes. Every soul, or atman, passes through a series of rebirths, either ascending through good karma, or descending through bad karma. *Karma* here refers to one's deeds, and these determine how a person will live in the next life. A life of violence and evil results in the soul returning in a body on a lower level, such as that of an animal. On the other hand, a life lived in righteousness, faithful to the true self and human nature, can be liberated from worldly existence and achieve union with Brahman. This path toward spiritual fulfillment is called the *dharma*.

This notion of moving up or down in the hierarchy of life has been connected to the caste system in India. Traditionally, the Brahmin (priests and scholars) are the highest caste, followed by the rulers and soldiers, the merchants and farmers, the peasants, and finally the untouchables on the bottom. These levels of society have resulted in much discrimination and oppression and have been opposed by a number of spiritual leaders. Gandhi, who condemned the practice of untouchability, insisted that all are children of God and saw to it that the Constitution of India forbade this practice. Gandhi justified his position from the Hindu ideal of *ahimsa*, nonviolence toward all living things. He then developed this into a political and social tool, "nonviolent non-cooperation," which in part helped India throw off the colonial dominance of Great Britain.

According to Hindu tradition, there are four stages in a harmonious life. The first is youth, where one assumes religious duties and begins study and service mentored by a guru. The second is that of marriage and devotion to family and the community. The third stage is for detachment from materialism and family and more concern for the wider humanity. And in the last stage, the person prepares the self for death, the passage to the unknown reality.

Integral to all stages of life is meditation (yoga being one form), attendance at temple rituals, and being active in community activities. Key in the rituals is *puja*, an act of worship to one's favorite deity. In the temple ones sees many beautiful statues of the gods and goddesses. The devoted dress these statues in magnificent garments, surround them with flowers, and present food to them, which sanctifies the food before it is eaten. During temple services, there is much community chanting of Hindu songs and many dancing rituals. Meanwhile some simply sit in meditation, while others pay their respects to the statue of their favorite deity. It is in temple that a person encounters "the Existent One" as well as many manifestations of the deity. Families also have such statues and altars in their homes and perform *puja* before sitting down to a meal blessed by the household deity. Because religion is viewed as part of life, there are rituals for getting up in the morning, bathing, eating, and going to bed.

The Ganges River is held to be sacred by the Hindus. When possible, the people of India hope to have their ashes placed in this river. Banares is, for many, a city of pilgrimage. The Ganges turns north here and faces the rising sun. The prayer of the faithful here at sunrise is to be enlightened by the Divine Sun and to die here, where one can break the bondage of rebirth and win eternal rest in paradise.

The closing of the Hindu year is marked on the night of the new moon near the cusp of October and November. Small lamps are lit to frighten away demons. The Hindu New Year is a time to celebrate, with new clothes, special foods, and light as well as serious prayer. It is also a time to settle all quarrels and forgive one's enemies. One of the biggest Hindu festivals is Durga Puja, held in the autumn to honor the mother goddess, the wife of Shiva. She is known under many names: Shakti, Durga, Parvati, and Kali to mention only a few. As Kali, she is associated with suffering from epidemics, earthquakes, and floods. As Durga, she is the loving mother and is honored with offerings, dancing, and a fire ritual. She invites all to come to her as they would their own mothers.

Many Paths to the Same God

Although the Hindu people, like all religious people, have had their prejudices and hatreds of others, their tradition holds that all religions are alternative and almost equal paths to the same God. They teach that we can take the path up the mountain that our culture teaches us, but we are all heading to the same summit. It is important to realize that the path is not God. Those that circle, trying to bring others onto their path, have stopped climbing! Here Truth is one and is called by different names.

The Central Affirmation

Huston Smith, a renowned expert on world religions, says the central affirmation behind their vast literature and elaborate ritual is "You can have what you want." On the face of it, this sounds rather easy—that is, until one asks the key question: "What is it you want?"

The Hindu tradition says we have four wants. The first of these is pleasure. Hindus do not see pleasure as evil; they tell followers to "Go for it!" Hindus often see the West as too puritanical toward pleasure and often too much in a hurry to really enjoy. The Hindu wisdom understands that each person who follows his or her desires will come to ask, "Is this all there is?" Pleasure is too trivial and narrow to satisfy the human heart, and we will come to the point of knowing that there is more to life than pleasure.

Hindu tradition says we have four wants

Once the limitations of pleasure are realized, individuals turn to the second great goal of life: success. Success brings wealth, fame, and power, which not only give personal satisfaction but also bring social recognition. Success can give us a sense of self-respect and dignity.

But success also has its limitations. It can render us defensive, competitive, and cut off from others to protect what we have. It sets us "over and against" instead of "with." In addition, we can never get enough success and become greedy for more. Moreover, success can also lock us into pleasure, into a world that is just too small for the human heart. Finally, success cannot satisfy because it cannot last. And no matter how much of it we have, the stark fact remains that "you cannot take it with you." (And no one can answer in the words of one comedian: "Then I won't go!")

None of this moves the Hindu to advise that these desires be seen as evil or that they be suppressed. Followers should go after them, albeit with prudence and a sense of justice. Still, these desires are to be seen as "toys," things from which we can move on as we mature.

An alternate path for the Hindu is renunciation. Here we don't mean rejection, but rather detachment or even the thrill of a higher call and level of living. The pursuit of pleasure and success no longer satisfy and much misery is found in futilely trying to hold on to them. One is drawn to a larger life where one's ego is renounced. Religion can then become important as a way of serving rather than winning, of giving rather than gaining.

Now the "wants" change: here people want to *be* rather than to *have*, to know the real truth of life, true joy, and pursuit of the infinite. The infinite is the reservoir of being that does not die: the center, the true self, where one is united with the Godhead. The true self is where the inner life touches infinity. As Thomas Merton, the great Catholic writer and bridge-builder between Eastern and Western religions, pointed out, God is found in the true self, where the self is imaged after the divine. He held that to find the true self, one must give up all masks, roles, and pretenses.

Hindu spirituality acknowledges our diversity of personalities and lays out four spiritual paths (yogas) that are linked to the four general kinds of persons. One path is reflective and takes the path to God of meditation, learning, and reflecting on the meaning of things.

Another path is more given to emotion and proceeds along the path of feelings, especially love. Here one gradually transfers one's strong love for things and others to God. Then God is loved as the basis of all. Many Hindus believe that the Christ is such a loving person, but they also see others, Rama, Krishna, and Buddha, in the same light.

A third path is that of work. This is for the active person, given to everyday affairs. Work becomes a devotion to God and is done with and for God. The person becomes an agent for the work of God and says: "Thou art the Doer, I the instrument." One thinks of Mother Teresa, who tirelessly worked for poor and abandoned people and said she was but "a pencil in the hand of God."

Finally, there are those whose path to God proceeds through experiment with the psyche. This path usually attracts those who are inclined to be scientific. Here the person carries out regular experiments in personal patience or overcoming addictions. Through yoga, various experiments are made with the body to control breathing and muscles to move toward inward contemplation. The Bhagavad Gita puts it this way: "Only that yoga whose joy is inward, inward his peace, and his vision inward shall come to Brahman and know Nirvana."

It has been said that the Hindu Temple is itself a metaphor for the spiritual quest. There one finds much beauty in the gods and goddesses, holy food, dance, song, and community. But ultimately all is but an illusion and one must turn inward to find where the human meets the divine.

Recently, I took a group of students to visit the local Hindu Temple and take part in the evening service. We were received with warm hospitality and taken on a tour of the magnificent statues of the gods and goddesses. Our host, the priest of the community, delighted us with stories from the Hindu tradition, and then we were asked to sit on carpets and listen to chants. We were deeply impressed with the gentleness, kindness, and deep spirituality of the members, whose ages ranged from young to old.

Buddhism

Buddhism began about five hundred years before the birth of Jesus. The first recognized Buddha, or Enlightened One, was Siddhartha Gautama (c. 480-400). Although highly revered, the Buddha is not seen as a god, but rather as an extraordinary man. Like so many religious leaders, Gautama was a reformer of Brahmanism, a religion that would come to be known as Hinduism. His followers saw him as a fully enlightened man, a great teacher who was born into the world for the happiness of all. He brought wisdom to the world and helped people to awaken and live fully human lives. He is neither the creator nor the savior, but does embody qualities that other religions associate with God such as boundless love, kindness, compassion, joy, and wisdom. Gautama was not born the Buddha, but became the Buddha through many trials, and his teaching can lead others to do the same.

Records of the Buddha's life do not appear until hundreds of years after his death and are symbolic and interpretive. Because there was no single biography, followers had to gather information about the Buddha's life from a number of sources. Gautama seems to have been born into a privileged family, and his father was a provincial ruler. There are stories of his miraculous birth and accounts of seers predicting that he would renounce the world and become a Buddha. His father was distressed by this and tried to protect his son from all suffering and pain so that he would not renounce the world.

Gautama was seen as a compassionate child, and there are stories of him nursing wounded animals back to health. When he was twenty-one, he married Yasodhara and she bore him a son. His father's efforts to protect his son were thwarted when Gautama's charioteer took him to a park where he saw an old man, a sick man, a corpse, and a meditating monk. The first three taught him that there was suffering in the world, and the monk suggested that there was a way to move beyond suffering.

Gautama was deeply troubled by the suffering around him and began to think that if he were to find a way past suffering, he would have to leave home and plunge into the darkness of the world alone. On the face of it, he seems to be deserting his wife and child, but there are traditions that say they eventually joined him as disciples.

Gautama became one of the many "wanderers" of his time and eventually joined two men who were masters of meditation. When he had learned what he could from them and was still not satisfied, he became an ascetic, living in the forest for six years, fasting, and sleeping little. Eventually he came to realize that he was called to the "middle way," the way between the sensual indulgence he had known at home and the severe austerity he had known as a forest recluse.

The turning point for Gautama came one night as he sat in meditation under a tree. Gradually the truth about the reality of life unfolded for him, and he became fully enlightened, a buddha. It was as though he had climbed to the top of a high mountain and could now see the expanding panorama of reality before him. Buddha not only came to see the truth of life intellectually, he experienced Truth.

For the rest of his years until his death at eighty, the Buddha taught the middle path to others. He began to gain followers, and when they reached enlightenment, he sent them out to teach others. Four different kinds of communities formed: monks, nuns, laymen, and laywomen; the latter two followed the teachings of the Buddha, but remained at home and provided food and other support for the monks and nuns. Monks and nuns left their families and lived a strict celibate life.

Why the sudden explosion of Buddhist followers? Like Jesus' gospel later, the teaching of the Buddha was good news. It invited people to a new and fresh way of living that was liberating. The Brahman religion of the time had become preoccupied with dogma and ritual and with many gods and goddesses. Buddha did not oppose any of this, he just said that they would not lead to the liberation of the human spirit. He bypassed the god-talk, the absolute beliefs, and the elaborate ritual and presented his simple four noble truths, which laid out the path to human freedom and peace. No longer would followers rely on gods to save them. Humans had within themselves the power to move beyond human craving and aversion.

To teach his way, the Buddha lived it. As he traveled he made his way of kindness and compassion accessible to all, especially outcasts. He liked to be in the trenches with people, asking them challenging questions, sharing his wisdom, and visibly showing them how to be peaceful and happy. He challenged the prejudices of his time and called people to move beyond self-centered accumulation to nonviolence and compassion. There are stories of Buddha settling difficult disputes and of his caring for sick monks who had been thrown out of their communities.

The Buddha died an old man, surrounded by his followers and assuring them that he did not need a successor. The teaching and the rules of discipline would see them through. They had all they needed within themselves to reach enlightenment and live a full life of service in peace. As one modern Buddhist woman puts it: "Material goods and position are simply impermanent. They do not last long. The only thing that lasts is inside you. If you have growth in your heart, you can go anywhere with freedom. Nothing can compare with being free from greed, hatred, and ignorance. But it is not an easy path."

After the Buddha's death, a council was called to gather the definitive teaching and rules of the great teacher for future generations. As was the custom at the time, these were all held in memory rather than put into writing. As the teachings spread, they began to develop into different traditions.

Three different traditions of Buddhism developed: the Theravada, which developed in Burma, Cambodia, Laos, Sri Lanka, and Thailand; the Mahayana, in Pakistan, Nepal, China, Korea, Japan, and Vietnam; and Tibetan Buddhism. Theravada Buddhism focuses on the historical Buddha and each individual following the teachings without any help other than from Buddha's teaching. Mahayana allows the mystical presence of Buddha, which can come to the disciple's assistance. Theravada seems more austere in its practice, whereas Mahayana appears designed more for the common person who seeks divine help. Tibetan Buddhism relies on the leadership and inspiration of the Dalai Lama. All three traditions agree that the enlightenment that the Buddha found exists within each person, that each is capable of becoming a buddha. Also common to all is the ancient chant: "I take refuge in the Buddha; I take refuge in the Dharma (teachings); I take refuge in the Sangha (community)."

Teachings of the Buddha

The teachings of Buddha are simple to understand but extremely difficult to live, sometimes taking many lives in the great cycle of life and death in order to achieve. The dharma, or the truth that Buddha taught, was not invented by him. Rather it is the truth of reality that has always existed and which the Buddha realized when he became enlightened. As one Bhikkhu (teacher) put it, the Buddha was like a scientist who discovered the laws of nature. Simply put, the Buddha discovered that suffering is integral to reality and that we can be liberated from it (by attaining enlightenment and nirvana) if we live a good life and purify our minds. The dharma is both a perspective on life and a way of life. It holds that everything in the world is impermanent (*annica*) and that aversion and craving lead to suffering. Health, beauty, friendship, and love are all passing. Only the "soul" or "self" truly lasts. Sickness, old age, death, war, and poverty are disagreeable or unsatisfactory (*dukkha*). The way to freedom from suffering lies in detachment and equanimity and the realization that one cannot control what happens. One must achieve "no soul," or "non-self," whereby one understands the inherent emptiness of all things and thus becomes free from suffering.

The Four Noble Truths

Buddhists see the four noble truths as the summary of Buddha's teaching. The first noble truth is that reality is ultimately unsatisfactory, filled with suffering. Everything is in flux. Nothing lasts, but will be inevitably lost. This is the Buddhist view of reality.

The second truth is that the cause of our suffering lies in our aversion and craving, in our holding on to things as though they are permanent. This ignorance of the nature of reality not only causes pain, anxiety, and grief but also can lead to greed, hatred, and other harmful states.

The third truth is that one can become free from suffering if one eradicates ignorance and the craving and aversion that stem from it. The clinging must stop, and the greed and hatred be rooted out. We must do good actions so that we can be free, happy human beings. Only then can we rise above the cycle of suffering and be free of endless rebirths.

And how does one stop clinging? Through the Buddha's eightfold path. Disciples often look at these paths as the eight spokes in a wheel, leading to the center—nirvana, the ultimate level of enlightenment. Each spoke is a path of "rightness," and together they cover every aspect of human living.

The first path is that of right understanding, which applies to the understanding of reality, a disciplined striving for correct knowledge and wisdom about cause and effect, the constant flux of things, and what is eternal. The second path is that of right-directed thought, or thought that cultivates loving-kindness and compassion rather than greed or hatred. It is thought focused on the holy path, the path of goodness. The third path is right speech, which avoids lying, cruelty, harshness, and gossip. Fourth is right action, which involves abstaining from violence, sexual sin, stealing, and harm to living things; the focus here is on acts of love and compassion. The fifth path is right livelihood, which avoids jobs and professions that harm others, such as fraudulent businesses and selling drugs, alcohol, or weapons. Paths three through five apply to the development of virtues. The last three paths apply to the development of beneficial mental states and are especially applicable to meditation. They are right effort, which directs one's attention away from attachment, hatred, and greed toward a wholesome mentality; right mindfulness, which is the discipline to become increasingly aware of phenomena occurring within and around us; and finally, right concentration, or the deep state needed to best meditate.

The path, though fairly simple to list, is extremely difficult to live. It may take many births and rebirths before a person reaches the inner goal of peace and freedom—enlightenment.

Many Buddhists join the skills they derive from meditation with their commitment to peace and freedom to advocate social justice, peace, and a better environment. In a world where many are caught up in a frenetic round of activity, the Buddhist way of stepping aside, moving within, and encountering the true self is attractive.

Catholics and Other Faiths

The Catholic Church traditionally described people from other religions as infidels, heathens, or pagans. Catholics viewed outsiders either with hostility or indifference and held that "outside the Church there is no salvation." This slogan was first applied in the early Church to heretics or those who did not accept the salvation of Christ. After Christianity became the official religion of the Roman Empire in the fourth century, the slogan was aimed at all non-Christians. It was assumed that the gospel had now been preached everywhere and that those who refused to accept it were rejecting salvation. Several medieval councils even went so far as to condemn those outside the Church, saying they would go to hell. This is what moved a charismatic Jesuit in Boston, Leonard Feeney (1897–1978), to fervently preach condemnation, and to get himself excommunicated for doing so!

In the Middle Ages, Thomas Aquinas posited exceptions to the slogan for those in deserted areas, but the real breakthrough came with the European discovery of the New World. Europeans discovered countless people who had never heard of Jesus. A major effort was made to convert these indigenous people, some at sword point. But one Spanish theologian, Juan de Lugo (1583–1660), dared to suggest that they could be saved by the faith they had in the God of their own religion. His view clearly did not prevail at the time, but it was voiced.

As we have seen in chapter 3, the Second Vatican Council made major breakthroughs regarding other religions. First, the Constitution on the Church extends the meaning of *church* to include not only the Catholic Church but also "all of humankind, called by God's grace to salvation." The council declared salvation is possible for not only Catholics but also all those who "seek God with a sincere heart, and moved by grace, try in their actions to do his will as they know it through the dictates of their conscience." In other words, any person, inside or outside religion, can be saved.

In the document on non-Christian religions, the council recognizes the common heritage that Christianity shares with Judaism and condemns anti-Semitism. It acknowledges the spiritual and moral truths that exist in

in other words, any person can be saved

non-Christian religions and points out their value to social life and culture. Deep respect for Judaism, Islam, Hinduism, and Buddhism and ongoing dialogue and cooperation are strongly encouraged.

Vatican II also made a historic breakthrough with regard to religious freedom. The Church had traditionally held other religions to be in error and therefore without rights. In countries where Catholics were a majority, the Church could suppress other religions, but when Catholics were in the minority, they insisted on equal rights. Fr. John Courtney, SJ, a champion of religious freedom, had earlier been silenced on the matter, but was given a voice at the council and, along with others, produced a historic document. It states: "The principle of the integrity of freedom in society should continue to be upheld. According to that principle, people's freedom should be given the fullest possible recognition and should not be curtailed except when and in so far as is necessary." The Church for the first time declared that religious freedom is a human right.

Interfaith Dialogue

Interfaith dialogue has progressed significantly in the forty years since Vatican II. John Paul II helped lead this progress. As a young person in Poland, he had close Jewish friends and was personally committed to condemning anti-Semitism and establishing good relations with Jews. John Paul II was the first pope to visit a Jewish synagogue in Rome. He lamented the Church's role in the Holocaust and made a pilgrimage to Auschwitz. He visited Yad Vashem, the Holocaust memorial in Jerusalem, and prayed before the Western Wall (Wailing Wall), inserting a note pleading for forgiveness in a crack in the wall.

John Paul II also reached out to Islam. In a 1985 address to fifty thousand young Muslims in Casablanca, Morocco, he said that Catholics and Muslims believe in the same one God and made points that are highly relevant in today's age of terrorism. He said: "Christians and Muslims generally have understood each other badly. Sometimes in the past we have opposed each other and even exhausted ourselves in polemics and war. I believe that God is calling us today to change our old habits. We have to respect each other and stimulate each other in good works upon the path indicated by God." John Paul II was the first pope to enter a Muslim mosque, where he prayed with the people and kissed the Qur'an as he would the Bible. He also visited Muslims in Indonesia and Tunisia, and intervened in wars in Lebanon and Bosnia. He was critical of the Israelis' treatment of the Palestinians and strongly opposed the Gulf War and the invasion of Iraq.

Early in his pontificate, Benedict XVI caused a firestorm over negative remarks he made concerning Islam. In a visit to Turkey, he began to mend fences by not emphasizing the lack of religious freedom for Christians in Turkey, but encouraging Turkey's attempts to enter the European Union and highlighting the great esteem and respect he holds for Muslims. Benedict also visited the famed Blue Mosque in Istanbul and prayed alongside his Muslim hosts.

John Paul met several times with the Dalai Lama, the leader of Tibetan Buddhism, and was on good terms with Buddhist, Shinto, and Zen leaders. On a trip to Thailand, he visited the Buddhist patriarch there and meditated with him before a statue of Buddha. In New Delhi he prayed at the tomb of Gandhi and paid homage to him as a "hero of humanity."

One of the most dramatic interfaith events was John Paul II's invitation to representatives of the world's religions to meet in Assisi in 1986 to pray together for peace. After 9/11, the pope convened another Assisi meeting, in 2002, where the participants prayed together and condemned violence in the name of religion.

John Paul II also had his critics. He was severely criticized by traditionalists for allowing himself to be blessed by a Hindu woman, permitting Hindu men and women to dance at Mass, giving communion to bare-breasted women in Africa, and greeting a voodoo priest in Benin.

In 2000, the Vatican released a document called *Dominus Jesus.* Many welcomed this statement for its strong position on Catholic tradition and its opposition to religious relativism (one religion is as good as another). Others saw the document as a setback for interfaith dialogue because of its condescending posture, its insistence that all are saved only by Jesus, its stand on the deficiencies for salvation in non-Christian religions, and its discussion of other defects in non-Catholic Christian communities.

Since Vatican II, interfaith dialogue and cooperation have been common for the Catholic Church. Officially and unofficially, there have been intense dialogues among church leaders and theologians. Perhaps more important, much sharing has occurred at the grassroots level among churches, synagogues, temples, and mosques as well as among families.

Student Reflection

"We used to take these amazing field trips with our teacher. On Sabbath we worshiped with Jews at a local synagogue. The prayers and readings were moving, and we were surprised to see both female and male rabbis leading the service. The people were hospitable and were eager to share their beliefs and show us their copy of the Torah. Another time we went to a Muslim mosque and were allowed to kneel on the rug for prayer and listen to the readings from the Qur'an. And the most interesting was the visit to the Hindu Temple, where we participated in an evening service where the community chanted and worshipped the gods and goddesses. They told us many stories from their religion. All this really opened my mind to other religions and to all the things we have in common."

Experts tell us there are four forms of interfaith dialogue. First, there is the dialogue of life, where we share our hopes, dreams, and problems with our neighbors in other religions. Then there is the dialogue of action, where we collaborate in actions for peace and justice. Third, there is the dialogue of theological exchange, where we share our beliefs and values with those from other faiths. And, finally there is the dialogue of religious experience, where we join in prayer and ritual, celebrating and worshipping together.

Conclusion

There can be no doubt that in our global era, a time of international co-operation and also of struggle and fear of terrorism, there is a need to understand and respect the diverse religious traditions around us. Much violence comes from ignorance, which causes hatred and bigotry. Respectful dialogue and cooperation can instead seek out the truth and bring all of us to the awareness that we are all children of God.

Activities

1. Over the semester, schedule visits to services at a Muslim mosque, Jewish synagogue, Hindu temple, or Buddhist temple. Ask a guide from the places you choose to tell you about their religion and how to participate in the service. In class following each visit, discuss your impressions.

2. Ask students from your college or university who are of faiths other than Christian to come to your class, share their beliefs, and report on their impressions of being in a Catholic institution.

3. Have teams prepare presentations on such figures as Gandhi, the Dalai Lama, Thich Nhat Hanh, Isaac Wise, Abraham Heschel, and Louay Safi.

Sources

Aslan, Reza. *No God but God*. New York: Random House, 2005.

Bea, Augustin. *The Church and the Jewish People*. New York: Random House, 1965.

Dupuis, Jacques. *Toward a Christian Theology of Religious Pluralism*. Maryknoll, NY: Orbis Books, 1997.

Fitzgerald, Michael L., and John Borelli. *Interfaith Dialogue: A Catholic View.* Maryknoll, NY: Orbis Books, 2006.

Harris, Elizabeth. *What Buddhists Believe.* Boston: Oneworld Publications, 1998.

Harvey, Peter. *An Introduction to Buddhism.* New York: Cambridge University Press, 1990.

Knitter, Paul. *One Earth, Many Religions.* Maryknoll, NY: Orbis Books, 1995.

Robinson, George. *Essential Judaism.* New York: Pocket Books, 2000.

Schoen, Robert. *What I Wish My Christian Friends Knew about Judaism.* Chicago: Loyola Press, 2004.

Smith, Huston. *The Religions of Man.* New York: Harper and Row, 1965.

6 A Sacramental People

Catholicism has always been noted for its symbols and rituals. Catholic services are known for "smells and bells," incense symbolizing worship and bells calling attention to the key moments of worship. Catholics are comfortable with pictures and statues of Jesus and the saints (even of God in Michelangelo's paintings), with wearing crosses and medals, and with elaborate rituals and processions. Recent visits to vast crowds of pilgrims at Lourdes and the shrine to Our Lady of Czestochowa in Poland reinforced this awareness for me.

One bone of contention for Protestants, especially Reformers like Ulrich Zwingli (d. 1531), was the Catholic appreciation for stained-glass windows depicting biblical scenes, statues, and rituals like the Mass. I once visited Zwingli's church in Zurich and was amazed at how bare and empty it was, featuring only the Bible on a stand. For the most part Protestants recognize two sacraments instead of the seven recognized by Catholics, and even these two at times are celebrated in a more minimalistic fashion.

Student Reflection

"I was raised Baptist and have always been taught that Catholics were idolaters. How do Catholics respond to this?"

The Sacramental Principle

Catholics, as well as people from other religions like Hinduism and many American Indian traditions, subscribe to the sacramental principle, that is, that the power of God can be experienced in the visible: in nature, people, material things, and rituals. I have often taken my students to worship at a nearby Hindu temple, and we are always amazed at the many wonderful and exotic statues of ornate and well-dressed gods and goddesses.

One of my friends, who is part Hopi, tells me that his people experience the power of the Great Spirit in the sun, the source of all life. For the Hopi, animals are part of the creative process: a chipmunk planted the seeds that became trees, and a coyote painted the colors in nature. The famous mystic Black Elk, of the Oglala Sioux, prayed to the Great Spirit: "Day in, day out, forevermore, you are the life of things." The Algonquins prayed: "The Great Spirit is in all things, is in the air we breathe. The Great Spirit is our Father, but the Earth is our Mother. She nourishes us; that which we put into the ground, She returns to us."

Other religions like Judaism and Islam prefer God to remain in mystery and though they can experience God in the inspired word and in rituals, they don't allow images or sacraments. When I take my students to worship at a synagogue, we notice that everything is centered on the Torah, which many Jews view as an inspired letter from their Father-God. And when we attend the Muslim mosque, we find only elaborate designs, and the worship service is centered on the Qur'an and prayers to Allah.

Symbols

Catholics believe strongly that the power of Christ can be experienced through symbols. Symbols are an integral part of life. Humans are likely the only creatures capable of making symbols, and we shape them to convey meaning. My granddaughter Marie is five and already she draws a house and stick figures to represent her "mommy, daddy," herself, and her baby sisters, Natalie and Lauren. These symbols show where Marie finds her security and happiness.

Symbols have a power all their own. Language uses words as symbols to convey meaning. Once you have learned a language you know how to use these symbols to convey what you want to say. For instance, the words "I love you" can generate powerful feelings. But if we don't know Spanish and someone says: "*Te amo*," the meaning escapes us. Phrases like "I promise you" or "I forgive you" or "Get out of my life!" can reach deep into our hearts and feelings. And then there are some mysteries of life that are beyond everyday speech, and we try to express them in the highly symbolic language of poetry.

Gestures are also symbols. A kiss can just say "hello" or perhaps be an invitation to intimacy. A hug can express a greeting, whereas a long embrace can express a more serious relationship. A pat on the back or a high five can make us feel proud of our achievements. And, of course, people can be symbolic. A medic arriving at an accident is a powerful symbol of rescue; a firefighter pulling up to a burning home symbolizes safety. A friend who shows up when we are in the hospital symbolizes love and concern.

Symbols have the power to draw us into the mysteries of life and reality. At one time the World Trade Center stood for the power of business and commerce in the United States. Then it was attacked on 9/11 in 2001, and for some time it stood for terror, vulnerability, and human loss. Now the open space where it once stood draws many into memories of loved ones lost, questions about why some people hate us so much, and fears that other catastrophes lie ahead.

On a recent trip to Poland, I observed piles of rubble that drew me into the horrors of the Holocaust. These were the ruins of the crematoria and gas chambers in Auschwitz, which were blown up by the German Nazis in an attempt to cover up their atrocities. They were just piles of bricks, but also extremely powerful symbols of the mystery of evil and human cruelty. They are symbols of the hatred that drove human beings to destroy millions of innocent lives with industrial efficiency. In a room there, one sees countless shoes of the victims, taken off just before they entered the gas chambers. Among these are many baby shoes and shoes of toddlers, as well as artificial limbs and canes! The meaning of all this, I must say, was beyond my comprehension, and to this day I am haunted by the experience of these symbols of death and destruction.

Sounds are also used as symbols to draw us into mystery. Recently I attended the burial of a marine killed in Iraq, the fiancé of one of my students. When *Taps* was played, I was drawn into the mystery of a life cut short and the grief of a lovely undergraduate; I experienced feelings of loss, patriotism, heroism, and the futility of war. I will never forget a similar ceremony when *Taps* was played at the cemetery near the beaches of Normandy. There were ten thousand white markers on the graves of those who died in the 1945 invasion that ended World War II. I was overwhelmed at the sight of the loss of so many young Americans and yet was inspired by their heroism and self-sacrifice. I can remember another sound, that of a siren, as we rushed a friend of mine off to a hospital for emergency surgery. Often when I hear a siren now, I am brought back to that experience and reminded of the anxiety, compassion for my friend, and fear that he wouldn't make it.

And we have our symbolic rituals. A dance can be a celebration of joy at a wedding or intimacy on an evening out. Thanksgiving dinner is a symbolic meal that can draw a family closer and provide a special time to share memories, greet each other with "what's going on?" and welcome new members with hugs.

We surround ourselves with powerful symbols, engagement and wedding rings, flags, photos, souvenirs, songs, all of which can have the power to conjure memories and put us in touch with deep feelings. How many of us wear something around our necks or on our fingers that are treasured symbols of loved ones past and present? The song laments, "You don't bring me flowers any more." The symbols of love are gone and so seems to be the love itself.

It is interesting to note that the word *symbol* comes from the Greek word *syn-ballien*, which means "to put together." It comes from the ancient Greek practice of making a contract or covenant. Each person in the agreement was given a piece of the same object. At any given time they could reconvene and match their pieces to show that each was a part of the original deal. The same applies to our use of symbols today. For a symbol to be effective, there has to be an agreed-upon meaning shared by the participants. Picture a couple celebrating their fiftieth anniversary at their favorite restaurant. They hold hands across the table, and the husband gently fingers his wife's diamond wedding ring. The symbolic ring puts them in touch with the mysteries of their lives together: the love, the struggles, the child raising. The ring has the power to draw them into fifty years of sharing in the covenant they began so many years ago and also gives them hope for more years ahead.

Sacraments, as we shall see, are similar: they are powerful and yet unique symbols that link us with the power of God and with our covenant with others. Sacraments are about communication with God and others. Sacraments are about community with God and others. And these profound and powerful symbols are concerned with propelling us into a way of life and action for others.

Religious Symbols

It has been said that we humans are religious by nature, that is, that religion has always been part of human culture. Studies in anthropology seem to bear this out. The root in the word *religion* is *religare*, which means "to be tied into." Humans have always been tied into the mysteries of the sacred, into the ultimate, in many cases into relationship with divine beings, or if you will gods.

As far as we know, people have always used symbols as a way to connect with the divine, to enter into the power of the gods. High in the Swiss Alps, altars and animal remains that date back to 180,000 BCE have been found in caves, suggesting that sacrifices were made in thanksgiving to the god of the hunt. Similarly there are thirty-thousand-year-old drawings in caves in France that suggest rites were performed to the "master of animals" to insure animal fertility and hunting success. The Masai, an ancient tribe that still dwells in East Africa, perform dances and processions to their god, whom they believe is manifested in the rain, the lush grasslands, and the lion. They make long pilgrimages, fasting along the way, to commune with the red god that they believe dwells in a volcano called Oldongo L'Engai. Today mosques, temples, churches, and shrines abound around the world, and countless religious symbols, including the crescent, the Star of David, and crosses, are used by a broad diversity of religions.

Jewish Symbols

Jesus, as we know, was Jewish, and his movement began as a reform of Judaism, so Jewish symbols are a part of the Christian system of symbols. For instance, the Jewish menorah, the candelabrum symbolizing that Israel is to be "the light unto nations," finds its counterpart in Christianity in the altar candles symbolizing that Jesus is "the light of the world." Shabbat, the Jewish day of rest and worship, is parallel to the Christian Sunday. The Passover Seder supper, commemorating the saving of the Jewish people from slavery in Egypt, finds its counterpart in the Mass in memory of the saving power of the cross. One of the oldest images of Jesus is that of the good shepherd, which ties his gospel image to that of the shepherd who became King David.

countless religious symbols are used

There are many symbols in the Hebrew Bible that are significant to Christians: the garden of Paradise, with the tree of knowledge, the eating of the forbidden fruit, and the snake; Noah's ark, the flood, the dove, and the rainbow; the burning bush, commandment tablets, manna in the desert, and the pillar of smoke; the temple with its altar, tabernacle, and the scroll containing the inspired Word of God. These were all Jewish symbols that drew the chosen people into the mysteries of their covenant with their god, into the mysteries of the creator and savior. These symbols eventually became part and parcel of the community that followed Jesus and were used to experience the power of the risen Jesus in their midst.

The Christian Sacraments

The closest Greek word to *sacrament* in the Scriptures is the word *mysterion*, which means the hidden plan of God to save the world, hidden in that it is difficult for humans to know or understand the will of God. Christian symbols draw us into this saving plan, into God's saving grace. In the Eastern Church sacraments are still referred to as "mysteries." The Latin word *sacramentum*, from which our word *sacrament* comes, was first used in a religious sense by Tertullian in the third century. He borrowed the term from the oath a Roman soldier made to be faithful to the emperor. Tertullian saw a similarity with baptism, where the convert in a sense takes an oath to be faithful to Jesus Christ. Augustine (d. 430) was one of the first thinkers to develop a theology of marriage and viewed marriage as a sign of God's grace. Aquinas (d. 1274) further enlarged our understanding of sacraments by describing them as signs, "instruments" if you will, that contain and cause the grace of Christ's saving action.

Aquinas' thoughts on sacraments eventually came out in the definition of the famous *Baltimore Catechism,* by which many of your grandparents were trained. Ask them what a sacrament is and they will probably be able to tell you: "An outward sign, instituted to give grace." Unfortunately, this "instrumental" approach often made it look like sacraments were "things."

Grace also was often thought of as a material "thing." This approach to sacraments was often mechanical, even cartoonish, and could at times approach the magical. For some, the sacraments were seen as huge pipes through which God's grace flowed into the soul. Small wonder why many simply lost interest in sacraments.

Contemporary approaches to sacraments have drawn from rich recent studies on language, symbols, culture, and religion as well as from new insights into Scripture, myth, and ritual. A major contributor has been Edward Schillebeeckx, OP, who describes sacraments in more intimate and personal language: sacraments are "encounters with Christ." He begins by describing Christ himself as the ultimate sacrament, the visible symbol of God's presence in the world. Sacraments, in turn, are visible encounters with Christ and thus with all his graces and powers. Along with seeing sacraments as dynamic encounters with Christ, theologians began to present a richer understanding of grace. Instead of seeing grace as mere "help" or as some kind of supernatural serum that was injected into us by the sacraments, modern scholars began to speak of grace as "the life of God," "the power of God," or "the energy of God." Here the actor in the sacramental encounter is God (Jesus Christ), sharing his saving life with us, moving our lives with divine energy. And the amazing thing is that God's grace is freely given (graciously), free of charge (gratuitous). Here sacraments are viewed as powerful symbols where we can have free access to the blessings of God and be more closely connected with God, other disciples, and indeed with all people.

Here is the hitch. None of this comes about automatically or by some kind of magic. Persons of faith must accept the grace of God in Jesus Christ, as they open their hearts to this life and energy. Hearts and lives that in faith are open and receptive, can receive new life and power from God. In this light, a sacrament can be a gift and privilege.

Sacraments, then, are powerful religious symbols, and Catholics believe that they can be deep experiences of the power of Jesus Christ. We can experience his welcoming friendship at baptism, the sealing of this relationship in Confirmation. We can know his nurturing and strengthening power in Eucharist. People experience his forgiveness in penance and his healing in the anointing. They can be made special sharers in his priesthood in ordination and be joined with him and their beloved in marriage. These are "the seven," and they are pillars of the Catholic experience of God and Jesus.

Baptism

For those baptized as adults, the experience is usually memorable. It was an important decision in that person's life and generally involved some kind of conversion. Much preparation was required, sometimes several years. The ceremony, which is the Church's initiation rite, is usually held at the Easter Vigil, where the community is celebrating the all-important resurrection of Jesus. The candidate is surrounded by family, friends, and a large community, intent on the ritual. Solemnly the person is washed with the waters of baptism, anointed, dressed in a white robe, and applauded by the community. The whole experience makes it quite apparent that this person is celebrating his or her new relationship with Jesus and his Church and will now be committed to the gospel way of life.

 Student Reflection

"I was raised a Methodist, but went to a Catholic high school because I wanted to play baseball there. At the school, I met a priest who was a teacher and helped coach the baseball team. I was really impressed by the priest and enjoyed the Masses he offered before the games. One day at Mass I said to myself, 'I want to be a part of this community—I want to be a Catholic.' After a year of instruction, I was baptized. I felt that this was really right. It was a deep spiritual experience for me."

Infant Baptism

Many Catholics are baptized as infants and therefore have no memory of the event. It is a sacrament that celebrates the new life, its covenant with

Jesus, and the initiation of this baby's life into the Christian community. Just as the baby, without realizing it, has already been introduced into a family, a nationality, and the human community, he or she is now introduced into the discipleship of Jesus.

The baby can certainly experience the care and love of its family. But the religious experience is profound for the parents, family, and parish. In faith they are witnessing the life and energy of God in Jesus touching this little life and are committing themselves "to be there" for this child in his or her search for God.

The Sacrament of Baptism

Like all things Christian, it all begins with Jesus Christ. He is the center of Christian life, as the savior, role model, and source of life and energy. It all began with people following Jesus as disciples and promising to live his gospel way of life, a way of love, forgiveness, mercy, compassion, prayer, and justice. Jesus, then, lives as the central symbol (sacrament) of God's gracious presence among his people, creating them and sustaining their physical and spiritual lives.

The main symbol in the sacrament of baptism is water. Water is so basic to our life. They say our bodies are made up of 79 percent water, and two-thirds of the earth's surface is water. Water is necessary for all life, including human life. Water nourishes; water sustains and cleanses; water also kills.

Given the importance of water, it is not surprising that it is an important religious symbol for spiritual cleansing, renewal, and rebirth. Washing the head of the new candidate is part of the ritual to initiate a new Buddhist monk. Muslims use ablutions to cleanse themselves for prayer. Hindus take ritual baths in the sacred Ganges River, and many have their ashes placed in these waters.

In Judaism, the religion of Jesus, water is used in creation stories to symbolize new life; the great flood symbolizes how sinners bring death upon themselves and how God saves the faithful. The Hebrews are saved crossing the Red Sea, while their enemies are destroyed by the same waters. The Hebrews then find freedom and their own land by crossing over the Jordan into the Promised Land. Ritual washing plays a large part in Jewish practice and ceremony, and bathing is the rite practiced to bring a Gentile into the Jewish faith.

Christian baptism seems to find its roots in the baptism of Jesus by John the Baptizer. Mark, the first gospel writer, tells his story in highly symbolic fashion. Mark begins his gospel with Jesus' baptism. John, who seems to have been a teacher and mentor to Jesus, was a rugged desert hermit. He came to the Jordan to call his people to repent their sins and lead them into the river to receive a ritual cleansing. John is portrayed as one who is preparing the way for Jesus by using his unique rite of baptism. Jesus comes to the river, stands in solidarity with those who want to change their lives, and accepts baptism. Suddenly, the Spirit of God comes to Jesus, and a voice from above is heard to say: "You are my beloved Son, with you I am well pleased" (Mk 1:11).

This historic, yet highly symbolic, story is written in the light of resurrection faith and reveals much about the early Christian beliefs regarding Jesus and his baptism. First, John's testimony shows that Jesus will baptize with the Spirit of God. When Jesus comes, he enters the water as a genuine human person, in solidarity with those coming for repentance. Jesus' baptism is an occasion where he realizes more than ever that he is loved by his God and, like every person, has a unique calling in life. Immediately after his baptism, Jesus withdraws to the desert where he is tempted like all of us. When he hears that John has been executed, he now knows it is time to begin his own mission to preach repentance, to heal, and to proclaim the presence of the kingdom of God. Immediately after that, Mark has Jesus begin to choose his followers and promise them that they will be "fishers" of people.

In this brief biblical story, Mark presents in miniature the main meanings of baptism. At the center is Jesus, the beloved Son of God. Baptism is a summons to repent for sin—literally to "retrace our steps" and return to the right path. Baptism is the free and gracious gift of God's grace and love. It is God's invitation to join the kingdom where love, mercy, and compassion reign and to join the Church, the people who promote the kingdom. Baptism is all about our own personal mission in life, where each of us uniquely spreads the gospel message in word and action. Let's examine each element of baptism in more detail.

Jesus. Often when I talk with students about being a practicing Catholic, we get into topics like going to church, learning doctrines, agreeing or disagreeing with the official church, even whether or not they like their pastor. While these are all issues connected to Catholicism, none of them is at its center. The center is a person, Jesus Christ. It all started when people answered Jesus' call to follow him, to relate to him as a close friend, to accept his gospel teachings, and to follow his way. They came to believe that Jesus was their God and Savior.

Of course, everyone is born as a child of God and receives life and being from God. But baptism is a new offer: to intimately relate to God through Jesus, God's Son. Baptism is a powerful symbol of God's power to shape the life we have received into a new life, a life with Jesus as friend, teacher, and healer. Baptism links us to Jesus and his community. So walking with Jesus of Nazareth, and enjoying his presence and power in our lives, is at the heart of what it means to be Catholic. Early Christians spoke of their new sect as "the Way." They were committed to a new way of life, one that was loving, merciful, forgiving, with a passion for peace and justice. So if we want to discuss practicing Catholicism, these areas are first and foremost.

Repentance. The word *repentance* is often a turnoff. It usually conjures up images of revival tent meetings or TV evangelists urging their listeners to turn away from their sins—and send money. But we can't dismiss the word that easily, because *repent* was one of the first words out of Jesus' mouth. The word comes from the Greek word *metanoia*, which literally means "beyond the mind," or we might say "getting a new outlook on life." It means changing our perspective, our direction, and goals. It means stopping, and then going in a new and more positive direction. It is not about beating our breasts, or guilt trips of wearing sackcloth and ashes. Repentance calls us to turn ourselves around and look for new horizons where we will find true happiness.

The most recent example of repentance for me was one of my students (we'll call her "Annie"), who experimented with crystal meth over the

Christmas break. She began hanging out with a drug crowd, and when they partied they got high on meth. Annie immediately got hooked and meth took over her life. She couldn't sleep, ate little, and began to look like a different person. She finally ended up in a homeless shelter and had it not been for one of the staff persuading her to get in a program, she probably would have died.

Annie spent three months in a recovery program, which was extremely difficult for her. Now she is out and for the time being is clean, but has tremendous urges to go back to her friends and get high again. Annie says that her twelve-step program is what keeps her going. She had to admit that she couldn't do this on her own, but had to turn herself over to the care of a Higher Power. She had to admit her addiction to herself, her God, and others and ask God to remove the defects in her that led her to drugs. She had to make amends with the people she had harmed and spend time in prayer and meditation to get closer to God and discover God's will for her and seek the power to carry that out.

Annie shows us what repentance is all about: turning to our God as the only way to overcome our defects and resolving with the help of God to take a new path in life. Baptism, similarly, is a symbol that a person recognizes his or her wrongdoings and sins and wants to "be made clean" by the power of God.

This might be helpful in case of adult baptism, but what about the baptism of infants who have nothing to repent? Traditionally, infants were thought to have original sin and had to be washed clean of this if they were to be saved. Today original sin is explained as the human inclination to sin. The baby is certainly born with human weakness and will in time give in to temptation. Baptism, of course, does not take this away, but it does act as a symbol that when the child eventually does need the help of God in facing evil, that help will be there—guaranteed. Baptism also demonstrates that the child is (we hope) surrounded by family and friends who will show up when the child is in need and will serve as role models.

Amazing Grace. Sacraments are a source of God's grace and blessings. Grace is the life and energy of God, which is shared with every child that is born. And we know that grace is abundantly available to everyone. The teen who tells his parents that he does not have to go to church because he can pray for God's blessing in the woods is right. The person who says that she does not have to tell a priest her sins in order to be forgiven is correct. God's life and blessings are available in many ways other than in the sacraments. In Paul's letter to the Romans, he says: "They are justified freely by his grace" (Rom 3:24).

And yet, for Christians, the sacraments have always been valuable because they symbolically promise an abundance of God's grace. The celebration of sacraments provides unique experiences of God's blessings at key moments of our lives. Of course, we can be one with God and Jesus as we pray at a family meal, but gathering with our family around the table of the Lord for Mass and communion can be a much more intense experience of communion with God. Yes, we can confess something we are sorry we did to a friend and be forgiven. But to celebrate the sacrament of penance with a priest that we trust and who listens, counsels, and prays with us can be a deeper connection to God's forgiveness. And we can take our beloved to the beach and exchange vows, but if we solemnly join our faith and vows before God in the sacrament, the experience can be much more profound.

In the sacraments, it is God who acts, enlivens, and gives. The word *grace* means "gift," and in the sacraments, God's life and power is given freely, gratuitously (if you will), and in abundance. All we need do is open our hearts in faith to it all.

Baptism is the beginning of this new, graced life in Jesus and his community. This way of life has its diverse attractions. In the case of Dorothy Day, she was drawn to the faith by those she saw in churches on her way home from the bars at night: they sat silently in the dark communicating with their God. She wanted that in her life. Gandhi, although he never became a Christian, was attracted to Jesus because of

the word *grace* means "gift"

his teachings on nonviolence. Thomas Merton, one of the leading spiritual writers of our time, left a party-going life and joined a monastery because he was attracted to the Catholic ways of prayer and service to poor people.

Thy Kingdom Come. As we saw earlier, the kingdom or reign of God was central to Jesus' teaching. Baptism is the sign of being a part of the kingdom, the place where love, compassion, and justice reign supreme. Baptism symbolizes becoming a part of the community of people, the Church, which is committed to those values. The Church should be a living and active symbol (sacrament) of these values. As a young woman who was raped and killed for helping Archbishop Romero in El Salvador once said, "The Kingdom of God is not in the sky somewhere. It is here among our people. We help God strengthen the kingdom when we struggle for peace and justice."

Not everyone chooses to be a part of a church or organized religion. In the United States, only about half of the population is so affiliated, and yet more than 90 percent say they believe in God and pray on their own. In some countries in Europe, the numbers of people who belong to a religion are quite low: 10 percent in France, 15 percent in Spain and the Czech Republic, 30 percent in Germany. Only Poland, with 85 percent, has a high percentage of participation in religion. Many people today say they are spiritual, but not religious. They choose to be on their own where religion is concerned.

But baptism does not symbolize going it alone. Baptism is about community. It's about belonging to a movement of disciples, accepting their tradition, learning from their Scriptures, celebrating their rituals, and living a specific way of life with others and for others. By definition, the baptized are an *ecclesia*, a specific gathering of God's people who live and act as a living symbol of God's power and presence.

And Church is much more than the hierarchy, the clergy, or the Vatican. The Church is a people. Church "happens" because, as Jesus promised: "For where two or three are gathered together in my name, there am I in their midst" (Mt 18:20). My most recent experience of this was during a late-night discussion with some of my students about how difficult it is today for young people to belong to a church. Suddenly we realized that in fact this *was* church happening right here in our midst. One of the students suggested that we join in prayer. Church can happen with your friends, in your family, at school, in your parish, and even worldwide as you reach out to help those in other countries. Baptism is about becoming a part of that community that celebrates the presence of Jesus and his power.

Mission. "What is your purpose in life? Why were you put here and what are you to accomplish?" Anytime I ask this, people look up and get quite serious. From time to time throughout our lives, we ask this ultimate question. No matter what job or career we have pursued, no matter how successful or not we have been, the question constantly returns. We all struggle to somehow get it right before we pass on.

Baptism helps us shape our answer. We are called to live lives for others, lives of love and caring. That is the purpose of life deep down. We are called to lives intimately caught up with our Creator and with others. Baptism provides a role model and friend to accompany us in Jesus. It gives us a road map for the journey in the Gospels. And it offers us a supportive community. Now that doesn't mean our question about what we should do with our lives is fully answered. We still have to search for our individual calling, our destiny. But baptism does give us a framework, a blueprint, a context in which we can work out how to best use the few moments in time that we have to make a difference.

Confirmation

The sacrament of Confirmation has a checkered history in Catholicism. In the early church, the initiation rite into the church was water baptism, an anointing with oil, and the reception of Eucharist. As Christianity spread, the anointing gradually got separated from the baptism and was reserved for the bishop to perform later on. Soon Confirmation took on a life of its own and became separated from baptism, a sort of rite of Christian adulthood or even a sort of "knighting" ceremony to don people "soldiers of Christ."

This has all changed since Confirmation was renewed and once again integrated in the Christian initiation of baptism and Eucharist. Now this sacrament, plain and simple, is viewed as a "confirmation" of baptism. Especially for those who have been baptized as infants and had no say in the matter, it is an opportunity to step up and agree to the baptismal vows and commitment. It is a time to say: "Yes, I know what it means to be a Catholic, and have lived as one for some time. Now I want to complete my initiation into the Christian life and say 'Yes' on my own."

But there are still problems. For many, Confirmation is celebrated in junior high or high school at a time of searching and questioning. Many lack the maturity or even the desire to step up and accept baptism. For many young people it is seen as a forced march under pressure from parents and peers, a commitment that soon becomes a vague memory. Many believe therefore that the Church should delay Confirmation to a later age, when there is sufficient maturity and a real desire to accept baptism

For the time being, Catholics make the best of it. They try to prepare the young people as well as possible and be satisfied that for many, the sacrament is at least a choice to ask for God's help to get through the often tumultuous years of adolescence. The sacrament symbolizes God's love and power at a time when the young Catholic needs it the most. Later we hope each will become more mature and able to make his or her own commitment to the Catholic faith.

Marriage

Many college students are apprehensive about marriage. They see the statistics that half of first marriages end in divorce and two-thirds of second marriages end the same way. Often they see how their parents have failed at marriage, and they have experienced the wreckage that can follow divorce. Or they have experienced the serious challenges that exist for blended families. This reality of marriage today has moved many young people (and older people as well) to simply live together. It has also caused many to wait until they are much older before they even think of marriage.

In spite of all the apprehension, most people still fall in love and want to be married to their beloved forever. Most young adults still want to get married in church in solemn ceremony and exchange their vows (which they generally take quite seriously) before the altar. At times this is for the sake of their parents, but still most young Catholics realize that there is some religious meaning to their marriage and pray they will be happy with their partner. They might even have heard that their marriage is a sacrament and have some vague idea of what that might mean. I say "vague" because it is not easy to understand the sacramental dimension of marriage.

Some Historical Background

The Catholic tradition on the sacrament of marriage has evolved over centuries. Since Jesus was a Jew, the Hebrew Scriptures provided the basis for Catholic thinking about marriage. For the Jew, marriage was a family matter, arranged and carried out by the family. It was not associated with the synagogue, temple, or priesthood. Genesis, written about 1000 BCE, shows that the Hebrews believed that marriage and procreation came from the hand of God. But they also realized that marriage had its dark side: they knew violence, abuse, incest, and infidelity were part of the human experience of marriage. The Jews allowed for divorce, but the right to request divorce was largely given only to the husband.

The ancient Jews did not accept the views of other religions around them that marriage mirrored the wedded gods with all their sexual antics and orgies. Nor did they view marriage as part of "the Holy." It was among God's created things, a place where one could share in God's blessings and creative powers. The Jewish prophets used marriage as a metaphor for the covenant between Yahweh and the people. Yahweh's willingness to forgive the infidelity of the people was often paralleled with the unconditional love of spouses. The Song of Songs celebrates the joy and fulfillment of sexuality and love.

for the Jew, marriage was a family matter

Jesus, the Jewish Reformer

Jesus, a devout Jew, set out on a mission to reform his religion and restore what he believed to be the authentic Hebrew traditions. In Mark, he is asked to take a stand on the heated controversy about the reasons for which a husband may divorce. Do the reasons have to be serious (Shammai's view) or can they be ordinary and everyday, like serving poor meals (Hillel's view)? Jesus seems to reject both views, which give few rights to wives. He quotes the Torah: "the two shall become one flesh." Then he takes a strong stand for the permanence of marriage: "What God has joined together, no human being must separate" (Mk 10:9). Matthew, written a generation later, describes the same teaching on divorce, but includes one exception: "unless the marriage is unlawful" (Mt 5:32). The exception reveals the diversity of traditions already developing in Christian communities, and the meaning of this exception has been debated over the centuries.

The Gospels reflect early Christian attitudes toward marriage. The nativity stories reveal Jesus as coming from parents who are loving, faithful, and courageous. John's gospel places the first of Jesus' miracles at a wedding feast at Cana. Paul generally reflects a patriarchal and somewhat tolerant view of marriage, and in the letter to the Ephesians (likely written by a disciple of Paul), the spousal relationship is likened to the covenant between Christ and the Church.

The early church held on to Jesus' value for marriage over and against Gnostic notions that marriage and sex were evil and Roman notions that marriage could be easily agreed upon and just as easily dissolved. The early church also struggled with pagan practices such as sexual orgies directed toward the gods and the acceptance of promiscuity. Often this led Christians to extremely conservative views on sexuality and to value virginity over marriage.

Augustinian thought helped form the basis for Catholic thinking on marriage and sex. Augustine opposed those who said marriage and sex were evils to be avoided and stressed that both are created by God and are therefore good. He wrote about the three "goods" of marriage: fidelity, children, and sacrament as a symbol of God's grace. At the same time, Augustine believed that sex had been tainted by the Fall and is therefore sinful even in marriage. Only procreation could justify sex.

As Christianity became accepted in the Roman Empire and then adjusted to later cultures of conquering tribes, there was little theological development with regard to marriage. It was not until the Middle Ages that marriage was actually declared to be one of the sacraments. Medieval church law dealt extensively with marriage, but did not view it as having the dignity of priesthood or religious life. Rather than being seen as a true vocation, marriage was for those who did not have a vocation to a life of celibacy or vows.

By the Reformation, the Church's view of marriage as a sacrament was challenged on all sides. The reformers denied that marriage was a sacrament under the jurisdiction of the Church and allowed for divorce. Rome took a strong, rigid stand for the sacramentality of marriage and against divorce. These views prevailed for centuries. In modern times, the views of Pius XI (d. 1939) were quite influential on Catholic thinking; marriage had a twofold purpose: (1) for the procreation and education of children, and (2) for mutual help and as a remedy for concupiscence (lustful inclinations). Though the pope had mentioned the value of partnership and love, those elements seldom made it into the instructions given to young Catholics.

The Second Vatican Council renewed Catholic thinking on marriage. Marital love was placed at the center, and procreation and mutual growth were set in this context. The council described marriage as a "community of love," an intimate partnership, and an authentic Christian vocation. It emphasized that marriage is a dynamic reality created by the two partners through a mutual giving of love and sharing of life. The grace of marriage is not thought of as help to avoid adultery and control lust, but as the living presence of Christ, needed to carry out a genuine vocation and call to holiness. Moreover, sex was no longer viewed as allowed for the sake of children, but as an integral way to nurture married love.

For Catholics today, marriage is much more than a legal contract; it is a symbol of Jesus' presence, gracing the couple with God's power. When marriage is a sacrament, the husband and wife join their faith together.

The couple wants their marriage to stand as a living symbol (sacrament) of their love for God, for each other, for the children they might have, and for all those they might touch with their lives.

Marriage is an unusual sacramental symbol because it is not a material thing like water, wine, bread, or oil. Here the symbol is the relationship between the couple themselves, the joining of two people's lives and their faith in God in a sacred union. Strikingly, the couple is the minister of this sacrament, not the priest. The priest is only a witness to their celebration of the sacrament of matrimony.

Marriage for Young American Catholics

Young Catholics often don't have such lofty things in mind when they choose to marry. They decide to marry because they have fallen in love. Romantic love, with all its emotional, chemical, and personal elements, is required in our culture before marriage would even be considered. Moreover, friendship is for many a prerequisite. Young people today want their mates to also be their trusted best friend, with whom they can share their lives. Children are not necessarily part of the equation. The personal elements of marriage are therefore much more important than the legal or religious aspects. For many, the Catholic and sacramental dimensions are rather vague. More that half marry someone who is not Catholic. Many young Catholics also choose to live together prior to marriage, in part to insure that all of these personal elements are really in place before they make a commitment.

The area of faith is also problematic for many young Catholics. At their stage of life, they are perhaps "on leave of absence," neither attending church nor too sure where they stand with regard to Catholicism. Often they agree to a Church wedding more out of tradition or respect for their parents.

Given all of this, one has to question whether many young Catholics really understand or even want the sacramental dimension to be a part of their marriages. Some advocate an alternative ritual for such young Catholics, one more suited to their mentality, where only later would they be asked to consider whether or not they wish their marriages to be sacramental.

Many suggest that the Catholic Church rethink its position on marriage in terms of present-day realities. Considerable money and effort is given to an annulment process that is used by only 10 percent of Catholics who get divorced. Often minimum resources are given to the all-important marriage preparation, and little if any provision is made in Catholic parishes for the pastoral care of marriages. Many Catholic couples quietly go their own way with regard to the use of artificial birth control, knowing they are not following the official position of the Church. Catholics who divorce and remarry without annulments, instead of being pastorally cared for, are alienated by being forbidden communion. These issues and many others such as child abuse, domestic violence, affairs, and consumer debt should be urgent pastoral concerns for the Catholic Church.

Holy Orders

Ordination to the priesthood needs to be discussed in the context of Christian ministry. In the early church, each disciple was committed to carry out the work of Jesus by virtue of baptism. Each was part of the "priestly people," and was guided and empowered by the Spirit of the Lord to serve the needs of the community. How that played out depended on the specific needs and the particular gift given to each disciple for service. There was no shortage of ministers such as we see today because ministry was based on an abundance of charisms, without concern for office, gender, or marital status.

Paul speaks of prophets who challenge those not living up to the gospel, teachers who spread the gospel word, and apostles who carry the message abroad and expand the Jesus movement. Even though positions of leadership gradually emerged, the first duty was to be a servant of others, to be a "church of equals." It was only in the late first century that we read in the pastoral letters of leadership by elders or presbyters. As for

the first duty was to be a servant of others

gathering, the communities assembled in house churches and the "table of the Lord" was presided over by a host or hostess. Gradually, however, this open house-church model was replaced with that of the Greek-Roman household, which was more patriarchal and hierarchical. After their acceptance into the empire, Christians took on more legally appointed offices and selected clerics to hold offices. The hierarchical and male model of ministry was well under way. "Power for" from the Spirit could easily slip into "power over" from authority.

Offices

The first mention of an early office, the deaconship, is described in Acts when the apostles select seven outstanding men to assist them. Though ordination did not appear until the second century, these men took up unique ministries in the early churches. This form of ministry was restored to the Church with the reforms of Vatican II and can include married men.

History reveals that for centuries deaconesses also existed in the church. While they did not have the same prestige as deacons, they made important contributions such as visiting the sick, serving at female baptism, and teaching. Key documents from the third and fourth century show their importance in the Syrian churches, and the Council of Chalcedon in 451 CE legislated that deaconesses must be ordained by the laying on of hands. Why the office of deaconess disappeared is unclear, but one can conjecture from some of the hostile remarks about deaconesses in papal and conciliar documents of the time that the "fathers" could no longer tolerate their presence and influence. There have been urgent requests to restore this office in our time, but the Vatican has rejected these.

Priesthood

There is no mention of priesthood, other than the Jewish priesthood, in the Gospels or in Paul's letters. Even Jesus was not a priest, because he was not of the tribe of Levi, nor did he designate any of his followers to be priests. The letter to the Hebrews refers to Jesus Christ as High Priest in that he offered himself in sacrifice. Acts and other early documents speak of presbyters, but these are elders who teach and preach and not leaders of liturgy.

The priesthood evolved gradually in the Church. For centuries when the Church was hidden, only bishops presided over liturgy. As the liberated church spread in the fourth and fifth centuries, there arose a need for local ministers of liturgy and pastoral care. In the Middle Ages, there was a major shift with regard to the priesthood. An ordained priesthood emerged, which was considered to be different "in essence and degree" from the priesthood of the faithful. This priesthood held special powers to consecrate Eucharist and forgive sins. Priests now began to be seen as separate from the people and the world, and celibacy was now made a requirement. The Protestant reformers made it a point to reject the priesthood, and in reaction the Council of Trent codified the medieval model of priesthood.

The Priesthood Today

In recent history the priesthood has taken many forms. After World War II the "worker priests" in France took jobs in the factories in an effort to reconnect with the working class. Some priests have been involved in the labor movement or have demonstrated for civil rights or migrant workers. Many priests have lost their lives living in solidarity with oppressed peoples. Once, visiting a tiny church in Nicaragua for Mass, I was moved by the number of pictures on the walls of priests who gave their lives for their people during the revolution. Notable were the six Jesuits who were murdered in El Salvador in 1989 for their efforts with the *compesinos*. So-called hyphenated priests combine their priesthood with work as chemists, writers, professors, psychologists, and other professions. There are priests who live in the bush country of Africa, traveling from mission to mission. Many live with poor people in Appalachia. And with the shortage of priests today, many have to work in two or more parishes.

The future of the priesthood is problematic. In this country the Catholic population has increased by twenty million since 1965, and yet there are now sixteen thousand fewer priests. Ordinations are half of what they were in 1965, and candidates for the priesthood are down by nearly two-thirds. Worldwide, the Catholic population has grown by half a billion since 1965, and yet there are fewer priests now than then. Seminarians are plentiful in Poland and in some African countries, but are scarce in America, Europe, and even Ireland, where they were once abundant. To add to the dilemma, cases of sexual abuse by some clergy worldwide has disillusioned and angered many of the faithful.

No one can predict the future of ministry. Some say a married clergy or the ordination of women would help. Others believe that more leadership roles will simply be turned over to the laity. One thing is certain, many Catholics today are deprived of the pastoral service they need and at times don't even have access to Mass.

Reconciliation

The sacrament of reconciliation (also called penance or confession) seems to have developed from belief in God's power of forgiveness as it was extended to so many by Jesus of Nazareth. As mentioned earlier, his was a call to repent for sin, and to all those willing to do this, he preached the good news of a loving and forgiving God. Jesus' Abba was not a person of vengeance and punishment, but a person of mercy and pardon. In the parable of the prodigal son, Jesus portrays his Father as one who runs down the road to celebrate the return of a sinner. Jesus also portrays himself as the good shepherd, rejoicing at finding a lost sheep.

In the early communities, the Jewish practices for atonement were observed: fasting, wearing sackcloth, prayers, and sacrifices at the Temple. As Christians separated from the Jews, they began to develop new rituals. Matthew's gospel tells of the practice of first confronting the sinner. If that failed, the person offended took one or two others along and tried again. If there was still no result, the community was informed and the sinner was set aside until he or she was willing to adopt new behavior (Mt 18:15-20).

Public penance first appeared in the second century. This ritual was for those who had committed serious sins like adultery, apostasy, or murder.

Usually the sinner was set aside, excluded from Eucharist, and required to do public penance outside the Church for several years until the community believed that the sinner had reformed. Only then could the penitent be readmitted to the community.

Private confession seems to have appeared in the Celtic churches in Ireland in the sixth century. Here sinners told their sins to priests and nuns, received counseling, and were given penance appropriate for the sin. This practice soon became popular and spread to the continent. At first it was condemned by Rome, but by the thirteenth century, private confession was approved and declared to be a sacrament. By now there were formulas to be used and only a priest could "hear" confessions. This form was made juridical by Trent, responding to the Protestant reformers, most of whom rejected penance as a sacrament.

Vatican II proposed a reform of reconciliation, and in the mid 1970s a new rite appeared. The dark confessionals were replaced with comfortable and friendly reconciliation rooms, where the priest could be talked to face-to-face or behind a screen. The priest, rather than being a judge, now represented the healing and forgiving Jesus. Scripture was read, spiritual advice offered, a meaningful penance given, and the priest prayed with the penitent for forgiveness. Three modes were suggested: private in the reconciliation room, at penance services, or a general absolution given to large groups without individual confession.

At first there was a great deal of enthusiasm for the new rite of reconciliation, especially for the great celebrations with general absolution. Soon narrow restrictions were placed on general absolution, and it is now seldom celebrated. Penance services, especially at times near important feasts, are still popular. Individual confession is not widely celebrated, except at retreats and renewal sessions.

in the mid 1970s a new rite appeared

 Student Reflection

"Private confession was popular during a campus ministry retreat that I made recently. Fr. Al, a much-loved elderly priest who lives in a dorm, came for the service and had long lines waiting to confess and celebrate the sacrament with him."

Anointing of the Sick

Until recently this sacrament was called extreme unction (the last anointing) and it was given before death. For many it was part of the classic Catholic sacramental cycle (baptism, marriage, and extreme unction). Today this sacrament, besides being a preparation for death, is also widely used for healing, both spiritual and physical.

The anointing is a powerful sacramental symbol of the healing power of Jesus Christ, which is so often demonstrated in the many miracle stories of the Gospels. About 20 percent of the stories in the synoptic Gospels are miracle stories, and a significant portion of John is concerned with miraculous signs.

Such incidents are unique to the Gospels. Nowhere else do we hear of so many miraculous cures attributed to one man. In Roman literature there are some accounts of cures by an emperor, and the Greeks went on pilgrimage to Epidaurus to receive cures from the god Asclepius. In the two thousand years of Jewish history covered by the Old Testament, there are only a handful of healings.

Unlike the magicians of his time, Jesus did not use formulas or lay claim to divinity. Rather, Jesus healed out of compassion and mercy to demonstrate that this is the kind of God Abba truly was. The Greek word for these actions is *dunemeis* or "acts of power," acts that clearly demonstrate the Spirit of God and the Kingdom is present in the world, wanting people to be whole and blessed. So radical were these actions for the poor and outcast that the Gospels tell us they were one of the main reasons his enemies plotted to kill him.

The early Christian communities believed the Spirit of the risen Jesus was still in their midst, as he had promised and continued to heal. Acts tells us that Peter healed a crippled beggar and a paralyzed man, and raised someone from the dead. The letter of James recounts how the elders anointed and prayed over the sick and brought them healing. This custom of anointing the sick and praying for healing lasted through the first eight centuries.

Then for a number of reasons—negative views about the body, devastating plagues, and a return to the notion that illness and disease were punishments for sin—interest in healing went into decline. The anointing became "extreme unction," part of "the last rites." Even the brilliant Aquinas avoided the topic of healing and viewed the gospel miracle stories as proof of Jesus' divinity. For the first eight centuries, the people could anoint, but now only a priest could perform these rites.

By the twelfth century, extreme unction was recognized to be a sacrament and from then on was administered before death privately by a priest.

Interest in Healing

There is a renewed interest in healing today. One of my graduate students, Teresa, is an expert on Healing Touch, a therapy that uses touch to influence the body's energy system and heal all aspects of the person. She gives workshops on Healing Touch to many health care workers, who apply these techniques in hospitals. In addition, many support groups use prayer to bring healing from grief, addictions, chronic illness, and disabilities. Many have turned to yoga, the Tao Te Ching, Zen, and other Eastern practices for holistic health.

The renewal of the Christian sacrament of anointing has reclaimed treasured traditions about the healing power of Jesus. On a recent pilgrimage to Lourdes, I was amazed to see hundreds of thousands of Christians from all over the world, processing, singing, and praying for healing. Most touching is the dedication of the many health care workers who volunteer their time to attend to the thousands of disabled pilgrims who come there to pray for inner healing and physical wellness.

The Christian sacrament of the anointing is now approached with an expectant faith for healing of the heart, mind, and body through the power of Jesus. No longer a private ceremony, anointing is a communal celebration, calling upon loved ones, families, even parish communities to pray with those seeking healing. The ritual includes songs, Scripture readings, prayers, and, of course, the anointing of those in need of healing.

Anyone whose health is seriously impaired may receive this sacrament now. This would include those who have a serious illness, the elderly, those about to undergo surgery, and those whose health is threatened by mental illness or addiction. There is a hope for healing on all levels: spiritual, psychological, and physical.

Now that this sacrament is celebrated widely, there is at the same time a scarcity of priests, who are the only ones allowed to administer it. In order that more people might benefit from the anointing, many suggest that lay hospital chaplains, Sisters, deacons, and even family members be permitted to administer the sacrament in the future.

Conclusion

We have seen that each sacramental symbol has its own history and tradition. Each sacrament is always a work in progress. Indeed, the renewal of the sacraments must keep pace with the complexities of our world, with its diversity and ever-changing needs. We have seen the need for change with baptism, Confirmation, ordination, reconciliation, and healing. If these sacraments are to remain relevant symbols of the powers of Jesus in today's world, their renewal must continue to keep pace with our changing world.

Activities

1. Hold a debate on what age would be appropriate for the celebration of Confirmation.

2. Invite a young married couple into the class to discuss the challenges they face as a couple.

3. Using clips from current TV programs, discuss the various attitudes toward marriage in today's media.

4. Invite an expert on Healing Touch into the class to discuss this movement.

5. Have an investigative team from the class interview some of the priests on your campus about their ministry and their hopes for the future. Then give a report to the class and follow with a discussion.

Sources

Chauvet, Louis-Marie. *The Sacraments*. Collegeville, MN: Liturgical Press, 2001.
Fischer, Kathleen, and Thomas Hart. *Promises to Keep*. New York: Paulist Press, 1991.
Hill, Brennan. *Exploring Catholic Theology*. Mystic, CT: Twenty-Third Publications, 1995.
Osborne, Kenan. *The Christian Sacraments of Initiation*. New York: Paulist Press, 1987.
Turner, Paul. *Confirmation*. New York: Paulist Press, 1993.

7 The Liturgy and Eucharist

My students have differing views

about going to church. Some say that at home they were required to go by their parents and once in college they just stopped going. Others attend campus services because they like the informality and the fact that the priests address the issues of young people. These students often say that when they return home, the liturgy is a real letdown. The reasons they give vary: it is always the same and gets monotonous; the sermons don't address their concerns; the people are not friendly and even give them looks about the way they are dressed; the music is not contemporary and few sing. Others find the liturgy at home pleasant: they like the priest and the people are friendly folks they have known all their lives. They enjoy this time for personal reflection and it means something to them to receive communion.

In this chapter we will first discuss liturgy: its development in the early Christian communities; some of the historical features that result in problems today; and what to look for in good, meaningful liturgy. Then we will look at the centerpiece of liturgy—the Eucharist. We will study some of the early views on Eucharist, examine how its meaning has changed over time and often amidst controversy, and then look at some contemporary interpretations.

Liturgy

The word *liturgy* comes from a Greek word *leitougia*, which means a public service done by the people (laity), or more literally "the work of the people." In the case of Christian liturgy, it means the rituals that are planned and celebrated by the community. Liturgy is the time when the community assembles to welcome, worship, pray, sing, listen, and receive communion.

Although this meaning of liturgy captures the grassroots notion of religious services and underscores that the Church is the people, it can at the same time be misleading. I say this because liturgy is really the work of God. In the Mass, first and foremost, God's power and grace move in the hearts of the faithful to give them what they need at the moment, whether it be strength to deal with difficulty, healing for physical or mental ailments or the loss of a loved one, forgiveness for sin, courage to avoid temptation, or clarity in making an important decision. Christian liturgy should be a powerful and intimate experience of God in the person of the risen Jesus Christ, in the community, in the words of Scripture, and in Eucharist.

Foundations of Christian Liturgy

Discussion of Christian liturgy begins with the "table ministry" of Jesus of Nazareth. As a devout Jew, he valued the custom of fellowship meals, where Jews assembled for prayer and the sharing of food. Here bread and wine were shared in the hope of growing closer to each other and to their God. But Jesus put his own unique stamp on such meals by including sinners and outcasts. He would dine with tax collectors, prostitutes, and the oppressed and impoverished. Apparently this irked some of Jesus' enemies, and they would whisper that he was nothing other than "a drinker and a friend of sinners."

So Jesus made it customary to share himself with others at meals, offering them love, compassion, and forgiveness. The Gospels tell us of many such meals. Once he stopped at the home of two friends, Martha and Mary, in Bethany. When Martha complained about Mary doting on his every word and not helping, he chided her and pointed out that listening is all-important (Lk 10:38-42). Here early Christians reflect on the importance of listening at the holy meals with Jesus and also note that women are to play a role at these meals. On another occasion, Martha serves Jesus a meal while Mary anoints his feet with oil and dries them with her hair. When Judas complains of the waste of money on the oil, Jesus remarks that the oil is for his burial (Jn 12:1-8). Earlier the two sisters had been present at the raising of their brother Lazarus from the dead (another example of the role of women in Jesus' table ministry and in the death and resurrection of Jesus).

Such meal stories abound in the Gospels. Zacchaeus, the hated tax collector from Jericho, dines with Jesus, turns his life around, and resolves to give half of all he owns to the poor and to repay his extortions four times over. Jesus dines at the house of Simon the Pharisee, and in the midst of this all-male meal, a lady of the night comes in, kneels at Jesus' feet, and proceeds to wash them with her tears and dry them with her hair. Instead of being embarrassed by her actions, Jesus rebukes the whispers of the men, welcomes her, and praises her repentance and love (Lk 7:36-50). Matthew tells of how tax collectors and sinners used to drop in at Jesus' house in Capernaum, which confirmed his reputation as a drinker and friend of sinners.

On a grander scale, Jesus is portrayed as miraculously feeding enormous crowds. On a number of occasions, he fed five thousand people with just five loaves and two fish. Even after his resurrection, Jesus continued to share meals with his disciples: Luke tells of a meal with two disciples after they fled from Jerusalem to Emmaus, and John recounts how the risen

Lord cooked breakfast for his disciples on the shore of the Sea of Galilee. Each time Jesus shares food and at the same time, himself, with others.

The last supper is central among Jesus' fellowship meals and serves as the basis for liturgy. The exact details of this meal are not available to us. The earliest account is given by Paul (1 Cor 11:23-26), which dates back to the instructions he received after his conversion around 40 CE (within a decade of the original supper). The gospel accounts vary in details and John's version is striking in that it contains no reference to Eucharist. Even the day the meal was celebrated is not clear. The synoptic Gospels place the meal at the time of Passover, whereas John's gospel places it before Passover. The accounts seem to be influenced by the theological reflections and liturgical practices of the time they were written. What is remarkable is that, after centuries of scrutiny from scholars, the accounts of the last supper are still viewed as having their source substantially in Jesus himself.

Simple Beginnings

The first Christian assemblies seem to have consisted of small groups meeting in house churches. A larger house would have held eight to ten, but if the community was a larger urban group, they might meet in a well-to-do person's villa, which would hold about fifty people. During the first few decades there were no gospel scrolls, and so oral stories about Jesus' teachings and miracles were told around the table. If there were someone present who had actually known Jesus, he or she would be an honored guest. Members of the community, who looked upon each other as brothers and sisters, would then celebrate "the breaking of the bread" in memory of Jesus, just as he had taught them. Jesus had promised his followers that he would be with them "all days" and that where two or three gathered in his name, he would be present among them. Aware that

oral stories were told around the table

they were indeed blessed by the presence of the risen Lord, they would rejoice and celebrate together.

Several years ago on a trip to Turkey with some students, we were surprised to find that there are still house churches. We were visiting Antakya, where the ancient city of Antioch was located, a place where one of the first Christian communities formed. It was here that Paul preached in the synagogue and outsiders first named converts "Christians." We arrived in the oldest part of the city near suppertime and were directed to a small house where Mass was being celebrated. As soon as we opened the door, people welcomed us and scrambled to get us chairs. The community consisted of about twenty people of all ages who were celebrating in a large room with beautiful murals of gospel scenes. The lively Mass was accompanied by guitars and ended with a strong rendition of "When the Saints Go Marching In"—in Turkish!

As soon as the Mass ended, everyone left save the priest, and we expressed our disappointment to him in not being able to meet his community. He said: "Oh, they just went out into the garden to get food and drink ready for you." We then went outside and were greeted with warm welcomes and friendly embraces. Through our translator we shared our stories and immediately felt a part of this little group of Christians half a world away from home. It was an experience we shall never forget. We now knew what Paul meant when he wrote about being one bread and one body (1 Cor 10:17).

There is little information about the early liturgies. The earliest account we have is about twenty years after Jesus' death. Paul is writing to the community in Corinth. He refers to the agape or love feast that the Christians held before the Eucharist and scolds those who do not share their food and those who drink too much. He then discusses the liturgy, which is patterned after the Lord's Supper and includes words of institution such as later appeared in the synoptic Gospels.

Another unusual testimony comes sixty years later from Pliny, a Roman governor in Turkey, in a letter to the Roman emperor Trajan. Reporting on "Christians," Pliny writes: "They were wont, on a stated day, to meet together before it was light, and to sing a hymn to Christ, as to a god."

He reports that they took an oath not to do evil actions and then departed, only to gather again later for a common meal. Pliny verified all this by torturing two deaconesses and described their rituals saying that they amounted to no more than superstition!

The *Didache,* an early first-century document, also refers to early Eucharist. Though the document avoids detail to protect Christians from persecution, it describes thanking God for Jesus and for the life and knowledge that he brought. It tells how the community gathered to become one as is the bread and acknowledge the glory and power of God through Jesus. In the prayer after communion, thanksgiving was given again for the knowledge, spiritual food, faith, and immortality gained through Jesus. The document calls for repentance and stands in anticipation of the Second Coming with the ancient prayer, "*Maranatha,* Lord, Come Again!"

Unlike today, members of the community did not often attend the Christian ritual out of obligation. Instead, they went because they wanted to enjoy the community, their "sisters and brothers." There was a strong bond of fellowship and faith that moved them to gather and tell stories about Jesus, to recall his teachings and miracles, to "break bread" in his memory (as Jesus requested at the last supper), sing hymns, and give each other a kiss of peace. We find in the early communities a "church of equals," where there were no distinctions between rich and poor, female and male, Jew and Gentile. The great appeal of the Christian movement was that everyone was welcome to enter this community of love. Who wouldn't want to join a family like that? Paul reflects this egalitarian spirit when he writes to the Galatians: "No longer Jew or Greek, slave or free, male or female, for you are all one in Jesus Christ" (Gal 3:38).

The early communities carried on Jesus' unique tradition of having women disciples, and thus women were able to lead in the communities and, if they were hosting the ritual in their house, lead the liturgy. The Scriptures mention a number of leading women disciples: Mary, the mother of Jesus; Mary Magdalene; Martha and Mary; Joanna; the Samaritan woman; Phoebe; Priscilla; Junia; and others. It needs to be noted that in the first century, there was no hereditary priesthood as there was in Judaism.

In fact, there was no priesthood at all. In the first few decades, early Jewish disciples also attended temple services, where there was a priesthood.

All this is in stark contrast to today's liturgy, and one begins to understand why some find going to church so problematic. The obligation to attend is often so rigidly enforced for some children and teens that once they are free to choose, they choose not to attend. The sameness and repetition of liturgy often turns away people who want more creativity and spontaneity. For instance, Latinos often join evangelical communities where they can move more freely and express their emotions. Africans at times return to their native religions where they can more freely be in touch with their customs and culture. It is common knowledge that Christianity failed in Asia in part because of the Church's refusal to adapt to their cultural and religious customs.

 Student Reflection

"As a woman, when I go to Mass and hear all the male images for God and see all the men in the sanctuary, it makes me sad and sometimes angry. Not being able to hear a feminine perspective in the sermon or watch a feminine style of celebrating is a real problem for me."

There is also the question of social class in our churches. Minorities and poor, handicapped, and homeless people often don't feel welcomed or comfortable. Martin Luther King Jr. used to say that Sunday in church was the most segregated day of the week! I work with homeless men who often tell me they don't go into Catholic churches because their appearance and clothes make them feel uncomfortable. I remember attending Mass in the cathedral in Managua, Nicaragua, on Easter. Most of the people were clean and well dressed. Then, a poor bag lady came in the back door. She looked embarrassed, and it took awhile before someone moved to make room for her in a pew. My thought was isn't it ironic that Jesus paid such special attention to the poor and outcast, and now they feel unwanted in our churches!

Attractions

In planning our services today, we can benefit by considering what attracted early Christians to attend. Foremost, they came to uniquely experience the presence of the risen Jesus Christ in their midst. Where pagan ceremonies celebrated the memory of dead heroes, Christians enjoyed the intimate presence of their Savior. He had promised to be with them "all days," and told them that where two or three gathered in his name, he would be in their midst. In faith, they knew they could vividly experience his presence in each other, in the stories about him, and in the bread and cup they shared.

Fellowship

The early Christians had strong bonds. They shared the privilege of following Jesus and the faith in his message. From him they had discovered "the Way," the path to meaning in life, personal happiness, and hope beyond death. In their communities they experienced Jesus' commandment to love each other as reality and they looked upon each other as brothers and sisters. At the table of the Lord, they experienced a friendship and intimacy like no other, especially as they drank what Paul called the "cup of fellowship" (1 Cor 10:6). They found a unique joy in being with other disciples, singing with them, fervently praying with them, sharing their faith and their gifts, and bringing their concerns for others to the community. The disciples viewed themselves as blessed, "the saints," a new priestly people gathered to worship their teacher and Savior. In the Greek culture, which deeply influenced Christianity, it is said that one hasn't really dined if one hasn't dined with friends. Liturgy was gathering with friends around the table of the Lord.

Eucharist

Of course the centerpiece of the early gatherings was Eucharist, the gift Jesus had given them, the privilege for which they were so thankful. Actually the word *Eucharistic* comes from the Greek word for thanksgiving. They came to thank God for Jesus' special presence among them in the bread they ate and the wine they drank. It was just as Jesus said: he would be with them all days and they were to gather for this meal in living memory of him. He had told them: "I am the bread of life. Whoever comes to me will never hunger and whoever believes in me will never thirst [....] I am the living bread that came down from heaven; Whoever eats this bread will live forever" (Jn 6:35,51).

The Evolution of Liturgy

Over the centuries many changes have occurred in the way Christians celebrate Mass. In order to better understand the reality we have today, let's look at some of these developments.

The most significant change came with the acceptance of Christianity in the Roman Empire by the fourth century. Soon after, it became the official religion of the empire, and the number of Christians exploded. The communities were extremely large, and so basilicas or Roman meeting halls were donated for church going. As we have seen, Christians formerly met in house churches, but in basilicas the opportunity for person-to-person intimacy became difficult.

We see this unwanted anonymity in many parishes today. Though I have attended my parish for years, I often marvel that there are few familiar faces coming down the aisle at communion. In addition, many of our smaller parishes, where such closeness is more available, are being shut down for lack of priests. Inner-city parishes, which often have a neighborhood closeness, are being closed because members are simply too poor to support the upkeep of the parish. At the same time, the Mass experience allows little time for interpersonal exchange. For many, Catholic ceremonies are more opportunities for personal reflection and prayer than for communal celebration.

Sameness

In the past there was a wide range of diversity in liturgy. Each area and culture had its own way of celebrating and there was much room for spontaneity. Divisions in Christianity expanded this diversity, but also hardened the Roman tendency toward uniformity. The first break that moved Rome toward rigidity occurred when the Eastern Church broke from the West in 1054. The second break, the Protestant Reformation, was far more significant. Now there were serious disagreements over the real presence in Eucharist, the priesthood, and even the value of the Mass itself. At least six different Protestant traditions about worship emerged, ranging from the conservative approach of the Lutherans to the radical positions of Zwingli to the need for utter freedom in worship by the Anabaptists. Anglicans and Episcopalians chose a middle road by adhering to traditional worship with the freedom to modify celebrations.

In response to these challenges and to preserve the Catholic tradition, the Roman Catholic liturgy moved toward central control and uniformity. The manner of worship that had evolved in Roman Catholicism over the centuries thereby solidified and became the norm. The development of the hierarchy and priesthood meant a top-down approach to authority and liturgy. The bishops and priests were now the "celebrants" and "said Mass" in Latin with their backs to the people while the community passively observed. Many said their private Masses on side altars. With the popularity of preaching in the Middle Ages, pews were installed where people could sit and listen. The advent of printing made it possible for uniform texts to be distributed and used worldwide.

When the church replaced the house, the altar replaced the table. What had been an assembly of friends in the Lord to commemorate his presence at the sacred meal became more the observance of a worship service, a reenactment of the sacrifice at Calvary. Little attention was given to the living presence of the Lord in the inspired Word of the Scriptures, and preaching about the Word became a lost art, except at retreats and parish missions. For many, Mass was attended out of a sense of serious obligation and was a time for quiet personal devotion.

Despite serious efforts at reform, discussed below, many Catholics are still negatively affected by this approach to liturgy. I recently attended

Sunday Mass in the cathedral in Krakow, Poland, the home diocese of John Paul II. I was struck by how little the huge throng of people participated in the liturgy, how faint the singing was, how few made any gesture at the kiss of peace, and the small number that received communion.

Liturgical Reform

Catholic liturgical reform began in European monasteries in the 1950s. There the study of the history of liturgy had revealed that the rite began with the people of the Church and should be restored to them. Liturgy should be more than a time for personal reflection; it should also be a communal celebration of Jesus' presence among his followers. Participation rather than passivity should be the watchword, and to allow more participation, Latin should be dropped and the Mass should be celebrated in whatever language the local folk spoke, whether it be Russian, Swahili, or English. Furthermore, as in the early days, Scripture should play a prominent role in the celebration of Mass.

These ideas percolated in the Church for a decade and then were officially accepted in Vatican II's document on the liturgy, the first document to be proclaimed by the council. Let's look at some of the major notions that were supported by this reform.

Foremost, the Church wanted to ensure that liturgy would be a strong force that would restore vigor to its members. To accomplish this, the Mass had to be adapted to meet current needs. In a now classic statement, the Mass was described as "the summit toward which all the activity of the Church is directed and the font from which all its power flows." In other words, we bring all that we are and have to the celebration of Eucharist, and open our hearts to God's grace to strengthen our faith and help bring the gospel of Jesus to the world in our daily lives. The Mass is essentially the work of Christ, bringing blessings to his disciples.

the Mass is essentially the work of Christ

Student Reflection

"The campus Mass is one of the high points of my week. I get together with my friends and we bring all our concerns about our personal lives, our families, our studies, and our activities. We listen to the readings, and usually the sermon applies the Scripture to our concerns. We pray together and receive communion. I always go away more focused on who I am and what my goals are, and I feel much closer to my friends and my God."

It was further stressed that the centerpiece of Mass is Jesus Christ. At Mass, Jesus is intimately experienced by those present, in the living Word of Scripture and in the Eucharist. In order to experience the risen Jesus' power and blessings at Mass, those assembled must open their minds and hearts.

Participation would be the key to liturgical renewal. Christians are reminded that they are all celebrants sharing in the priesthood of Christ, led by the presiding ordained priest. And to enable participation, the Mass must be simple, intelligible, in the language of the people, and adapted to their culture. The prayers, symbols, and singing must be such that the local folk could understand them and enthusiastically join in. This meant there would from now on be much diversity and creativity introduced into the Mass. It would no longer be in Latin or the same throughout the world.

The Changes

Your parents probably remember the many changes in liturgy more than any of the other moves made by Vatican II. Churches had to be redesigned. For many centuries, churches had long rows of pews facing the high altar, where the priest "said Mass" facing the wall. The sanctuary was blocked off by a communion rail, which the faithful would approach and kneel before to receive communion. Now the churches were reconfig- ured, often in a round or horseshoe shape, with the altar in the middle and the priest facing the people. The community became aware that this was their Mass, led but not dominated by the celebrant. The Church was once again seen to be "the people," and thus they were encouraged to join in the responses, sing the songs, listen intently to the readings and the homily, share the kiss of peace, and share communion at the table of the Lord. Members of the community were to help plan liturgy, welcome people as they arrived, join in the readings, give commentaries, bring up the offerings, and distribute the Eucharist. Once again liturgy was to be the assembly of the people to celebrate the presence and power of Jesus Christ in their midst.

I can think of two experiences of Mass where I was deeply moved to see how liturgical reform is affecting some people today. The first was in Nicaragua in a little homemade barrio church. The small neighborhood community welcomed me and my students for Sunday Mass, proudly showing us their picture of Archbishop Romero, who they viewed as a saint and a martyr, as well as the large photographs of young priests who had been killed by the government during the revolution for standing by their people. The Mass was simple, led by a rather scruffy veteran missionary who wore sneakers with his vestments. The people had been through much oppression and violence and they gathered in thanksgiving that the revolution was over. They listened intently to the Scriptures, carried on a lively dialogue with the priest during the homily, and sang their native songs with great emotion. At the kiss of peace, each person in the community went to everyone else and gave a loving *embrazo*. Even though we were strangers, we were made to feel like honored guests. The reception of Eucharist was solemn but joyful, and after Mass the people shared a simple meal and a fruit drink with us on the side of the church. We held their babies, joked with their children, and had a delightful time. This for me was truly "Eucharist," thanksgiving, and a profound experience of the presence of Jesus in this community.

The other experience was during a trip to Tanzania with some of my students. On Sunday our guides took us to a village church. Inside it was decorated in natural materials from the area, and over the altar was a huge mural of Jesus with a mountain and the wild animals of the area.

Before Mass we were welcomed by the young African priest and the local people. Some were dressed in simple Western clothes and others wore native costumes of bright colors. The Mass was in Swahili and followed the traditional format. The priest would stop at points during the homily and explain in English what he was telling his people. The singing was delightful, with the community swaying and making native sounds during the local songs. The kiss of peace took about ten minutes, for everyone was embraced. It was so great to see all the children run over and hug us. There was great peace and joy in the experience, and we had a sense of a strong Christian bond with these folks even though we were from afar. I went away wishing that more of our churches in America would take time to show such creativity, spontaneity, and intimacy in their Masses!

There is so much to be gained by attending a church that works at their liturgy, and young people often "shop around" for such parishes. Many look for communities that welcome them as young people, address their issues, and sing songs that are contemporary. They want time to reflect on their goals and their personal journey during this crucial time of development. They want to listen to the Scriptures read well and with feeling, and hear homilies that are interesting and relevant. They search for communities that know how to worship their God. They look for communities that are plugged in to the issues of the world and that look for ways to be of service to those in need of charity and justice.

The search for such liturgy at times takes young people outside the Catholic churches. Some of my students worship in the new mega-churches. At these churches, there is a large staff ready to serve them. There is a coffee bar where people gather before and after the service to meet new friends and share with old ones. With more than three thousand in attendance, the service is packed and much use is made of technology for images and sound. The sermon takes about half an hour and is a well-prepared multimedia presentation (sometimes dramatized) on a current issue and how it relates to Scripture and life. Small groups meet and discuss the spiritual life during the week. Funds and food are regularly raised for the needy, and

small groups discuss the spiritual life

trips are organized to spend several weeks helping people in underdeveloped countries.

Often these mega-churches are rather secular and show little appreciation for the age-old traditions of the Church. Some place little value on the Eucharist. Some of my students say these churches can be trendy and superficial at times. But still the Catholic Church could learn much from these communities about how to build community and celebrate Christian liturgy.

Many think that liturgical renewal has come to a standstill. Some time ago, the Vatican said there was to be no more experimentation and thus put a hold on any further creativity. Central control in Rome has brought about a return to uniformity throughout the world. Attendance at Mass has fallen to less than 50 percent in the United States, to 15 percent in Spain, and single digits in Germany and France. Even Ireland has seen a sharp decline in Mass attendance.

If liturgy is to once again be vital and attractive, there will have to be more room for contemporary symbolism and relevant ritual. There will have to be more variety and diversity in Catholic celebrations. Many think that Catholic liturgy will have to become more inclusive. Often women feel excluded by the dominance of male leadership at Mass, at the exclusive language used in the rituals, and by the overemphasis on male imagery for God. As mentioned before, minorities and poor, handicapped, divorced, and gay and lesbian people often feel uncomfortable in traditional churches.

Eucharist

Eucharist or Holy Communion began with a simple yet unfathomable gesture. A young preacher and healer, Jesus of Nazareth, took bread and wine in his hands the night before he died and shared it with his friends, saying that this food was indeed he. He asked them to repeat this meal in his memory.

The gospel accounts of Jesus' words and actions at this meal vary. Mark, the earliest gospel (written around 70 CE), has Jesus pass the cup to the disciples before he says, "This is my blood." Mark and Matthew (written about 80 CE) have Jesus refer to "my blood of the covenant," while Luke and Paul both use the phrase "the new covenant in my blood." Luke's account differs from the others when it describes a ritual in which cups of wine are shared twice.

In Mark, Jesus talks of his blood being shed for the multitude, while Matthew writes about the blood being shed for the forgiveness of the sins of the multitude. Luke merely has Jesus say, "my blood which is shed for you." Only Luke and Paul speak of Jesus' request that this be done in his memory. And only Mark and Matthew quote Jesus as saying that he will not drink wine until the coming of the kingdom, although this eschatological notion seems to be captured in Paul's phrase "until he comes."

In spite of these differences, there is a remarkable consistency in all the synoptic accounts of the last supper. Jesus' disciples are present at meals solely for them; there is a meal within a meal; blessings and thanksgiving are given over the bread and cup, and Jesus uniquely identifies himself with both. The passing of the cup to all is also extraordinary and original to his meal.

Early Eucharist

The followers of Jesus shared this meal and celebrated his presence in their midst as their friend and Savior. As we have seen, small groups of early Christians, often at the risk of their lives, gathered secretly in homes for what they called "the breaking of the bread."

Xavier Léon-Dufour, a noted biblical scholar, points to two early traditions of Eucharist. The older appears linked with Antioch and stresses Jesus' request for remembrance. It is Hellenistic and Jewish and sees Eucharist as a gift from Jesus and a sign of the covenant. The later tradition appears more Jewish and apparently originated in Jerusalem. There is a parallel between the body and blood and the emphasis on blessings, expiation, sacrifice, and cultic ritual. John's tradition is more a last will and testament and focuses on the death and the importance of love and service, symbolized by the washing of the feet. In time all these traditions interlocked in one.

As we have seen, the Eucharist has simple and often secretive beginnings. Once Christianity was accepted, the celebration of Eucharist became public and throngs of Christians gathered for magnificent liturgies in basilicas. From then on, Christians celebrated Eucharist in grand cathedrals as well as simple country churches. Christians received Eucharist aboard ship, on dining room tables, and even on the fenders of jeeps in the midst of battle. For two thousand years, Jesus' followers have experienced a unique encounter with Jesus' presence and power through the sacrament of Eucharist.

Controversy

From the beginning, Eucharist was controversial. The Gospel of John reflects this when Jesus says that he is the living bread and many walk away from him as a result. Later, those outside the Church attacked Christians for their beliefs in this sacrament. Many Romans were outraged at the "atheism" of Christians, who did not properly honor the Roman deities or the divinity of the emperors, but instead paid homage to a Jewish peasant who had been crucified as a criminal. Belief in Jesus' resurrection and presence at these community meals was considered absurd. Many Jews were enraged at Christians for claiming that Jesus was the messiah and was worthy of worship. Enemies of Christians spread stories that their gatherings were acts of cannibalism, of actually eating flesh and blood. There were even stories spread about how Christians were sacrificing babies and holding bizarre sexual orgies at the so-called last supper.

There were also problems with Eucharist within the Christian communities themselves. The Gnostic communities, groups who placed a high value on wisdom and intelligence, and who eventually were deemed heretical, held matter in contempt. Their dualism, which held that only the spiritual could be from God, prevented them from accepting the Incarnation and any sacramental approach to God. They could not accept that

Jesus could be bread and wine. Another movement, the Arians, denied the divinity of Jesus and did not accept that he was worthy of worship in Eucharist. The Docetists denied the true humanity of Jesus, and their position also held implications for Eucharist. But on the whole, within the orthodox tradition, there was no questioning that Jesus was present in the Eucharist.

Different mind-sets affected the way people interpreted Eucharist. The early Fathers were largely Platonic in their views, which meant that reality existed in abstract forms and ideas. Reality was thus perceived through the mind's grasp of the essence of things, rather than through the senses. Applied to the Eucharist, what appeared to the senses to be bread and wine mattered little. The essence was what mattered, and the essence was the body and blood of Christ. From this perspective, there could be little problem with the notion of the real presence.

A shift to this Platonic philosophy brought challenges to the understanding of Eucharist. First, the Western tribes that swept through Europe brought with them a stark realism about everyday life and looked at Eucharist through this lens. Second, the West's struggle with Islam brought them into contact with Aristotle's philosophy, which had been preserved by the Arabs. Here reality was seen in terms of matter and form and was perceived through the senses. Finally the reforms of Charlemagne brought about scholarship wherein theories about Eucharist could be compared and discussed.

The Monks of Corbie

A Saxon monk named Paschasius Radbertus wrote the first theological treatise on Eucharist around 830 at his monastery in Corbie. In teaching about Eucharist to his monks, he took a rather traditional view, explaining that salvation was brought about by communing with the risen body of Christ, the exact same body that was born of Mary. Paschasius tended to interpret the real presence literally, and some of his contemporaries thought his views bordered on cannibalism.

Paschasius' colleague at Corbie, Ratramnus, wrote another treatise. He was not so realistic and viewed the real presence in terms of "sign" and symbol, more of a spiritual presence perceived in faith. Communion was with the spirit of Jesus Christ, rather than literally with his body and blood.

Not much was made of these two opposing views at the time, but the terms of the age-old controversy regarding Eucharist had been set. Was the presence of Jesus real or symbolic? The Western tribes, who by now prevailed in Europe, favored the more literal view of Paschasius.

As we have noted, there were different patterns of thought with regard to the "real presence" of Jesus Christ in the Eucharist. For some the presence of Jesus was purely spiritual, while for others it was real flesh and blood. These controversies tended to shift the emphasis to the elements of bread and wine and away from the meaning of the Lord's Supper as a total event. The elevation of the host and chalice became the central event at Mass for many, and for others Eucharist could be carried in a locket on a trip as one would a good luck charm. Believers were often distracted from the notion of "communion" with each other and with the Lord and from how Eucharist connected with their daily lives. Many felt themselves unworthy to receive.

 Student Reflection

"We were told in second grade that in our first communion we were going to receive the body and blood of Jesus. I was frightened at the thought. I told my father and he really did not know what to say. I remember being very confused. I think kids that young are very literal and that communion should be delayed until they can understand better."

Berengar of Tours

Controversy over the meaning of Eucharist lay dormant until the eleventh century. At that time Berengar (d. 1088), a scholar well versed in Aristotle's grammar and dialectic, revived the symbolic approach of Ratramnus. He believed that Christ was present in the Eucharist only in a spiritual sense. He ridiculed those who said the bread and wine were changed into the flesh of Christ and maintained that these were only symbols of the reality of Jesus' spiritual presence.

Berengar's views stirred the Roman authorities, and meetings were held to address his position. On two occasions, Berengar was required to sign an oath that he believed in the real presence. On the first occasion, the oath was so literal it later became an embarrassment. It stated the true body and blood were present at the consecration in such a way that "they are physically taken up and broken in the hands of the priest and crushed by the teeth of the faithful, not only sacramentally but in truth." Fortunately the second oath was more nuanced and used Aristotle's notion of substance and accidents, noting that the bread and wine were "substantially changed" into the body and blood of Christ at the consecration. This laid the foundation for the term *transubstantiation,* which was first used in 1215 against the Cathars, who scorned the material world and thus challenged the presence of Christ in something as disdainful as bread and wine.

The Rise of the Universities

The medieval universities provided a forum for scholars to examine Eucharist and soon many treatises appeared. For most the move was away from a literal and toward a philosophical approach to the real presence. Thomas Aquinas, the most brilliant of the theologians at that time, gave authority to the term *transubstantiation,* explaining that the substance of the bread and wine changed while the other characteristics remained the same. His explanation is still prevalent today in official documents like the *Catechism of the Catholic Church.* Among the faithful, the literal approach still held sway, and Eucharist was often seen as a relic to be worshipped or carried about in processions.

The Beginnings of the Reformation

In the fourteenth century, John Wycliffe (d. 1384), a theologian and fiery church reformer at Oxford, argued that the Scriptures alone should be the source of Church authority. This led him to contend that such things as papacy, priestly powers, and terms like *transubstantiation* had no validity because they were not found in the Bible. For Wycliffe, holiness, not ordination, was required for liturgical leadership, and such leadership should be open to the laity. Though Wycliffe's positions were condemned at Oxford in 1381, he had laid the foundation for sixteenth-century Protestantism. John Hus (d. 1414) brought Wycliffe's teaching to Bohemia and expounded on the Englishman's position against transubstantiation. Hus was censured, excommunicated, and then burned at the stake. His execution put a century-long chill on the debate over Eucharist, but Hus had predicted that within a century someone would rise up and these reformed views would prevail.

Martin Luther, a young Augustinian scholar of Scripture, appeared on the scene roughly a century after Hus was executed. Unwittingly, this young monk ignited the Reformation, which would tear Western Christianity apart. His ninety-five theses, which he posted for debate, challenged the selling of indulgences. Here people paid money to ensure that their departed loved ones would be freed from their sins and punishment in purgatory. Unscrupulous monks and priests had made a major industry of indulgences and raised huge sums of money for Rome. Luther denied that either the pope or the Church had the authority to grant such indulgences, and he railed against the superstition and corruption that surrounded this practice.

In 1520, Luther raised a number of objections to the commonly accepted Eucharistic theology of the time. He questioned having Masses said on behalf of the diseased, which had become a major source of income for the clergy, some of whom said many Masses a day. Luther challenged the term *transubstantiation,* objected to the cup being denied to the laity at communion, and denied that the Mass was a sacrifice.

Arguing that the Scriptures were the sole authority for Christian beliefs, Luther eventually opposed an ordained priesthood and denied priestly powers. He denied the saving power of the Mass, teaching instead that faith alone could save and that Mass was only a sign of God's offer of salvation. He called for Eucharist to return to a simple service resembling the last supper. And Luther rejected transubstantiation as pagan metaphysics, but surprisingly insisted on the literal approach to the real presence. Luther wrote: "Whoever eats this bread eats the Body of Christ. Whoever crunches this bread with teeth or tongue crunches the Body of Christ."

More Radical Positions

Other Protestant reformers went beyond Luther's position on Eucharist. Ulrich Zwingli (d. 1531), a bombastic Swiss preacher in Zurich, rejected the belief that any material thing could play a role in salvation and challenged Catholic teachings on sacraments as well as Eucharist. Zwingli abolished the Mass and taught that Jesus could not be present in the Eucharist because he was in heaven. Eucharist was simply a spiritual communion, not the reception of the real presence. Luther and Zwingli actually debated these matters and never came to agree. Luther told his followers to avoid the "Zwinglian way" at all costs.

John Calvin (d. 1564), a major figure in the Reformation, proposed a moderate version of Zwingli's position on Eucharist and thus laid the foundation for much of contemporary mainline Protestant Eucharistic theology. Calvin held that while the Lord's Supper could strengthen the faith, it could not play a role in salvation. Calvin took a hard line, insisting that the teaching on transubstantiation was perverse, that belief in consecration was sorcery, and that viewing the Mass as a repetition of Calvary was blasphemy. He understood the real presence as a faith union with Christ but not as a contact with his body. For him, the outward signs of bread and wine held little significance, and he agreed with Zwingli that Christ's body was in heaven and could not be present in the Eucharist.

The Catholic Response

The Catholic response to the reformers was slow in coming. In 1545 the Council of Trent was called to address these issues, and after meeting in fits and starts, the council finally reached its conclusions almost twenty years later in 1562. By this time the churches had become separated beyond recovery. Trent answered the reformers' views on Eucharist definitively: Jesus is "really, truly, and physically" present in the Eucharist; the Mass is a sacrifice and its merits can be applied to the salvation of the living and the dead; the Lord could be worshipped in the elements; *transubstantiation* was an apt term to describe what happened at the consecration, and only ordained priests could celebrate Mass.

Contemporary Views

The Catholic understanding of Eucharist has profoundly deepened over the last half century. Modern biblical, theological, and historical research has provided a wealth of new understanding of the texts and how the Eucharistic celebration has evolved. Study of the ancient Christian writers has given us information about the Eucharistic tradition that was not available during the great debates of the Middle Ages and the Reformation. We now have a far richer knowledge of symbols, sacrament, ritual, sacrifice, priesthood, and real presence.

The recovery of a vigorous understanding of the Resurrection has been key to a better understanding of the real presence for both Catholics and Protestants. Certainly communing with the risen Christ rules out the literal views of chewing flesh and blood, placing the experience in the area of the spiritual and of faith, and yet seeing it as nonetheless "real." In addition, a renewed awareness of the presence of Christ in the living Word of Scripture, in the community, and throughout the world, places Eucharist in a larger context. It links Eucharist not only to worship but also to the command to love each other and to be concerned and active regarding hunger, peace, and justice. Eucharist becomes a meal to be shared, lived, and linked with service to others, not something to be argued over and received. People want to receive because they long to be in union with Christ. Eucharist should be a personal and communal sharing of Jesus, not a source of division. Many Catholics think that depriving the faithful of communion should not be used as a punishment, whether it is for a divorce or for the way one votes in an election.

The Crisis in Ministry

Today there is a growing shortage of priests in the Catholic Church worldwide. This has serious implications for Eucharist. Many Catholics do not have the opportunity to participate in the celebration of Mass and have to settle for communion services. As the clergy decline in number, it is unclear who will lead Catholic liturgy. Will permanent deacons play a more prominent role? Will there be a change in the celibacy law so that married clergy can officiate? Will women be given a more central role in liturgical leadership? Could Catholics return to the house churches of old, where the "domestic church" of families would become the setting for liturgy? Some envision the joining of parishes, with the clergy celebrating Mass as circuit riders or only showing up on occasion to consecrate hosts for communion services. Many hold that such a narrowing of priesthood is hard to reconcile with the early church's experience of Eucharist. No one can predict the future, but we do know it will call for wise and decisive leadership to face this growing crisis.

Ecumenical Progress

Tragically, the very sacrament of Eucharist, which Jesus gave his followers to experience unity with him and each other, became the ground for serious division within the Church. To heal these divisions, serious theological dialogues have been held between Protestants and Catholics since the Second Vatican Council. They were the first such discussions since the Reformation and achieved some outstanding breakthroughs in understanding.

International dialogue between Lutherans and Catholics produced an extremely significant document in 1967 called *Eucharist as Sacrifice*. Here are expressed basic beliefs about the meaning of Eucharist that are acceptable to both Catholics and Lutherans.

In these dialogues both Lutheran and Catholic theologians have found much common ground with regard to the real presence. The Lutherans agree that Christ is present in many ways: in people, baptism, Scripture, and preaching, and that Christ is present in Eucharist, "whole and entirely, in his body and blood, under the signs of bread and wine." They say they affirm the real presence rather than attempt to explain it, and that it takes place by the power of the spirit through the Word.

The Catholic theologians explain their position on the Mass as sacrifice in ways acceptable to Lutherans. Protestants have traditionally objected to the Catholic view that at Mass the priest offers the victim in sacrifice to God. Lutherans have always been concerned that this view wrongly tries to add to the work of Jesus Christ at Calvary. In answer to this, Catholic theologians agree that Christ's sacrifice is unrepeatable, that reconciliation exists only through the cross, and that at Mass we do not offer Christ, but he is the one who offers us the celebration of Eucharist.

Understandably, the sticking points in these ongoing discussions between Lutherans and Catholic have been the ordained priesthood and intercommunion. In the 1970s there was a move toward co-celebration between priests and ministers as well as extraordinary experiments with inter-communion. In recent times, however, there have been regressions in these areas. The Catholic Church has hardened its position on the need for a celibate male clergy and has forbidden Protestants from receiving communion at Mass. Thus the theological agreements have not translated into real, everyday ecumenical experiences.

Much progress has also been made in dialogues between Anglican and Catholic theologians. Traditionally the Church of England's views on Eucharist are similar to those of Calvin, rejecting transubstantiation but at the same time avoiding Zwingli's complete rejection of the real presence. Today Anglican views on the real presence range from ones similar to the Catholic position to those who see Christ's presence alongside the bread and the wine. The Church's rejection of Anglican orders in 1896 remains a huge obstacle to finding common ground on the Mass. Still there has been progress in the mutual understanding of the sacrificial aspect of Mass and acceptance of the real presence. The practice of the ordination of women in the Anglican and Episcopalian churches has become a serious obstacle to further dialogue.

In 1982 the World Council of Churches published *Baptism, Eucharist and Ministry*. This document is the centerpiece for future dialogue on Eucharist because it establishes common ground on the basis of solid biblical scholarship, a more accurate account of history, a united concern for social justice, and a desire for Christian unity. It has helped move the churches to get beyond hundreds of years of scandalous division toward an era of unity. All that is needed now is vigorous leadership to move ahead on more practical and pastoral levels.

Another example of progress is the agreement reached between the Catholic Church and the schismatic Assyrian Church of the East. Here Rome recognized the Eucharistic celebration of this church, which uses an ancient Eucharistic prayer that does not have the traditional words of consecration. This seems to indicate that the Eucharistic real presence comes about in the midst of the entire Eucharistic prayer and not simply through the recitation of a formula.

Conclusion

Faith in Jesus Christ remains the centerpiece of the Christian tradition. Although Christians still differ on how Jesus is present in Eucharist, they share faith that he is present. Many of these controversies are now history, and Christians stand at a point where sharing in Eucharist can bring them closer to each other. People of all churches can now continue to honor his memory and experience his presence in the breaking of the bread.

Activities

1. Form investigative teams to attend Lutheran, Episcopalian, Baptist, Methodist, Presbyterian, and non-denominational services. Compare

notes on the attitudes toward and reception of communion at these services.

2. Conduct an e-mail interview with your parents, brothers, and sisters on the value (or lack of value) in attending church and ask about their interpretations of Eucharist. Share the results in class.

3. Design a class liturgy that would appeal to college students today.

Sources

Bradshaw, Paul. *The Search for the Origins of Christian Worship.* New York: Oxford University Press, 2002.

Caban, Allen. *Patterns in Early Christian Worship.* Macon, GA: Mercer University, 1989.

Dupre, Louis. *Symbols of the Sacred.* Grand Rapids, MI: Eerdmans, 2000.

Hurtado, Louis. *At the Origins of Christian Worship.* Grand Rapids, MI: Eerdmans, 1999.

Kilmartin, Edward. *The Eucharist in the West.* Collegeville, MN: Liturgical Press, 1998.

Pecklers, Keith, ed. *Liturgy in a Postmodern World.* New York: Continuum, 2003.

Walton, Janet. *Feminist Liturgy: A Matter of Justice.* Collegeville, MN: Liturgical Press, 2000.

8 Women and the Church

Women's struggle for equality

in our society and our churches is not new. In most cultures throughout history, there have been examples of women, usually from the wealthier classes, who have found opportunities for a better education, participated in the professions and arts, or filled positions of leadership. Historically, there appears to be an ongoing cycle in which women make social progress and then gradually return to subservience.

The ancient cultures surrounding Jesus experienced this cyclical advancement of women. In the Hellenistic period, which included Jesus' time, women gained many rights in domestic, social, and economic spheres. Spartan women set records in the Olympic foot and chariot races just decades before the time of Jesus. Greek women also distinguished themselves in music, medicine, arts, crafts, and the professions.

They held positions as writers, philosophers, and priests in the cults and mystery religions of the day.

Roman women in Jesus' time were not as fortunate, for they lived in a patriarchal culture that gave males supremacy in the home, in divorce law, and in sexual activity. At the same time, some elite and wealthy women were exceptionally well educated and were successful in business, politics, medicine, and the arts. Some women served as priests in cultic groups and held other posts within the Roman religions.

Jewish Traditions

The Jewish culture of Jesus' time witnessed a long history of various attitudes toward women. The Jewish Scriptures, which developed over a thousand years, reflect a wide range of perspectives. The earliest account of the creation of Woman, for example, says she comes from Adam's rib and is given to him as a helper. She is then easily led into evil by the serpent and persuades Adam to follow her. In a later, more advanced story, both woman and man are created in the image and likeness of God, and both are blessed and commissioned by God.

In the Jewish Scripture, God is often portrayed with masculine imagery: as a warrior defending his people, a vengeful punisher of his people for their infidelity, a father extending love and care to his children, and a husband displeased with the infidelity of his spouse (the chosen people). Conversely, there are many instances where God is described as a woman: a loving mother, a nurse caring for her children, a seamstress clothing her people, and a midwife bringing forth new life. The Canaanites passed on their goddess traditions to the Hebrews, whose Babylonian exile moved them to incorporate a devotion to the goddess of fertility in their rituals. The powerful prophets Isaiah and Jeremiah condemned such images, and subsequently the Jewish feminine images of Yahweh moved into the wisdom tradition, with the celebration of Lady Wisdom.

The social structure of Judaism was largely patriarchal, but even so, great women like Sarah and Rebecca were honored as "mothers of Israel."

Miriam, the sister of Moses, was a prophet and one of the leaders of the Exodus, and Deborah was a formidable prophet and judge who brought God's word and justice to her people. Alexandra was a powerful queen of Israel who led her people to peace and prosperity just seventy years before Jesus was born.

Women in Jesus' Time

Although it is true that Jesus was Jewish, there were many versions of Judaism surrounding him and a wide range of attitudes toward women. There were, for instance, the Essenes, who were celibate and avoided women; the Sadducees, who had a number of wives and could dismiss one or another easily with divorce; and the Herodians, who had a history of violence toward their women. Jews at that time argued over the roles of women in society and religion, and Jesus seems to have taken part in those disputes. Examples include the gospel stories in which he is asked his view on divorce and in which he protects an adulterous woman from being stoned to death.

In general, women in Jesus' time were in a subservient position. Their identity was largely derived from their family roles as wife and mother. As young daughters, they had few rights, were allowed few personal possessions, and were not permitted to keep money earned for work. When they came of age at twelve and a half, they were usually handed over to become a wife for a sum of money and were then considered the husband's property and servant. Fathers who were desperate for funds were permitted to sell their daughters as slaves.

Women at that time belonged in the home and were seldom seen in public. Should they have to go outside, their faces were covered, and they were not permitted to speak to anyone, especially a man. In the rural areas, with which Jesus was more familiar, the women were permitted to work, but never alone with a man. (Such customs are still practiced in some Arab countries today.)

Women were closely monitored to protect the bloodlines and inheritance laws of the "chosen people." Because women were considered weak and seductive, safeguards were placed on their behavior. Meanwhile, men enjoyed a degree of sexual freedom.

In the family, women were expected to be obedient servants and could rightfully expect in return protection, shelter, food, sexual relations, health care, and a decent burial. Fathers, who could expect more respect from their children than their mothers, were permitted to have several wives.

Divorce laws in the Jewish culture favored men: women could seldom sue for divorce and had few legal rights. Men could divorce their wives for reasons ranging from the serious, such as infidelity, to the trivial, such as bad cooking. Widows could not inherit and were placed under the authority of their male in-laws.

In religion, women were kept in the background. They were not given circumcision, the sacred sign of the covenant, and with rare exceptions were not instructed in the Torah, and therefore did not carry out the religious teaching of their children. They were not obligated to make pilgrimages to Jerusalem, and if they did, they had to stay in the lower court of the Temple. Generally, women were segregated in the synagogues and did not read at services. Nor were they permitted to be priests who prepared and offered sacrifices in the Temple. The main reason for this was that women were considered to be regularly "unclean" because of menstruation and giving birth.

Much that is documented about the role of Jewish women at that time is filtered through the eyes of male authors, so we don't have a complete picture of what occurred in daily life. It is likely that many Jewish men held women in respect and that many Jewish women struggled for justice and equality. There were no doubt reformers who were influenced by some of the more liberal views of the surrounding Greek and Roman societies and who wanted to restore the best of the Jewish traditions toward women. Jesus of Nazareth was one such reformer.

Jesus' Views

The Gospels, as we have seen, are based on memories of Jesus' life and teachings. He was clearly remembered as a reformer and an innovator on issues involving women. Jesus grew up in a Jewish family and was raised for most of his youth by his mother, whom he supported with his work as a craftsman. His mother, Mary, who is revered in the Gospels, was no doubt a major influence during the thirty years he spent at home.

In his public life, Jesus confronted the patriarchal system of his day. He never viewed women as property or servants, but insisted that every person was a child of God. There is no indication in the Gospels that he saw women as inferior or was wary of them as weak or seductive. On the contrary, he addressed all of the taboos of his day about women. He spoke to women and healed them in public, defended them when they were oppressed as prostitutes or disabled, and freely taught them his message along with men. He especially reached out to widows, who were then an oppressed class, honoring their small but generous donations in the Temple. On one occasion, he compassionately addressed a widow in public and restored her only son to life.

Jesus taught that both mother and father were to be equally honored. Lovingly, he took little girls as well as little boys to him and held up both as examples of the Kingdom of God. He befriended Martha and Mary and taught them in their own home. He engaged the Samaritan woman at the well in conversation and sent her off to convert her town. Jesus' first miracle was done at the bequest of his mother, Mary, and another early healing was done to Peter's mother-in-law. These and many other stories are based on memories of how Jesus honored women.

Jesus challenged the unjust divorce laws of his day and refused to identify himself with those who were either liberal or conservative in allowing men to divorce. For Jesus, marriage was a sacred covenant blessed by God, and he taught that both men and women had to honor this commitment as long as they lived. He also insisted that lust had its source in men's hearts and thus challenged the traditional notion that women's seduction was the cause of sexual sin. He had no fear of the taboo of touching the dead girl's body, but miraculously brought her back to life. Nor was he uncomfortable when the "unclean" woman touched his cloak in public to seek a cure for her constant hemorrhaging. At first put off by a request from a Gentile (non-Jewish) woman that he cure her daughter, he quickly seems to have realized his bias and healed the young woman.

Jesus also reveals his reverence for women in his parables. He tells the story of the virgins who are prepared for the wedding feast, to show that both men and women participate in the reign of God. In Matthew's judgment scene, women and men equally come together for the days of fulfillment. The story of a woman putting yeast in bread tells of a female disciple spreading the word of God. And in the magnificent story of the woman searching for a lost coin, Jesus portrays God as a woman seeking out a lost soul. As Jesus weeps over Jerusalem and the difficult times ahead, he uses a female image for himself as he says: "How many times I yearned to gather your children together, as a hen gathers her young under her wings, but you were unwilling!" (Mt 23:37).

Women Disciples

Jesus not only challenged many of the Jewish traditions regarding women but also, in one instance, he moved radically beyond them. Jesus chose women disciples, and there was no precedent for that among Jewish teachers and leaders in his day.

Much has been made of Jesus' choice of twelve male apostles, even to the point of justifying an all-male hierarchy and priesthood. In fact, the significance of the twelve is problematic in that the Gospels present varying lists of names. There are no accounts of apostles being replaced other than in the case of Judas, and little or nothing is known of their missions other than that of Peter. It is possible that the twelve are given as symbolic heads of the "new" tribes of Israel and that this symbolism developed in the post-Resurrection period. It is also recognized that the term *apostle*

Jesus chose women disciples

broadened under Paul and others to signify those who were truly passing on the tradition of Jesus.

Leading Women Disciples

The New Testament provides us with a number of examples of women followers of Jesus. Women accompanied Jesus in his work, were closely present during the key events of his death and Resurrection, and were prominent in the early communities.

Mary, Jesus' mother, was asked for her consent to bring him into the world. Her Magnificat puts her in the tradition of the prophetess Hannah, the mother of Samuel, and gives voice to her concern for the poor. It is Mary who orchestrates the first miracle at Cana, an event surrounded by sacramental symbolism. She bravely stands beneath her son's cross, and here Jesus joins her with his beloved disciple to begin the new community and work in partnership to continue his mission. Mary is also part of the community formed at the Pentecost, as the church is symbolically born in the Spirit.

One of Jesus' closest disciples is Mary Magdalene. One of the Gnostic gospels even says that she was his favorite. Although tradition has portrayed her as a converted prostitute, there is absolutely no evidence for this in the Gospels. This designation seems to come from a later pope who confused her with the unnamed woman who washed Jesus' feet and dried them with her hair. The Gospels tell us that Mary was a woman of means who financially supported the work of Jesus after she had received one of his miraculous cures. The high level of her ministry is clear from the role that Mary is given at the foot of the cross and as the first witness to the risen Jesus in John's gospel. As a result, the early church described Mary as "the apostle to the apostles."

The Gospels also tell us of two close women friends of Jesus: Martha and Mary. Jesus reminds Martha that domestic tasks are not as important as listening to the Word of God. In John's gospel, Martha provides table service and is a key figure in the resuscitation of her brother Lazarus. Martha hears from Jesus himself that he is the Resurrection and the life, and she responds by declaring her faith in him as Messiah and Son of God, all key beliefs of the post-Resurrection faith. These stories clearly reveal memories of the importance Jesus gave to women and the central roles they had in the early communities.

Martha's sister, Mary of Bethany, is portrayed as a key disciple. Ignoring the taboos of the time, Jesus came to her house, taught her, and defended her right to accept his message. Just before Jesus' death, Mary anointed his feet with an abundance of her best perfume and dried them with her long, flowing hair. It is striking how Jesus follows her example and washes the feet of his disciples at his last supper in John's gospel. Mary of Bethany certainly provides a striking symbol of women disciples carrying out sacramental ministry in the early communities.

As was discussed in an earlier chapter, there is strong evidence that women also served in key ministerial roles in the early Christian communities. Priscilla, who worked closely with Paul, the apostle, is an outstanding example. Paul acknowledges in his letter to the Romans that Priscilla and her husband, Aquila, risked their own necks to save his life. Priscilla was one of the founders of the community at Corinth and a major player in Rome and Antioch. There was also Junia, whom Paul said was distinguished among the apostles, and Phoebe, who led the church at Cenchrae. Tryphosa, Julia, and many other women are named in the New Testament as leaders of communities and disciples who acted as early preachers, teachers, and leaders of liturgy. Clearly, the Scriptures give solid justification for women to be at the center of Christian ministry.

Some Outstanding Christian Women

Throughout the history of the Church, there have been many outstanding examples of women playing significant roles. Early on, in the third century, Perpetua, a young wife and mother from Carthage, North Africa, was arrested for professing her faith in Jesus. Her father, still a pagan, kept bringing Perpetua's anxious little son to the prison and begged her to recant, but she wouldn't give up her faith in spite of the pain these visits brought her. She was condemned to death and was thrown to the wild beasts in the coliseum. For many early Christians, who lived in danger because of their faith, Perpetua stood as a courageous and sacrificing hero.

In the sixth century, Scholastica, the sister of Benedict, one of the founders of monastic life at Monte Cassino, established a convent near-by and helped set up the foundations for religious life for women. In the fourteenth century, Catherine of Siena (d. 1380) spent her youth tending outcasts with diseases and serving poor people. She later became a strong political force, writing letters to princes and Church officials and urging them to cease their wars and violence. She became so influential that she was able to persuade the pope to leave Avignon and return to Rome. After doing this, the pope sent her as his emissary to settle the civil war in Italy. Narrowly escaping an attempt on her life, Catherine was instrumental in bringing peace to her area. Summoned to Rome, she then served another pope in bringing about Church reforms and worked on high-level political matters for the Vatican. Pope Paul VI in 1970 declared Catherine a Doctor of the Church.

Teresa of Avila (d. 1582) was born as the Protestant Reformation was beginning and played a key role in reforming Carmelite convents. She journeyed throughout Spain, opening new convents that were exemplary houses of prayer. Teresa faced resistance to her reforms from her own order and was even charged by the infamous Inquisition. Her writings on the mystical life are classic, and in September of 1970 she was de-clared the first woman Doctor of the Church, shortly before Catherine was declared.

Elizabeth Seton, the first canonized American saint, was born just before the signing of the Declaration of Independence. She was born into a well-to-do New York family and married a wealthy shipping merchant, having five children with him. While in Italy, Elizabeth's husband lost his business and died of tuberculosis. Soon after that she was converted to Catholicism and opened a small Catholic school in Baltimore. Eventually Elizabeth took religious vows and founded the Sisters of Charity. She died at age forty-seven, a pioneer in Catholic education.

One of the most outstanding Catholic women in modern times is Dorothy Day. A college dropout, she went to work as a journalist in New York City. After a love affair, an abortion, a failed marriage to an older man, and a common law marriage wherein she had her beloved daughter, Tamar, Dorothy was converted to Catholicism. After meeting Peter Maurin, a dedicated social activist, she joined him in starting the Catholic Worker Movement, which campaigned for poor people and opened houses and soup kitchens for homeless people. Through their newspaper, they promoted labor rights and nonviolence. Even though Dorothy said she never wanted to be canonized because she wanted to be taken seriously, her cause was opened in 2000.

And then there is Mother Teresa of Calcutta, who is known worldwide for founding homes for the dying, clinics for lepers, and orphanages for abandoned children. Mother Teresa is discussed in depth in chapter 9.

These are only a few examples of women who have given outstanding service to their Church.

The Women's Movement

The roles that women assume in the Church today are in part influenced by the women's movement. The sea change we see today began in Europe and the United States in the nineteenth century. In the United States, women like Susan B. Anthony and Elizabeth Cady Stanton led the women's movement. For four decades, Anthony traveled throughout the United States, stumping for women's right to vote. It was only fourteen years after her death in 1920 that women were finally permitted to vote in this country. She and Stanton were also strong advocates for women's rights in divorce and for temperance laws to alleviate the economic and even physical abuse that women received from their drunken spouses.

In the 1960s a new wave of the women's movement, sometimes called "women's liberation," appeared in this country. This movement went beyond women's rights and advocated the freedom of self-determination.

Many women wanted to go beyond the roles and jobs assigned them by society and become free to develop themselves in an environment of equality. Women wanted access to all arenas: professional, military, sports, and ecclesiastical. As a result of their efforts, women have made significant strides in the armed forces, law, medicine, corporate life, and higher education.

Student Reflection

"I heard about 'women's lib' from my mother. She said that at first she got caught up in it and at college she and her friends burned their bras and marched for women's rights. Now she feels that women have gone too far and are too preoccupied with male bashing and wanting to take the power from men. I think the women's movement is no longer needed because women are equal today. I haven't experienced any inequality because I am a woman."

The modern women's movement has often blamed patriarchy for gender inequality and oppression. They claim that top-down male hierarchies have been established in society on all levels from home to office to church. These structures are often based on archaic beliefs that women are inferior to men, that they are too emotional, romantic, and even seductive to be trusted with positions of responsibility. Women's difference lies in the physical: they have been designed to have children and to assume the primary responsibility for feeding and raising them.

Patriarchy establishes the dominance of men over women. "Father knows best" and is "head" of the family. In this structure women should be obedient, submissive, serving. They are, as indicated in 2 Genesis, "helpers" of men. Like all good servants, women should know their place and stay there. And for most traditionalists, their place is in the home, the kitchen, and the nursery, doing "women's work."

women have made significant strides

 Student Reflection

"My father is a good man, brought up on a farm and has worked hard all his life. But he sees himself as being in charge, and when he comes home tired from work, Mom and the girls are supposed to wait on him. Wow, did we have some wild sessions at home over these issues! I love my father, but I certainly don't want to marry a man with his attitudes."

Variations in the Movement

In recent times, women have discovered that their search for equality is challenged by factors other than gender. Women of color face two obstacles: their gender and their race. They have expressed themselves in womanist literature that reflects struggles different from white women in more secure economic situations.

Groups of women in developing countries recognize that they face gender, racial, and cultural barriers unique to their situation. For example, a considerable literature has appeared from *mujerista* authors, expressing the oppression experienced by women in Latino cultures.

The Women's Movement in the Church

The women's movement has affected most churches and religions and some advances have been made. With the exceptions of the Orthodox and Hasidic communities, the Jewish religion has women rabbis. Many Protestant churches have ordained women in positions of ministry, and women have been ordained to the priesthood in the Anglican and Episcopalian churches. Some Anglican provinces have women bishops and the Episcopalians in the United States now have a woman presiding as bishop.

The official Catholic Church has adamantly opposed the ordination of women. Since the 1970s many Catholic women have protested this decision. The Catholic Church has lost many talented women to other churches over this issue, although some have decided to become ordained by people they consider legitimate bishops and function in the Church despite the excommunication they face for doing so. Recently, ordinations of Catholic women have been carried out in Europe, Canada, and the United States. In this country, the Women's Ordination Conference has been a strong advocate in this area. But among their number are many who say that they would not want to be ordained into the priesthood in its present hierarchical, male-dominated condition.

The protests have come from different quarters of the Church. Women who have participated in their husband's deacon training program often complain they are unfairly denied ordination to the diaconate. Despite centuries of early church deaconesses, and requests by the American Canon Law Society and many clergy in this country, the Vatican's answer remains no.

Women in the Church have various complaints. Many protest the constant use of male images for God, when the Scriptures provide a number of female images; in response, some have recovered goddess images for their spiritual practice. Others object to the pervasive use of exclusive language in the liturgy of the Church. Still others are offended by the dominance of males in leading liturgy, preaching, administering the sacraments, and holding positions of authority in the Church.

A related phenomenon is the appearance of many women's circles. Some are book clubs or discussion groups; others are formed for prayer, liturgy, or social action. Often these are actually faith communities where women feel more at home than they do in their parishes. Some see these circles as the basis for a new energy and spiritual power among women.

Student Reflection

"I belong to a women's group in my dorm. We have a special bond as Christian women at our meetings on Wednesday evenings. We read current items, discuss whatever we want, and pray together. Church really 'happens' for us at these meetings. Recently we have started to volunteer at a soup kitchen once a month, and the experience of being with homeless women and prostitutes has given us lots to talk about."

Many groups of religious women also oppose their treatment by the official Church. Many of the Sisters took Vatican II reform seriously and worked arduously to update their congregations and offer their members excellent educations. Often the Vatican and the local bishops thwarted their efforts. As a result, these congregations have been unable to present a clear picture of their goals to new recruits. In addition, many conservative bishops are dismissing well-educated and progressive Sisters from their dioceses after years of dedication. Kenneth Briggs, in his new book, *Double Crossed,* takes the position that the Vatican and many in the hierarchy have indeed betrayed the nuns in America, and as a consequence many congregations are facing extinction. Many believe that only when these groups disappear will we awake to all the work they have done around the world and understand that their passing will leave the Church in dire straits.

Many Catholic women have also experienced what some call the "stained-glass ceiling" of the Catholic Church. Well-educated women have found that they are able to go only so far in the Church, and are usually stopped by doors marked "authority" or "living wage." As a result, they have moved to other churches, to nonprofit organizations, or to their own practices, where they can use all their talents and make a decent salary. Some continue to attend parishes where they feel nurtured, but others have left the Church.

On the other hand, there are many Catholic women who are satisfied with the situation in the Church today. They feel that they have ample opportunity to carry out work for the Church in many areas and have no desire for ordination or to assume official leadership roles. There are also those who, while disappointed with the official Church, choose to stay because they treasure the Catholic tradition and the experience of "church" in their local community. Some believe they have enough to do with raising their families or in their jobs and professions without getting involved in these ecclesiastical debates.

Official Catholic Positions on Women

The Vatican has had several significant encounters with the women's movement. On an international level, the Vatican battled with women's groups over abortion and birth control at the 1994 UN Conference on Population and Development in Cairo and the 1995 World's Womens Conference in Beijing. Intra-church confrontations have occurred over the Vatican's resistance to using inclusive language in liturgy and the Vatican's successful efforts to keep U.S. bishops from writing a pastoral letter on women.

On the positive side, John Paul II did make some efforts to bring women into the perennially all-male Vatican offices. He appointed the first woman as a superior in a Vatican congregation, the first woman to head a papal academy, and the first women to serve on the International Theological Commission, which advises the Vatican on doctrine. Some women laud the pope for his teaching on male/female complementarity, his value for life and family, and his strong devotion to Jesus' mother, Mary. Others thought that the Roman appointments of women were tokenism and that the pope remained a strong traditionalist regarding women.

The Teachings of John Paul II on Women

In 1988 John Paul II published a significant document on women called *On the Dignity of Women*. In it the pope points out that Vatican II committed the Church to reading the signs of the times to discover what God is calling it to do. Further, John Paul notes that Vatican II acknowledged the fullness of women's vocation and influence, as well as their equality with men, a historic turning point. Deeply steeped in the Scriptures, John Paul reminds us that women and men were both created in the image of God and acknowledges the feminine images of God in the Scriptures. He urges women not to give up their unique characteristics in an effort to liberate themselves from male domination.

The pope describes how Jesus was such a unique promoter of women's dignity and vocation, citing many gospel examples of his compassion and concern for women. He recognizes that Jesus did in fact choose women as his disciples, an unprecedented choice at that time. At the same time, he insists that Jesus was deliberate in calling only men to be apostles, thus establishing that only men can act at Eucharist in the person of Christ. Although he is thankful for the "feminine genius" and for all the fruits of "feminine holiness," he is adamant that we not change the "immutable truth and values" of Jesus.

In 1995, on the occasion of the World Conference of Women at Beijing, John Paul wrote a letter to the women of the world stressing that the Catholic Church wants to do its part in upholding the dignity, role, and rights of women. He thanks women for being good mothers, wives, daughters, sisters, and workers in every area of life. He thanks vowed women, and then writes: "Thank you, every woman, for the simple fact of being a woman!" He points out that women's insight enriches the world and helps make human relations more honest and authentic. In an unusual section, the pope recognizes that members of the Church have prevented women from fulfilling themselves, and he says: "For this I am truly sorry." He hopes that the Church will commit itself to the attitude of Jesus and the Gospels and set women free from every kind of exploitation and domination.

The pope then gets specific and calls for real equality in terms of equal pay for equal work, protection of working mothers, fairness in career advancement, and equality in the area of family rights and citizens' rights. The pope recognizes the significant contributions that women are making in all areas of life. At the same time, he vigorously denounces the sexual violence and oppression to which so many women are subject. He expresses his admiration for women who are dedicated to fighting for women's dignity and rights.

In the same year that John Paul wrote this letter to women, he presented a document reiterating the Church's ban on the ordination of women. Here he repeats the earlier position of Paul VI that Jesus chose only men apostles, and the Church in choosing only men for the priesthood is in accordance with God's plan. He points out that in doing this Jesus wasn't just making a cultural decision in accordance with the practices of his time, a decision now subject to change with the modern culture. No, Jesus was making a "free and sovereign" decision to choose men apostles to be the foundation of his Church. He points out that Jesus did not even choose his own mother for the apostolic mission or priesthood, and this in no way cast a shadow on her great dignity. Although recognizing the presence of women disciples in the Gospels and early church, women cannot be ordained. He points out that this is no longer open to debate, nor is it simply a disciplinary matter. John Paul is firm: "Wherefore, in order that all doubt may be removed regarding a matter of great importance, a matter which pertains to the Church's divine constitution itself, in virtue of my ministry of confirming the brethren (cf. Lk 22:32), I declare that the Church has no authority whatsoever to confer priestly ordination on women and that this judgment is to be definitively held by all the Church's faithful."

New Feminist Interpretations

Women scholars and theologians have now taken their place in the academic arena and are providing new and valuable insights into the Christian tradition. Women biblical scholars have been studying the Scriptures, reclaiming many formerly ignored feminine emphases, and at the same time revealing patriarchal biases that underlie the Scriptures. After all, the Old and New Testaments were largely written from the male perspective and for thousands of years have been studied and interpreted from the same perspective. It is time for a fresh look at these Scriptures from a feminist perspective, a perspective that is committed to the full equality and dignity of women.

Women scholars have also been working hard at giving a new look to the Christian tradition. They have provided exciting new insights into the God question, Christology, the Church, and sacraments, as well as original views on moral questions, especially those touching on social justice. There are now many female voices speaking from the experience of poverty, oppression, and violence and calling the Church to new responsibilities and commitments. One can only imagine the implications if the entire Christian tradition was studied and re-interpreted from a female perspective.

Next, we provide an overview of developments in feminist theology and address some of their implications for the Church.

The God Question

As we have seen, the Vatican acknowledges the presence of feminine images for God in the Scriptures, and at the same time insists on the universal use of masculine images as well as gender-exclusive language in liturgical celebrations and official documents. Women theologians challenge this and call for a more balanced use of feminine imagery and language in the Church. They offer not only an acknowledgment of feminine imagery, but also in-depth studies that call the Church to a more balanced and inclusive approach to the God question.

The fact that 1 Genesis proclaims that women and men are made in the image and likeness of God has tremendous implications for renewal in the Church. This is the place to start, and this acknowledgment of the sacredness and equality of the sexes provides a critical perspective on the development of the patriarchal, oppressive structures that also exist in the tradition.

Carl Jung (d. 1961) tells us that the feminine (anima) and masculine (animus) are blended in each person. The two complement each other, and each dimension of sexuality makes a distinct contribution. For the person of faith, the feminine and masculine have their source in the Creator, and both are needed if we are to authentically understand the ultimate, Mystery we call God. Jung also teaches that the human mind is shaped by hereditary factors as well as tradition and carries within it archetypes that are part of the collective unconscious. In other words, each person is born with a mind that has already been shaped by millennia of imagining. We are born already influenced by humankind's profound experiences and deepest longings. The archetypes we carry within us enable us to explore the mysteries of life. We might also say that the many religious myths are really embodiments of these archetypes and reflect the perennial human search for answers to ultimate questions.

Women biblical scholars have reclaimed the goddess images that influenced Judaism, figures like Ashtar, Isis, and Tiamat, which they encountered from the Abrahamic roots, their contact with the Canaanites, and their time in Babylon and Egypt. These female images were operative in Judaism until they were suppressed by the prophets, and then they were transformed into the wisdom tradition, with the eternal and powerful Sophia and the divine Lady Wisdom at its center. Whereas, most female images have been rejected as "pagan" by the patriarchal tradition, they now can be recovered as rich and fruitful images of the feminine dimension of the deity. In the same way, the feminine images in Roman and Greek religions (especially the Hellenistic mystery religions that have so many parallels in Christian tradition) and the emphasis on the feminine in the Gnostic communities offer rich insights into the Mystery we call God.

As we know, the Hebrew culture developed over millennia amidst social structures that were largely patriarchal. Patriarchy gradually pushed the female aside and by the time of Moses, the predominant image was Yahweh, often portrayed as a king or father. As the one God belief began to dominate, all the characteristics of the other gods and goddesses were subsumed under Yahweh, who would encompass Sky God, Storm God, Warrior, Creator, Lawgiver, Punisher, and Redeemer. Even though the prophets used some female images of God, the male images prevailed and thus the priesthood and leadership roles in government, education, and households were placed in the hands of males. Yahweh was now the God of the fathers and the Father-God.

The Female Images of Old Europe

Marija Gimbutas, a well-known archeologist, has gathered thousands of symbolic artifacts from Neolithic village sites, from a period she calls Old Europe (7000–3500 BCE). These items have revealed the rituals and themes of a female-centered religion, where the universe is viewed as the living body of the Mother Creator. It is she who gives meaning to the mysteries of birth, life, and death and of all that exists. All living things take part in her divinity. In this world, there is a striking absence of domination and warfare, and there is a balanced social order wherein women play key roles. This is in marked contrast to life in the male-dominated Indo-European tribes that overran these areas in the fourth century BCE, tribes noted for their violence and brutality. Gimbutas points out that these feminist cultures existed for thousands of years, until they were replaced by patriarchal cultures with warrior deities. Gallic and Celtic cultures held onto remnants of these female images of God well into the fourth century of the Christian period, when Roman Catholicism suppressed them. Homage to the Earth Mother was gradually replaced by devotion to the Blessed Mother and female saints.

Trinity

Women theologians have pointed out the excess of male imagery in the Trinity, where the Father, Son, and Spirit all seem to be male. Some try to moderate this by using terms like Creator, Redeemer, and Comforter. Others reclaim the ancient Syriac and Eastern traditions, where the Spirit is addressed as female. There has also been more emphasis placed on the bonding and relational aspects of the Trinity, which are strong feminine values. From this perspective, the communal life within God is characterized by equality, partnership, and interaction.

Christology

Women's voices have provided many new interpretations of Jesus Christ and his mission. These voices are not only from scholars but also "from below," from women who have experienced oppression within their church and the world and who look to Jesus for liberation. Western women have viewed Jesus as one who confronted the patriarchal and hierarchical structures of his time and who is now with them in their similar struggle. Black womanist writers believe that they were often bypassed by the civil rights movement and look to new views on Jesus to address their issues.

Mujerista authors, speaking from the Latina experience of women in the Americas, hold that liberation theology did not include their struggle for freedom and now look to Jesus in their struggle. More recently women's voices are being heard from Asia, Africa, and Eastern Europe, seeking a Savior that will accompany them in their unique search for equality.

Some women express discomfort with the traditional stress on the "maleness" of Jesus, because maleness was so often used in the past to justify oppression. Black women point to "slaveholding" Christianity, which could worship the Lord Jesus on Sunday and at the same time "own" people and treat them as inferior. They point to Christian communities who saw no contradiction between the Christ they worshipped and segregation and the exclusion of black women in their churches. And they note how many black women are caught in a male-designed welfare system that keeps them in a position of powerlessness.

Latina women point to the male image of Christ the King that was used by the conquistadores to subject whole peoples to genocide and servitude. They signal liberation theologians that present Jesus as a liberator but fail to confront the machismo that so oppresses women in their cultures. This male force has allowed men to abuse women, desert them, and subject them to inhumane working conditions, often in cultures that consider themselves to be Christian.

Other feminist theologians reject the "metaphysical Christ" so prominent in the early councils of the Church. They point out that much of this perspective is based on Hellenic philosophy, where women are seen as inferior, and which requires that salvation comes only if a male God becomes a male savior. Many insist that in the Incarnation, God became "human" rather than "male," and that Jesus represents the best of what it means to be human, a person who lived and died for love, compassion, and equality. Jesus thus represents the wholeness to which all women and men are called. If Incarnation refers to the embodiment of God, then this should include the female body, which is uniquely life giving, feeding, and nurturing. This reclaims an earthy Jesus, who touched and healed bodies and challenged the sexual taboos of his time. Women speak of a sensuous Christ, who makes women proud of their bodies, confident in their beauty, and insistent on respect of their dignity. This is a Christ who values the intuitive, is comfortable with relating and intimacy, and who can be discovered in new ways in the female experience.

Some Latina theologians are not so put off by Jesus' maleness, but value the historical Jesus as a strong and courageous leader who stood up for the freedom of women. He is a Savior who walks with them in their struggles, as well as a good role model for the men in their society. Others favor focusing on the Christ of faith, the risen Jesus who now transcends sexuality. This glorified Christ is viewed as being in solidarity with women, a spiritual presence that empowers them in their struggle for liberation. They see this Christ in the face of women of all colors and backgrounds who suffer poverty, degradation, or subjugation from their government, from neocolonial policies, or in their own families or religious communities.

Redemptive Suffering

Some women theologians challenge the traditional Christian notion of the redemptive power of suffering. They observe that the belief that Jesus saved us from our sins through suffering has often been used to teach women to stoically and patiently accept their suffering as God's will. This can create passivity in women and stand in the way of their fight for liberation.

 Student Reflection

"That reminds me of my grandmother. She was abused by my alcoholic grandfather and her priest always told her to 'just offer it up.' She always seemed so helpless and like she had given up on happiness here and just wanted to be in heaven."

Women also challenge some interpretations of the belief that Jesus is the new Adam, who saved us from the sin of Eve. Here women are often portrayed as wily seductresses who lead men astray. They should therefore stay in the background, stand by their men, and allow men to lead them and save them from their weakness and sin. This has led some women to believe that they have to bear the sins of others the way Jesus did and even allow themselves to be sacrificed as victims of domestic violence or unjust labor practices.

In response to these beliefs, it is proposed that suffering, for Jesus or others, is caused by evil people and systems, not God's will. Therefore, women should be made more aware of the social, economic, political, and religious evils that suppress them. They should be encouraged to reject and resist such oppression, rather than to passively endure it. Here Jesus is viewed as a fellow sufferer who took the side of the oppressed, condemned the oppressors, and was crucified for his actions.

This view of Jesus Christ as a companion-sufferer is central in much feminist theology. Whether they are victims as abused wives or daughters, homeless bag ladies in the worst areas of a city, girls forced into prostitution, or abandoned mothers in a barrio, they pray to Jesus as the source of their strength and courage to go on. The literature reveals a deep faith that Jesus is walking with a young teen working long hours in a sweatshop, an outcast lesbian, or a young mother with AIDS. Women who search for clean water and food for their children in Korea write about the power they receive from Jesus. Workers in an orphanage in Nicaragua tell of seeing him in the faces of disabled children. Stories from nursing homes reveal that the elderly and dying find hope and strength in experiencing the Spirit of Jesus with them. And this does not seem to be the image of the suffering Jesus, but rather the experience of Jesus affirming them, helping them deal with their pain. This seems to be a Jesus Christ who saves in suffering and from suffering rather than through suffering.

In what has become an avalanche of Christian women's writing, there is also the perspective that Christ's mission should not be restricted to victims and outcasts. A Christology is also needed that addresses women who live comfortably and have good opportunities for work and education. Not enough theological reflection has been done for women who have good marriages, but feel overwhelmed by the responsibilities of homemaking and mothering. And who is Christ for working mothers or professional single women? Who is Christ for women in the military, the corporate world, or the fields of law, medicine, sports, education, and other areas? These women are diverse and need a Jesus Christ who offers them wholeness and calls them to generous service. They call for the Church to address more dimensions of women's vocations than the motherhood and virginity mentioned in the papal teaching on women.

Women theologians have reclaimed the prophetic image of Jesus, seeing him as a person who proclaims as blessed the poor and out-cast, condemns those who lay heavy burdens on their backs, and frees people from whatever imprisons them. Many women, whether "imprisoned" by the stifling routine of the suburbs, the monotony of schoolwork, the squalor of the barrios, the environmentally degraded villages of Eastern Europe, or the refugee tent cities in Africa, look to Jesus for a strengthening presence. Many have been inspired by him to rise up and confront the dominating and unjust institutions around them. They have experienced "woman power" and "woman church" as they organize and fight for respect and dignity in their cultures and religions. They see Jesus as the "prophet of Sophia," with her mission to spread a creative, relational, and joyful message. They identify with Jesus' movement of compassionate healers, people who left their patriarchal families and trades and lived as brothers and sisters, a discipleship of equals. They view the Spirit of Jesus as one that transcends race, gender, and sex and is available to all.

Feminist Views on the Church

Vatican II gave many women a new perspective on the Church. They were attracted to the biblical description of Church as "the people of God," because it included them. They rejoiced when they heard the council proclaim "a Church of equals" and were delighted with John XXIII's goal to restore the Church to its original vision of a community following Jesus' unprecedented choice to have women and men disciples. Women heard that the Church was now willing to read "the signs of times" to discern its present mission and presumed this would include the signs made by the women's movement. They now saw themselves as part of a Church dedicated to the world, in solidarity with the oppressed, and dedicated to restoring justice. This gave many women hope that they could now count on the Church to address the many areas where women were oppressed. Women were excited that they could now receive more visibility in the Church as leaders, catechists, lectors, Eucharistic ministers, professors of theology, and counselors. They were now full-fledged members of a "priestly people" and were willing to do their part in fostering the reign of God.

The new emphasis on community when discussing the Church has appealed to many women. Women often have special gifts for relating and bonding and know that they have a great deal to contribute in this area. Women also approved of the Church's newly placed value on the heart as well as the head, on power *with* over power *over,* and on the experiential and emotional to balance the rational. This was a more balanced and holistic approach to mission that was more compatible with the style of many women, a more balanced approach to mission. Words like *cooperation, collaboration,* and *consultation* attracted many women to the Church because these were their preferred modes of operation.

Resistance to the Old Ways

Those who have embraced this new vision of Church are resistant to any return to a Church that is top-down, hierarchical, and absolute with centralized authority. Women have been able to work effectively with bishops who embrace the new vision, but there has been considerable tension when leaders revert back to the "do as I tell you" mode of authority. Sisters' congregations, in their efforts to renew and revise their own dress and way of life, often clashed with the Vatican and local bishops. Individual women who

[Vatican II] gave many women hope

found themselves in a position of dissent were punished. Organizations promoting women's issues or women's ordination were marginalized. Recently, a number of conservative bishops, committed to restoring the traditional ways, have been appointed to dioceses. This often means progressive Sisters and laywomen who have spent decades serving the Church in its renewal efforts are fired.

The Ordination Issue

The ordination of women remains a flash point for many women in the Church. The Vatican has spoken a number of times on this issue and considers the matter closed. Many women (as well as men) consider the matter still open to debate. As we have seen, the official Church's teaching hinges on Jesus' decision to choose only men apostles. These men apostles are the foundation of priesthood and so there is nothing the Church can do if it wants to remain in line with the will of Jesus. Moreover, the priest stands "in the person of Christ," the Bridegroom, and must therefore be a man.

Biblical scholars and church historians have other views. Biblical scholars are unanimous in saying there is nothing in the New Testament to oppose the ordination of women. As for the twelve apostles, there are challenging questions. Though the Gospels maintain a strong tradition for an apostolic mission, the list of apostles' names varies from one gospel to another. As mentioned earlier, the apostles in the Gospels vote to replace Judas, but after that none of them is replaced when they die. With the exception of Peter, we know little about the mission of each apostle. In addition, in the New Testament the word *apostle* has a variety of applications, at one time referring to Jesus, at another to Paul and Barnabas or other disciples; and the word is also used to describe an office of ministry in the early church.

There are also complications with the notion of priesthood. We know that neither Jesus nor the apostles were priests in their Jewish religion. The Christian priesthood, largely inherited from Judaism, seems to have evolved in the second century. Later it was influenced by the clerical structures of the Roman Empire. As a result, it is difficult to ascertain the "will of Jesus" regarding the priesthood. We do know, however, that he did not accept the taboos of his time against women and that he made the unprecedented decision to select female disciples. All of these points and others need to be addressed in any future discussion of woman's ordination. Fr. Bernard Haring, one of the leading theologians at Vatican II, maintains that arguments against the ordination of women are flawed. As for women standing in the person of Christ at Eucharist, he sees no problem with that because it is the Spirit who actually transforms the bread and wine.

Conclusion

The role of women in the Church will be one of the central questions affecting the future of the Church. As the clerical system of priesthood continues to decline, there will be a need to move in a new direction. If a council considers questions of renewal in the future, it will hardly be simply a gathering of twenty-five hundred men as it was during Vatican II. Consideration will have to be given toward having an equal number of women. Of course, this is problematic because in the present system authority in the Church is synonymous with ordination, and women cannot be ordained. The Vatican must continue to introduce women into its congregations, and bishops must proceed to appoint women to leadership positions, such as pastoral associates and diocesan officials. But until Church authority can be separated from ordination or until women can be ordained, women will not be able to hold positions equal to men. If women were given equality in the Catholic Church, the future Church would have a different look indeed. Imagine the changes that would mean in ministry, liturgy, moral teaching, and justice concerns. Imagine a Vatican III with women equally represented.

Women Martyrs

Throughout the history of Christianity, many women have been willing to sacrifice their lives for their beliefs. In the early church, there was Perpetua, a well-to-do young mother who, while still nursing her baby, was threatened with death if she did not give up her belief in Jesus. Her prison diary reveals the intense struggle she endured as she faced the choice of giving up her family and even her newborn baby if she refused to offer sacrifice to the Roman gods and deny her Christian faith. Perpetua chose to be a faithful disciple. She was condemned and sentenced to be torn apart by wild animals in the arena.

Tekla, a woman who was converted by Paul the apostle himself, took on an apostolic mission to spread the gospel to others. She was threatened with rape, with being sold into prostitution, and with execution, but refused to give up her ministry. Eventually, she was publicly executed in the arena.

In our own time there have been many women who were martyred for their faith. In 1942, Sister Edith Stein, a Carmelite nun who had converted from Judaism, was gassed and cremated at Auschwitz. The Gestapo arrested Sister Stein from her convent in Holland in retaliation for the Christian rejection of Nazism in that country.

In 1980, three Sisters, Maura Clarke, Dorothy Kazel, and Ita Ford, along with a lay missionary, Jean Donovan, were arrested, sexually abused, and murdered by the Salvadoran military for their work serving poor people in the name of Christ during the civil war in El Salvador.

In 2005, Sister Dorothy Stang, an American Sister who for years defended the Brazilian rain forests and stood up against the developers who oppressed the poor people there, was murdered. Her actions for gospel justice moved one logger to hire two hit men to shoot Sister Dorothy in cold blood. She died reading the Scriptures.

These are just a few of the many women who have chosen to stand with Jesus and his teachings and have had to pay with their lives for this decision.

she died reading the Scriptures

Activities

1. Do a survey of women's groups on the Internet and discuss in class the range and diversity of these groups.

2. Have a team survey and analyze advances women have made in the professions, corporate life, and the military.

3. Invite a woman Protestant minister, Jewish rabbi, or Episcopalian priest into class to discuss her experience of ministry.

4. Hold a debate on whether or not women should be ordained in the Catholic Church.

5. Visit a church where the service is led by an ordained woman and discuss your reactions in the next class.

Sources

Beattie, Tina. *New Catholic Feminism*. New York: Routledge, 2006.

Carmody, Denise. *Responses to 101 Questions about Feminism*. New York: Paulist Press, 1993.

Chittister, Joan. *Job's Daughters: Women and Power*. New York: Paulist Press, 1990.

Douglas, Kelly Brown. *The Black Christ*. Maryknoll, NY: Orbis Books, 1994.

Eigo, Francis, ed. *Discipleship of Equals*. Villanova, PA: Villanova University Press, 1988.

Fabella, Virginia, and Sun Ai Lee Park. *We Dare to Dream: Doing Theology as Asian Women*. Maryknoll, NY: Orbis Books, 1990.

Isherwood, Lisa. *Introducing Feminine Christologies*. Cleveland: Pilgrim Press, 2002.

Schneiders, Sandra. *Beyond Patching: Faith and Feminism in the Catholic Church*. New York: Paulist Press, 1991.

Schüssler Fiorenza, Elizabeth. *In Memory of Her*. New York: Crossroad, 1994.

Tamaz, Elsa, ed. *Through Her Eyes: Women's Theology from Latin America*. Maryknoll, NY: Orbis Books, 1989.

9 Modern Catholic Social Teaching

The modern Catholic Church's

teaching on social justice comes to us through official documents and grassroots actions. In this chapter we discuss both, examining the history of official Catholic social teaching and then two lives that offer outstanding examples of the teaching: Mother Teresa and Cesar Chavez.

The start of official modern Catholic social teaching is usually credited to an encyclical letter by Pope Leo XIII in 1891. Catholic social teaching continues in the present time with three encyclical letters by Pope John Paul II. Official teaching also comes through documents produced by bishops' conferences, and here we limit our discussion to two notable documents produced by U.S. bishops' conferences, one on peace and one on justice.

Modern Catholic social teaching evolves and changes with time. It arises out of historical situations and is produced by scholars prevalent at the time of the writing. These scholars serve as consultants and authors of documents to which popes affix their names and authority. Hence, Catholic social teaching is always contextual, reflecting the issues that are pressing at the time. And yet throughout there is a consistency in values and themes that can often be applied to current situations.

A Brief Historical Overview

Leo XIII

Leo XIII (d. 1903) was a highly intelligent, aristocratic scholar, who was well trained in Thomistic philosophy and well informed about the social theories prevalent in late-nineteenth-century Europe. He writes as an embattled witness, still smarting over the collapse of the Papal States in 1870, the loss of Church authority to that of State, and the deep divisions in Christianity left by the Reformation. Leo's Church was largely a European-dominated institution that accommodated colonialism but opposed the Enlightenment's scientific advances as well as individualism, democracy, and secularism. The French Revolution's destruction of the Church and slaughter of its clergy and leaders made revolution-generated notions about liberalism, freedom, and equality anathema to the official Church. The pope before Leo, Pius IX, had condemned liberalism, and aside from a few voices, like that of Bishop von Kettler (d. 1877) in Germany and Cardinal Manning (d. 1892) in England, the Church was not involved in social justice issues. It was thus courageous for Leo to step into the social arena and share the Church's view. His liberal perspective on the Church's role in social matters, however, would not become mainstream until the Second Vatican Council in the 1960s.

Leo was comfortable with medieval Christendom's hierarchical model of Church and State, where both institutions worked together for the personal salvation of all. In this model, the Church provides the State with the natural and divine laws, the unchanging truths needed to achieve eternal happiness. Duty is key: the State is duty bound to listen to the teachings of the Church and each citizen is duty bound to obey the Church and listen to "the justly constituted authority" of the State.

The Church of Leo's time opposed what it considered to be two conflicting extremes: (1) individualism, democratization, and liberal capitalism, which were jointly blamed for the rebellion against Church and State; and (2) collectivism as seen in the rise of socialism and communism in Europe. Leo's world was in the midst of an Industrial Revolution, where greed often enslaved the working class in grinding poverty and produced their class struggle with the wealthy owners of capital, a struggle that was aggravated by atheistic Marxist theories. Many still placed the Church on the side of absolute power and capital, and Leo wanted them to see that the Church was concerned about workers.

Leo took a courageous, Catholic stand for human dignity and denounced both socialism and capitalism for the dehumanization they were producing. He supported a right to private property, a just wage, and a right for workers to organize, and he recognized a need for state intervention on behalf of those who were struggling. Most important for the future of Catholic social teaching, Leo took a stand against those who said religion was private and had no business meddling in economics or politics. He loudly proclaimed that Christ's message of compassion and justice had direct bearing on the social oppression of the time and that the Church had every right to be a player in these issues.

Leo's perspective had its limitations in that it was top-down or hierarchical and relied heavily on the medieval philosophy of Thomas Aquinas. Nonetheless, it gave voice to a strong, much-needed Catholic position on social justice. The pope was showing communists, who took the position that religion was irrelevant and a crutch for the weak, that religion could be a force for justice in the world.

Pius XI

Forty years later, the Church's perspective on the socioeconomic scene of the time was again voiced, this time by Pius XI in 1931. The context had changed dramatically: The First World War had devastated Europe. Liberal capitalism was in a shambles with the Great Depression. Communism had rooted itself in Russia with the revolution, and its Soviet Union was suffering under the ruthless dictatorship of Joseph Stalin. Fascism was on the rise under the dictatorship of Benito Mussolini in Italy and with Adolf Hitler's popularly elected Nazi Party in Germany. The world was on the brink of cataclysm.

Pius (d. 1939) denounced the entire socioeconomic order of this time and proposed a new social order based on Christian principles. He also defended workers, who were desperately affected by the Great Depression, and reasserted a right to a just wage and to private property. To deal with class struggles and the abuses of capitalism, Pius advocated the estab- lishment of hierarchical vocational "orders" similar to medieval guilds. Some saw this as advocating profit sharing and co-partnership or cooperative ownership in industry. Others saw Pius' proposed orders as archaic and a reaction against the fascism in his own country. The pope's views did seem to advocate a Christian social order that seemed implausible in a modern, diverse, and global world. Though his proposals for a new social system were largely ignored, Pius made it clear that not only love but also justice were necessary for any proper reconstruction of the social order. He brought justice into the mission of the Catholic Church and advocated that the laity lead social reform efforts. In his day, Pius was recognized by many Catholics as an advocate for poor people and a champion of the common good.

John XXIII

In 1958, John XXIII (d. 1963) took the church and the world by surprise, bringing a new image to the papacy and a new voice to the cause of peace and justice in the world. John was jolly, urbane, friendly, and genuinely likeable. He came to the world, not in judgment, but as a brother, filled with hope and optimism. The Church had come through a horrific world war, was witness to the ongoing cold war, and had something to say to the world.

John's two encyclical letters, on social progress and peace and justice, received serious attention worldwide, even from Church critics. The pope wrote passionately about international inequality and economic oppression and presented a well-developed discussion of human rights. He also voiced the Church's concern about the dangers inherent in the nuclear arms race between the Soviet Union and the United States.

Pope John did not speak on high from a Church that was far-removed from world problems and yet ready to offer simplistic solutions. John spoke as an elder brother concerned about all the world's people, especially the oppressed. He taught in the name of a community of followers of Jesus and he witnessed to the gospel message of love and service. He called for freedom, the interdependence of people, and the need for solidarity with those who struggle against oppression. He spoke of the value of socialization and moved from the former language of obligation and duty to a new language of freedom for development. All the while, John was preparing a worldwide council that would be dedicated to renewing the Catholic Church, bringing it into the present, alerting it to "the signs of the times," and relating the Church to the modern world.

As we discussed earlier, the Second Vatican Council presented a renewed image of the Church as a people committed to following the example of Jesus and bringing his message of love, peace, and justice to the world. Several documents from this council are particularly relevant to social justice. The key document is *The Church in the Modern World*, which embodies Pope John's desire to see the Church as a loving servant of the world's needs. Here it clearly states that the disciples of Jesus are in solidarity with the world in which they live: "The joys and hopes, the grief

John spoke as an elder brother

and anguish of our time, especially those who are poor and afflicted, are the joys and hope, the grief and anguish of the followers of Christ." The document commits the Church to an ongoing reading of the "signs of the times" to discern how and where God is calling it to serve. The Church solemnly declares its belief in human dignity, its solidarity with human community, and its involvement in bringing justice to human activity. The views expressed are practical and address specific areas of marriage and family, culture, economics, politics, and peace.

The other council document of social import concerns religious freedom. Here the Church takes a new perspective on religious freedom, asserting that human dignity demands that no one be forced to act against his or her conscience, especially in their choice of religious belief.

Paul VI

Pope John died after the first session of the council, but the council continued under the guidance of his successor, Pope Paul VI (d. 1978), until its work was accomplished. After the council, Paul wrote a significant encyclical on development that addressed the duty of the Church to aid all people, of all nations, in growth and progress. The world in the 1960s was undergoing exciting advances in communication and rapid growth in industrialization and trade. Wealth for many was increasing briskly. The two great powers, the Soviet Union and the United States, were locked in a nuclear arms race that brought humankind to the brink of Armageddon during the Cuban missile crisis. The Vietnam War kept the globe tense, while the assassination of John F. Kennedy left it stunned. Severe oppression and injustice weighed down the Third World as its people and resources were manipulated and exploited by the First World. Dictators in Central and South America and Africa were oppressing the masses, subjecting them to widespread poverty and violence.

Paul had worked with poor people in Italy and championed the cause of workers. In his encyclical on development, he emphasizes the integral connection between the Christian faith and the pursuit of social justice. He expands the notion of development to include a right of individuals and communities to write their own history and develop their own potential and talent. He stresses that the goods of creation are meant to serve the needs of all and expresses indignity over the appalling conditions that many in the developing world face; he urges governments and international organizations to address these inequities. Paul emphasizes the notions of the "preferential option for the poor" and "solidarity," which are derived from Jesus' concern for the poor and the outcast, and these notions would later profoundly affect the formulation of liberation theology. In some of Paul's other writings, he takes a strong stand on equality and participation, shows concern for the environment, and explicitly states that the Church's message must be one of peace, justice, and liberation.

The Roman Synod on Justice

In 1971 bishops from around the world gathered in a synod to discuss the Church's commitment to justice. By now global inequities and economic oppression had grown into enormous problems. Seventy-five percent of the world's resources were being consumed by one-third of the world's population. The superpowers were spending enormous sums on the arms race as hunger, disease, and poverty spread rapidly. A population explosion in poorer countries was overwhelming their already overexploited resources; development was seriously degrading the global environment; and in the Third World, millions of people were being displaced from the land that sustained them.

Notable at this synod was the presence of many bishops from countries with widespread poverty and oppression. They could address these problems firsthand.

The bishops' document calls attention to the systemic injustices throughout the countries of the world and the need for Christians to move beyond their concern for personal salvation to commit to work for justice. Their now classic statement strongly connects faith with justice: "Action on behalf of justice and participation in the transformation of the world fully appear to us as a constitutive dimension of the preaching of the gospel." Also significant is the Church's unique admission that it too has injustices within it and must address these before it is to witness to justice in the world.

John Paul II

Pope for nearly twenty-seven years, John Paul (d. 2005) was one of the most influential church leaders of the modern era. His visits to some hundred countries gave him global visibility, and his dedication to justice and poor people was profound. His leadership spanned key years in the twentieth century and even some in the twenty-first.

Student Reflection

"Pope John Paul II was the only pope I ever knew of and I was a fan. He was an actor and skier when he was young, and he really knew how to talk with young people. My older brother went out to a youth rally in Denver, where they saw the pope and heard him talk. He said that John Paul was really great."

John Paul wrote three significant encyclicals on social justice. In the first, in 1981, he reflects biblically and in his typical personal manner on the dignity of human work. His days as a laborer in Poland under the German Nazi regime, his personal meetings with workers in other countries on his travels, and his vigorous participation in the Solidarity movement's struggle for labor unions in Poland against Soviet opposition all gave John Paul firsthand experience with the plight of workers. He knew that work had too often become a commodity and workers, mere pawns in the hands of wealthy industrialists. In response, John Paul composed a useful, contemporary theology of work, which explains the structural injustices that workers can face. This led John Paul to his serious critique of the rigid systems of capitalism and communism, both of which, he contends, unjustly give money and property priority over people. The pope focuses on the human rights of workers and stresses solidarity with them, obviously referring to his commitment to the Solidarity movement among workers in his Polish homeland.

In 1987 John Paul returned to the notion of development, especially addressing problems in the Southern Hemisphere (Central and South America, Africa). In this encyclical, he is critical of the West's liberal capitalism and the East's communism and shows how their rivalry had deeply hindered progress in the Southern Hemisphere. John Paul also notes the signs of the times: communist regimes dominating nations and brutally repressing uprisings, revolutions in Central and South America caused by repressive governments, and world markets exploiting poor people and the environment in developing countries. He points out that, although the world should be concerned about tensions between East and West, we should also be concerned about the growing inequities between the First World in the Northern Hemisphere and the Third World in the Southern. The pope further notes the insufficient attention paid to the new Fourth World, which grows as even people in wealthier nations fall into extreme poverty. The global situation has become such that a minority are getting richer, while a majority are getting poorer. John Paul deals vigorously with these new crises, critical of all sides contributing to the widespread injustice and suffering. He elaborates the notions of structural sin and the preferential option for the poor, attacks materialism, and addresses issues of overpopulation and environmental degradation.

Finally, in 1991, John Paul wrote once more on social justice. Here he speaks strongly against atheism and socialism, commenting on the recent collapse of communism, a change in which he played a significant role, especially in Poland. He continues to be critical of liberal capitalism and the kind of market economy that oppresses the poor and needy. He is also critical of welfare systems that treat poor people as objects and prevent them from participating in economic productivity. Though John Paul does not feel it is the Church's responsibility to suggest economic models, he insists that the Church play a key role in the struggle for justice.

Catholic Social Teaching

When early Catholic social teaching attacked "liberalism," it was aiming at the modern movements of capitalism, industrialism, and democracy. The Church perceived these movements as being falsely utopian, materialistic, and oppressive of the Church and the working class. Pius XI called the Church to listen to its official teaching and to return to the tried-and-true methods of guilds. Pius used the "principle of subsidiarity," which holds that nothing individuals can do for themselves should be taken away from them and given to the community. Neither should functions of lesser groups be taken over by larger and higher institutions.

Leo XIII was more modern in his approach and urged workers to organize and to work for protective legislation. Leo held that all had the right to possess property, but that this right had to take into account the needs of one's neighbors and of the community. Pius XII moved further in recognizing the modern world and recommended turning to new methods of social reform and democratic political structures.

It was at Vatican II that the Church, instead of being threatened by the modern world, clarified its role in relation to this world. Popes John XXIII, Paul, and John Paul II furthered developed the Church's position on human rights and the proper use of private property.

Underlying the earlier Catholic social teaching is an adherence to "natural law." The scholastic interpretation of natural law comes from Thomas Aquinas. Here, an eternal law or plan exists in the mind of God for all eternity and is an immutable source of all truth and value. This law is apprehended and articulated as "natural law" by human reason. Both State and Church play a role in enforcing natural law. The State, of natural origin, plays the role of regulating human behavior, punishing offenders, and providing for the common good. The Church, of divine origin and therefore superior to the State, possesses revealed truth and directs persons and institutions to their ultimate goal, the supernatural.

Leo XIII was more modern in his approach

Catholic Social Teaching in the United States

Catholic social teaching gradually made inroads into Catholic thinking in the United States. Several decades after Leo XIII's encyclical on social justice in 1891, Fr. John A. Ryan (d. 1945), a professor of theology at the Catholic University of America, published *Distributive Justice,* which analyzes the U.S. economy from the point of view of Catholic social teaching. Father Ryan went on to become a leader in Catholic social reform and in the labor movement in this country. Many of the reforms he advocated became part of Roosevelt's New Deal.

In the 1940s, Monsignor George G. Higgins became the point man for American bishops on social issues and labor relations. He worked tirelessly in both areas for fifty years and in 2000 was awarded the Presidential Medal of Freedom by President Clinton. Another "labor priest" was Fr. Charles Owen Rice, who for at least fifty years wrote a regular column on labor relations and marched in picket lines with Pittsburgh steel workers, along with his mentor, Fr. James Cox. Rice marched to protest the Vietnam War and marched with Martin Luther King Jr. to protest bigotry. The Jesuit priest, Fr. John Corridan, was another powerful advocate for Catholic social teaching. The film *On the Waterfront* is based on his dangerous fight for reform in the longshoreman's union and against the corruption and organized crime on the New York waterfront. He also served as associate director of the Xavier Institute of Industrial Relations, along with another Jesuit activist, Fr. Philip Carey. Finally, there was Dorothy Day, who along with Peter Maurin, founded the Catholic Worker Movement and spent most of her life supporting labor causes and serving poor and homeless people. We will discuss her in more detail later. These are some of the heroes of Catholic social teaching. Unfortunately, this teaching did not enter into mainstream Catholic life in America.

With the advent of Vatican II and its emphasis on social justice, more effort went into social reform. After the council, the U.S. bishops began to make statements on hunger, racism, prison reform, gun control, care of the elderly, and other social issues. They also established the Catholic Campaign for Human Development, which since 1969 has funded many low-income empowerment projects in the United States and works to educate Catholics about the root causes of poverty. The American bishops also oversee Catholic Relief Services (CRS), which was founded in 1943 to assist poor people around the globe. CRS now serves on five continents and in ninety-nine countries, providing direct assistance in emergencies and helping people work toward their own development. Recently, CRS provided relief services to earthquake victims in Pakistan, flood relief to people in Northern India and Sri Lanka, and summer camp for young people traumatized by the recent war in Lebanon as well as some seven hundred volunteers to assist in that crisis. CRS continues to provide assistance to tsunami victims and massive assistance to HIV/AIDS victims in Africa.

Significant Catholic Bishops' Statements

In the last two decades, the American bishops have published two extremely powerful documents on social issues. The first was the 1983 pastoral letter on peace, led by Archbishop Joseph Bernardin, who also designed the well-known "consistent ethic of life." In this document the bishops honor the pacifist position and the just war theory. They point out that pacifism is based on the teachings of Jesus and that the early church aspired to follow it. In their discussion of the just war theory, the bishops focus on the use of nuclear weapons as deterrence. They condemn the use of such weapons on civilian targets and can see no justification for the "first strike" use of nuclear weapons. In addition, the bishops cannot see how nuclear war can remain limited, and yet they do not close the door on the retaliatory use of nuclear weapons.

In 1986 the U.S. Catholic bishops wrote a powerful document on the relationship between the American economy and Catholic social teaching. Significantly, the bishops did not look to Rome for answers, but instead established a lengthy dialogue with experts from many fields and heard testimony from many Americans living in poverty. Next, the bishops studied the Scriptures and contemporary theology. They were then ready to call their people to a conversion in matters of economic justice and to state their solidarity with poor people.

The bishops urge participation and partnership to end unemployment, poverty, and the loss of private farms, and they call for an end of U.S. economic domination in the Third World. The bishops wisely do not claim to have all the answers, though they do have cogent suggestions for U.S. economic reform. They speak in solidarity with marginal and powerless groups in the United States, take a stand for human rights, and call for a shift in moral priorities to favor the one out of seven Americans who are poor. This was not just another Church document, but a well-researched and powerful statement that even caught the concerned attention of the Reagan White House.

Today the American bishops continue their commitment to social justice. They support the rights of workers and are critical of trade agreements that impede the development of poor countries and endanger the environment. Recently they entered the current discussion on immigration, noting the contribution that migrant workers make in this country, and urged that they be treated with dignity and paid fair wages.

The Progression of Catholic Social Teaching

Although the official Church documents on social justice try to give the impression of continuity in perspective, it is easy to detect many major changes in perspectives as the teaching develops. Like any body of thought, Church ideas evolve over time as the situations and scholarship upon which the documents depend advance. Mistakes are corrected, outdated solutions are set aside, and new ideas are introduced. In the following, we briefly discuss some of these advances.

First and foremost, one detects shifts in philosophical outlook in the documents. The early documents rely heavily on nineteenth-century Thomistic scholasticism with its static notion of natural law. Here the Church adheres to the design of all things by God. This design is unchangeable; hence, the Church strongly advocates that all persons and institutions follow this design. As time passes, the documents become more existential in outlook and recognize the changeableness and relativity of reality. There is a shift from the classical mode where things remain static and unchanged to a historical consciousness that admits change and evolution. As the complexity of reality is faced, the Church is less likely to advocate simple solutions to the world's social problems.

Another development regards dualism, which separates the natural from the supernatural, the secular from the sacred. From a dualist perspective, the Church speaks from one aspect (the supernatural) to the other (natural). Here the Church stands outside the world looking in and offers solutions from the supernatural point of view. The early Church documents here are suspicious, even condemnatory, of modern movements for freedom, equality, democracy, individualism, and science. To the "worldly" reader, the Church seems cut off, removed from the real world, and thus not fully capable of addressing its concerns.

Later documents, especially those after Vatican II, are more holistic and see reality as one, containing both natural and supernatural dimensions. God and the spiritual are within all things; the world is graced; and solutions to its problems can be found within, not from some outside or heavenly source. As one theologian put it, "Outside the world there is no salvation." Moreover, the secular world is recognized to have its own solutions to economic and political problems. Rather than proposing solutions, the Church urges society to create just solutions using its own expertise.

Another important shift is toward the Scriptures as a primary guide. Earlier documents tend to use the Church's tradition as the main source of guidance and apply this tradition with a certain infallible authority. In later documents, a contemporary approach to Scripture is used and the gospel teaching of Jesus is central.

One also sees a shift in the way the Church or the papacy views itself. In earlier documents, the Church is defensive, absolute in its teaching. The Church and papacy here are monolithic, infallible, and clearly capable of offering solutions to injustice. As time passes, Vatican II renewal provides the Church with the new image of a pilgrim people searching for how to provide the world with the gospel perspective and eager to do what they can to serve the cause of justice. The Church admits it is also on the journey, with its own injustices to heal. One notices a shift from top-down solutions to dialogue with others, including those outside the Church. Human experience is gradually recognized as a real source of truth. Here absolute norms are not as easy to come by and conscience begins to play a more prominent role in decision making.

Another shift is from the language of duty and obligation to a discussion of rights, personal and communal development, and even liberation. The Church, rather than being an institution that requires obedience, is a community dedicated to helping people develop their potential and be free. It is a community in solidarity with all people, especially those who are poor and oppressed. Governments are viewed not so much as rulers of the masses, but as protectors of human rights and agents of empowerment.

Finally, the papal voice changes dramatically as one reads these documents. Earlier popes spoke as authoritative teachers from afar, removed from the world, but confident that the Church had the needed solutions. In contrast, the popes from John XXIII on spoke as people who had firsthand experience with oppression and who are in solidarity with those suffering oppression. They spoke more as elder leaders, concerned not only about their own Catholic people but also about all people. Instead of speaking as distant teachers, they speak as pastors, encouraging people and nations to propose their own solutions for inequity and oppression. They speak in the name of Jesus Christ and his gospel teaching, offering the Church's support and action for peace and justice. Most importantly, they provide their own Catholic people with insights, ideals, and tools to work heroically in the trenches for the poor and outcast so loved by Jesus.

Some Key Notions in Catholic Social Teaching

Throughout the history of Catholic social teaching, certain key themes have emerged and evolved. It is useful to note and explain these themes, so that Catholics may more readily incorporate them into their faith life.

Human Dignity

The dignity of the human person is the foundation for Catholic social teaching. The Hebrew Scriptures reveal that life comes from God, that the human person was created by God in the divine image (Gen 1:27) and comes from the earth, but bears the breath of God as life (Gen 2:7) and is crowned with a glory a little lower than God's (Ps 8:5). The human person was created as a companion and partner for the Creator God. The Christian Scriptures teach that humans are children of a loving Abba God (Mt 5:43-45), children of the Kingdom of God (Mt 10:14), and are blessed, loved, and sought out by their Abba God when they stray.

Unique to Christianity is a belief in the Incarnation, an astounding reality wherein God actually became a human person in Jesus Christ and revealed the union between the divine and the human for all time. Jesus himself was the embodiment of a loving, caring God and treated others with love and respect, especially the poor and outcast. Then, with the greatest act of love in history, Jesus offered his life on a cross to bring salvation to all people.

So from the Catholic point of view, human dignity is intrinsic to being a human person. It is not something you earn by climbing up a social or economic ladder. Nor is it a matter of some being more "dignified" than others because of their skin color, bank account, or success. For Catholics, every person is born with human dignity and carries that dignity throughout life.

It was this belief in human dignity that filled the early Christians with joy, eager to spread the good news to all at the risk of their lives, and to care and share with each other. Throughout history, Christians have often acted heroically based on their belief in the sanctity of human life. It moved St. Francis (d. 1226) to kiss a leper and serve the poor. It drove Frederick Ozanam (d. 1853) to champion and serve the cause of poor people in nineteenth-century France and to found the still-vibrant St. Vincent de Paul Society. This belief helped Gandhi to stand up for his Indian people who were oppressed by the British. It gave Cesar Chavez (d. 1993) reason to devote his life to fighting for better conditions for migrant workers. It motivated Dorothy Day (d. 1980) to open shelters for the homeless, soup kitchens for the hungry, and to challenge all those who promoted violence and war, and it inspired Archbishop Romero (d. 1980) to risk and ultimately lose his life for his people in El Salvador.

Human Rights

Catholic social teaching lays human dignity at the foundation of human rights. Earlier popes spoke of the rights of workers to organize and receive a just wage, but emphasized obligations. John XXIII presented a whole list of human rights, which he insisted were "universal, inviolable, and inalienable." In 1979 John Paul II spoke to the United Nations and extended the list to include life, liberty, security, food, clothing, housing, health care, rest, leisure, freedom of expression, education, thought, conscience and religion, family life, property, work, a just wage, and others. It is now clear that the Catholic Church stands firmly for the human rights of all people. The Church, which earlier had been threatened by human freedoms, now fully embraces them and agrees with the Universal Declaration of Human Rights promulgated by the United Nations in 1948.

The Link between Faith and Justice

Catholic faith is directed to God, neighbor, and self. It includes a concern for one's own salvation and that of others. To be other-centered requires both love and justice. With love or charity we address the immediate needs of others; with justice we address the causes of injustice and seek solutions. Both are needed. In this country we benefit from the work of many, especially our religious Sisters who have established hospitals, schools, and orphanages. But we also need religious figures like Martin Luther King Jr. and Cesar Chavez, who are dedicated to achieving civil rights for their people. Many social activists like Dorothy Day and Oscar Romero were dedicated to meeting people's immediate daily requirements and also to advocating for their rights and demonstrating against their oppressors.

The dualism of the past often separated the material from the spiritual to the degree that the Church was only responsible for the spiritual needs of its people. The Catholic Church often took an otherworldly approach and stayed aloof from economics and politics. In modern times, the Catholic Church has come to realize that it lives and serves in the world, and that its gospel message has something to say in secular affairs. That is not to say the Church should try to run the government or tell people how to vote. But it should be a voice in the world, crying out and acting for peace and justice. As a Church, it can rightfully critique political and economic matters. This was made clear when John Paul II took a strong stand against the war in Iraq. He was not forcing his views on others, but felt he clearly had the right to voice them.

In contrast to dualism, which separates religion from public affairs, there is the other extreme, which uses religion to advance political or economic causes. The imperial Romans justified their persecution of Christians on the grounds that they were following a false and superstitious religion that did not honor the emperor's divinity. The Crusaders invaded the Holy Land ostensibly to save it for Christians and focused their violent campaigns on the hatred of "infidels" (Jews and Muslims) and the desire to gain territory and trade routes. The conquistadores justified their conquest of the New World and decimated its indigenous people with the belief that they were inferior and could only be saved by converting to Christianity. Slavery in this country, a system of forced labor fueling an immense cotton business among other things, was justified by the belief that blacks were the cursed descendents of Ham in the Bible and were created by God to serve as slaves. And the most dramatic example we have today of the improper use of religion to justify a cause is 9/11, in which Muslim extremists believed they would go directly to Allah if they flew planes into buildings and killed thousands of innocent people in a devastating jihad against Western "Satans."

Catholic social teaching attempts to properly integrate the life of faith with a concern and action for justice. On the one hand, it is critical of faith

[The Church] should be a voice in the world

that is otherworldly and completely private. And on the other, Catholic social teaching, as it has developed in our time, avoids telling the world what it should do about sinful structures like sweat shops, torture chambers, and slavery, which exist around the globe.

The 1971 Synod on Justice said that justice was "constitutive" (made up of) of preaching the gospel. A thumb and four fingers constitute a hand. If one of these digits is missing, the hand is still a hand, but it is not whole. Likewise, the life of faith constitutes a concern and action for justice. Without these, one still has faith, but not a faith that is whole.

In a Church today that is so divided between progressives and traditionalists, turning faith to acts of justice can provide common ground. There is nothing like working together for handicapped, homeless, and abandoned people to help us put aside our disagreements about doctrine and Church issues and get down to what gospel life is all about—serving others.

Solidarity

The human person is a social being and is not meant to live in isolation. Catholic faith teaches that everyone is my neighbor and that as children of God, we are all sisters and brothers. This often conflicts with American culture, which lauds the self-made individual, who stands coolly apart from the crowd. But realistically, we are not self-made. We are helped and assisted in becoming ourselves by the affirmation, recognition, and encouragement of others. Our human dignity and rights are offered and protected in community and there is an interconnection among individuals and nations. Mutuality, cooperation, and collaboration are important elements in life. Christian life has always been lived and celebrated in community, and therefore Catholicism in its parish structures and its rich tradition of religious life has a great deal to teach the world about living well together, sharing, and caring for each other.

Paul VI pointed out that little progress will be made in development unless we commit in solidarity to the development of all people. For him this means that rich nations must care for poor ones through taking direct action, establishing fair trade, and ensuring that no one is left behind when decisions are made.

For John Paul II, solidarity means to commit to the common good, to be devoted to the good of each individual and to all. It means seeing not only other people but also other nations as our neighbor. It precludes domination and oppression of other people or nations. He sees solidarity as a virtue that must be part of our personal conversion.

Student Reflection

"This realization of the power of solidarity hit home when I volunteered in prison ministry and met people my own age who had lost family and security through addictions or bad choices. I was able to give to them, but I really think that they gave more to me!"

Preferential Option for the Poor

Although Catholic social teaching has always given special consideration to the poor, the strong phrase "preferential option for the poor" was not used in official writing until John Paul II.

The phrase arose out of Latin American liberation theology and is drawn from the notion in Hebrew Scripture that God constantly hears the cry of poor people, that God is indeed partial to poor people and became one of them in Jesus Christ. Liberation theology advocates that theology arises from poor and oppressed people and that the Church should be their special advocate.

The Roman Catholic approach to this "option" stands back from the more radical views of liberation theology and does not advocate that theology or social change come solely from the bottom up. Generally, Catholic social teaching does not see the "preferential option for the poor" as an exclusive option, or one that says God and the Church should favor the poor. Special choices are made for those with special needs, just as parents do for their child with special needs. These choices are not to imply that parents love the child in need above the others. The American bishops explain that the wounds of poor people hurt everyone and that by giving them preferential treatment you help heal the entire community. Others explain the option by saying that the effect of any Church or civil decision on poor people should be the first consideration, which is not the usual procedure when city planning or parish budgets are drawn. One example of such a "preferential option for the poor" is the story of the great English Cardinal Manning of the nineteenth century. When he discovered that poor children in London needed schools, he set aside his plan to build a new cathedral and instead spent the money to educate these children. He said, "Could I leave twenty thousand children without education, and drain the funds of my flock to pile up stones and bricks?"

The Common Good

Commitment to the common good flows from the fact that Christians are called to be other-centered. The common good is the sum total of social conditions that humans need to be fulfilled. Commitment to the common good resists individualism, where each person is out for him- or herself, and also challenges collectivism, where the individual has little freedom. Concern for the common good means being a team player, aware that what is good for the group is good for the individual. In other words, it involves understanding that working for better health care for poor people improves health care for all, just as working for a higher minimum wage prevents crime and makes our streets safer for each individual.

The problem here is trying to define the common good. It looks different if one lives inside a gated community and is concerned about privacy and security than if one lives in a neighborhood with substandard housing and street crime. Catholic social teaching tries to take a middle view by stressing that it is up to the State to protect the common good. Not an easy task if the State is supported by, voted for, and controlled by those with power and money. That is why Catholic social teaching eventually turns to the language of development and liberation, because each person must be free to reach his or her full potential and use his or her talents. State protection of human rights becomes essential here, and the oppression of certain segments of society is rejected. One of the most powerful statements of Vatican II, which according to Sr. Mary Luke Tobin was influenced by the few women present at the council, states: "With respect to the fundamental rights of each person, every type of discrimination, whether social or cultural, whether based on sex, race, color, social condition, language or religion, is to be overcome and eradicated as contrary to God's intent."

Sinful Structures

For the last thirty years, Catholic social teaching has pointed to sinful structures that threaten individual liberty and the common good. Some of these structures stem from convictions on the part of individuals and groups that then turn them into laws and oppression. For instance, the precolonial system of legalized slavery resulted from the belief that blacks were inferior and even created to serve others. This prejudice continued into the post–Civil War period and became the reason for the Jim Crow segregation laws. In Nazi Germany, the conviction that Jews and homosexuals were inferior and were holding back the advancement of the superrace resulted in the infamous work camps, which gradually devolved into camps designed for the efficient, industrial extermination of "enemies" of the superrace. Or more recently, the leaders of Enron, fueled by greed, set up sham investment systems that inevitably collapsed, causing hundreds of individuals to lose their life savings.

John Paul II wrote eloquently about such sinful structures, noting that they are first set in motion by greed or the drive for power and then take on a life of their own and crush many people in their path. Whether we speak of nations, corporations, prison systems, international trade agreements, or world monetary systems, structures can be designed to destroy or to build up, to crush or to promote human dignity. To resist and oppose sinful structures, the Church holds up the gospel values of love, justice, and concern for others, and encourages participation, collaboration, and equality as the social structures are put in place. With its beliefs in creation and Incarnation, the Church can promote a commitment to human dignity that stands in opposition to sinful structures.

Such a commitment can be life-threatening, as evidenced by the death of Sr. Dorothy Stang, who was murdered for her resistance to the destruction of the rain forests and the oppression of poor people in Brazil, or by the assassination of Archbishop Romero for his public condemnation of the repression of his people by the Salvadoran government.

Sharing and Caring for the Earth's Resources

The Catholic belief in creation means its social teaching holds that God provides everything, from the air we breathe, the water we drink, and the food we eat to the resources we use for energy, housing, and clothing. We believe there is plenty for everyone, yet thirty thousand children die daily of malnutrition and millions do not have good drinking water, clean air, or land suitable for growing food. The United States has 6 percent of the world's population, yet uses 40 percent of the world's resources and produces the world's largest amount of pollution. The United Nations maintains that one-third of the world's people live well and are improving their lifestyle, while two-thirds live in poverty and sink deeper into degradation each year.

Catholic social teaching takes a strong stand against such inequities and warns that these imbalances can only lead to further violence and wars. It insists that the goods of creation be shared by all; it stands against oppression, whether from nations, corporations, or trade agreements that favor rich people by crushing poor people. However, the official church's top-down approach to leadership put it at odds with liberation theology's bottom-up approach, which works closely with poor people to

God provides everything

resist oppression. This is what led to the clash between Pope John Paul II and Archbishop Romero. Ironically, although the pope actively supported the Solidarity movement among Polish workers, he could not accept Romero's solidarity with the struggling *compesinos* in El Salvador.

As for care of the earth, though several mentions had been made in Church documents, the issue was not firmly addressed until John Paul's message on World Peace Day in 1990. The pope's message expresses alarm at the severe degradation of the earth and its resources and emphasizes that this is a moral crisis that is devastating the human family and threatening world peace. The pope makes a strong plea for people to link their religious beliefs with the crisis of environmental degradation. In response to the pope's plea, many national bishops groups produced their own documents on ecology. We will discuss this connection between the Christian faith and care for the environment in detail in chapter 10.

Our churches still have a long way to go before they become a force in the movement to save the earth. The jury is still out as to whether or not today's college students will take responsibility here and become part of the many solutions needed to have a safe and healthy environment for themselves and their children.

Peace Issues

For more than a century, the Church has been issuing social teaching, and in that time there have been numerous revolutions and local wars, two cities destroyed by nuclear bombs, and two cataclysmic world wars. During the Second World War alone, nearly sixty million people lost their lives and twelve million were killed in a holocaust surpassing anything ever before seen.

Christianity received its teaching on peace from Jesus himself, who taught his followers to turn the other cheek and love their enemies. In the early church, Christians were not permitted to engage in warfare. Once they became accepted into the Roman Empire, the theory of the "just war" was composed by Augustine, based on the writings of the great Roman orator, Cicero. As Vatican II pointed out, the Church has a strong presumption against war and allows war only if it is waged to protect human dignity and human rights. The necessary preconditions include legitimate authority, just cause, war as a last resort, reasonable hope of success, proportionality, right intention, and no direct attack on noncombatants. Many today believe the possibility of nuclear holocaust precludes the use of the just war theory.

John XXIII was especially effective in his pleas for world peace and in urging people to live in harmony and share the goods of creation. Paul VI emphasized that peace was linked with justice and acknowledged the possibility of a just revolution. But John Paul II often promoted peace and urged people to struggle for justice nonviolently. Although he adhered to the just war theory rather than pacifism, John Paul condemned the Gulf War, and before his death, took a strong stand against the United States waging war in Iraq.

The Church's view on pacifism has evolved. Pius XII, for instance, strongly opposed conscientious objection. Vatican II, on the other hand, supported pacifism and conscientious objection, provided they are based on morals and are not simply indifferent to the rights and duties of others. As we saw earlier, the American bishops contributed significantly to Catholic social teaching on peace and voiced support for those who in conscience choose not to participate in war. There has been among some religious leaders a strong commitment to pacifism. These include Gandhi, Martin Luther King Jr., and Dorothy Day. Other leading advocates of nonviolence in this country were Walter Wink, Daniel Berrigan, Gorden Zahn, and John Dear.

Some Heroes for Social Justice

Mother Teresa of Calcutta

In our time Mother Teresa of Calcutta is the person best known to college students for her work for the oppressed. Although she was given more to direct and personal action than to political work, she developed institutions around the world that promote human rights in health care, security, jobs, education, care for the elderly, and human dignity.

Though Mother Teresa spent most of her life in India, she was born and raised in Skopje, Yugoslavia. She was baptized Agnes Bojaxhiu in a Catholic Albanian family. Her mother, Drana, was a strong-minded, deeply religious woman, who taught her daughter that each person is a child of God. Young Agnes was obviously influenced by her mother's bringing the local poor to their dinner table and by her dedication to tending the sick and dying in their neighborhood. Her father, Nicola, was a shrewd merchant who owned a construction company. His strong commitment to Albanian independence may have cost him his life, for it is thought that he was poisoned at a political conference when Agnes was only eight. He also taught his daughter to share everything she had with others.

Agnes was an attractive, fun-loving girl who was active in her Jesuit-run parish. Through the Jesuits she became extremely interested in mission work in India. On the advice of the priests, she signed up for the Loreto Sisters, which had schools in India. Oddly, they sent her to Ireland to learn English, and then after only two months, sent her to India, where she spent several years in the beautiful motherhouse in the Himalaya Mountains. In 1931 she took her vows as Sister Teresa and was sent to teach in a girls convent school in Calcutta. Strangely, this nun who is known for her work with the poorest of the poor spent nineteen years teaching geography to Indian high school girls. She was much loved by the girls, who called her "Ma," and as one of her students reported: "Through her words, the love of Jesus and the remembrance of his sacrifice was branded on our souls. We understood the beauty of sacrificing ourselves in turn for him."

Although Teresa lived a cloistered life at the convent school, she periodically glimpsed the extreme poverty and suffering around her during brief visits to the city. Eventually, she wrote her mother with good news: she had become headmistress of the school! But she received the reply: "Dear child, do not forget that you went out to India for the sake of the poor." Then in 1943, the Japanese began bombing the city. The girls were sent home and the school suddenly became a refuge for the area's displaced and poor people. Teresa now gained firsthand experience serving desperate people. Then in 1946 Muslims and Hindus began slaughtering each other in Calcutta. Food was cut off from the school, requiring Teresa to go out amidst the blood-drenched streets and the carnage to bring food back to the school. Teresa began to realize that her calling was to be out in the streets among suffering people.

Amidst all this, Teresa came down with tuberculosis and was sent to the motherhouse to recover. She says she realized on her train ride there that it was God's will that she leave the convent and move to the slums to serve poor people. Once she regained her health, Teresa applied to leave her Order and was given permission to live as a nun under the authority of the local bishop. She went off in the simple sari of an Indian woman, with a few coins in her pocket, anxious and lonely at first. Some of the local priests thought she was "cracked," and the archbishop said he would "give her a year."

But they underestimated the might of this little Sister. She saw the face of God in the eyes of the hungry, the naked, those dying in the gutters alone. She was determined to be "a pencil in the hand of God."

At first Teresa took small steps. She had no experience with either the harsh urban life or with abandoned poor people. She started with what she knew: education. And on a vacant lot she began to teach street urchins their letters by drawing in the mud. She also taught them hygiene, by giving them soap and showing them how to wash.

Teresa began to understand how abandoned poor people felt. On one occasion she stopped by a convent and asked if she could eat her simple lunch outside. She was directed to eat outside under the back stairs.

Eventually things improved for Teresa as she was given a room in a home for the elderly and was joined by some of her former students. The tiny group of women worked with street kids and gradually raised enough money to open some simple schools. Her charming offer to donors was difficult to turn down: "I am going to give you a chance to do something beautiful for God."

Gradually they gathered abandoned and undernourished babies into an orphanage that they opened. Teresa urged women not to abort because she was willing to take their babies. She and her "sisters" would be "carriers of God's love" to these little ones.

Next Teresa and her followers began to gather those who had been left to die in the gutters. She tried to hail cabs and rickshaws for them to be carried to her apartment, but she was shunned. Eventually she was evicted from her place for bringing all these undesirables home.

But things always seemed to work out for Teresa. She was given an abandoned Hindu temple that had become a hangout for vagrants and thugs. She and her Sisters cleaned up the foul-smelling place, took on the toughs that hung out there, and opened her now famous Home for the Dying. She welcomed everyone, no matter what their religion, and honored their differing rites for the dying. Actually, their care was so good that many recovered and returned to normal life.

Teresa's next move was to offer care for the many lepers in the area. Because they were not allowed in the city, she purchased vans to drive to their colonies. With new antibiotics, many of these lepers were cured and returned to society. Teresa provided professional health care for the lepers as well as job training and even helped them publish their own newspaper. Many were helped to regain self-respect and independence.

Teresa was learning of the great power of endurance among poor people and was coming to understand what Jesus meant when he said they were "blessed." She grew to admire their courage, wisdom, and faith. At the same time, she was teaching many of the rejected about the power of God's love and how it can overcome any suffering, any cross.

In the early 1960s, people began to hear about Mother Teresa, who now had her own order of nuns. Her first speaking engagement was in, of all places, Las Vegas. From there she visited other areas of the United States and Europe.

In 1965 Mother Teresa went global, beginning with a home for the dying in Venezuela and eventually opening homes in 125 countries. She tirelessly promoted her work and found her message could move everyone, from Cambridge dons to military officers to cardinals to financiers.

In the late 1960s, a skeptical English journalist reluctantly agreed to interview her. Much to his surprise, Teresa overwhelmed him with her spirit and turned him to religion. The book he wrote about her, *Something Beautiful for God*, and the videos he made of her work helped her become an international celebrity. Eventually she was honored with awards from the Vatican, Cambridge University, and the White House, to name only a few. In 1979, she received the Nobel Peace Prize.

Mother Teresa believed in spreading God's love and did not hesitate to ask anyone to help her.

Although ailing with a heart condition early on, Teresa continued with her mission to poor and dying people until the end. She became a force in the world such as we see only once in centuries. The end came suddenly and with a certain irony. She died on the day of Princess Diana's funeral, a woman whom she had mentored when her marriage was going bad. Mother Teresa had encouraged Diana to give of herself in love to the needy of the world. Both women, different in background and appearance, were mourned worldwide at the same time. John Paul, speaking at her beatification, said: "Let us praise the Lord for this diminutive woman in love with God, a humble gospel messenger and a tireless benefactor of humanity. In her we honor one of the most important figures of our time."

Cesar Chavez

Cesar Chavez is another outstanding example of someone who took Catholic social teaching to heart. Cesar was born in Arizona in 1927, but his roots went back to Mexico. His grandfather and namesake, Cesario, had moved as a homesteader from Mexico to the Gila Valley, where he built the family hacienda, or farm. Cesar, along with his fifteen brothers and sisters, was first raised in a small house behind the grocery store, garage, and pool hall run by his parents, Librado and Dorotea. Eventually Cesar's family bought forty acres but were swindled out of their land and had to move back to the grandfather's hacienda. Little Cesario helped on the farm and was happy as a child, except in school where he was treated as inferior and punished because he spoke Spanish.

Drought and rising taxes forced the family to abandon the farm, and they packed up what they could in their old Studebaker and headed for California. The family began working as migrant workers, living in dilapidated sheds with sagging beds and thin mattresses. As they moved from farm to farm, they encountered the same metal shacks, outdoor latrines, poor food, and endless hours of backbreaking labor.

They usually received $2 a day per family for their work, with more for grape picking. Sometimes they were not paid at all, and if they complained, the owner would call the police and have them arrested. Cesar had to grow up fast and work as an adult would. He had little time to play or have fun.

Cesar soon learned about racial prejudice. The migrants were not allowed to enter the Anglo side of town and would be refused service in many of the restaurants. Signs on businesses read "White Trade Only" or "No Dogs or Mexicans." Cesar was learning to distrust white people and at times would confront those intimidating his family.

Schooling for Cesar was sporadic and poor. He counted thirty-seven different schools in his family's travels, and he felt largely unnoticed and poorly treated in most of them. The migrant children always had to sit in the back on benches instead of at desks and were punished if they spoke Spanish. Cesar dropped out after eighth grade.

Cesar continued the backbreaking work of the migrant throughout his teen years and then joined the U.S. Navy in the early part of World War II. In the navy he encountered the same grinding prejudice and was only allowed to mop decks. The whole experience was bad for Cesar, and once on leave, his anger overflowed when he refused to sit in the Mexican section of a movie theater. He was arrested, jailed briefly, and left resolved to break free from the migrant life after he was discharged from the navy. In 1948 Cesar married his beloved Helen and they worked for a while as migrants. For a time he tried being a lumberjack with his brother and later got a job in a lumberyard.

Cesar's life changed when he met a priest, Fr. Donald McDonald. Fr. McDonald taught Cesar about the economics of farm work, gave him the facts of how unfair it all was, and took him around to show him farmworkers on strike. The priest encouraged Cesar to read Catholic

Cesar had to grow up fast

social teaching, books about the labor movement, and the writings of St. Francis and Gandhi. He showed this young Mexican American how the growers, banks, corporations, and the state and federal governments were all contriving to oppress migrant workers.

Next Cesar met Fred Ross, a community organizer who helped Mexican Americans in Los Angeles. Ross offered Cesar a job and mentored him on organizing and advocating for the migrants of his area. At first Cesar was quite shy, but as he gained confidence, he was sent to San Jose and then Oakland to advocate for Mexicans there before returning to his home in the San Joaquin Valley.

After ten years as an organizer, Cesar decided to work on his own in order to have more freedom to form unions for the farmworkers and take on the growers. It was a hard decision because he would no longer have a paycheck coming in, but he made the leap, even turning down job offers from the Peace Corps and AFL-CIO. He moved his family to Delano and opened a small office in a garage behind his small rented house. His brother Richard, a carpenter, helped support Cesar's family. And Cesar's wife, Helen, kept working in the fields to earn extra money. This freed up Cesar to drive his old car around the state to gain new union members. He often had to beg for gas money and food, but this put him in touch with the great generosity of the poor people who helped him.

Cesar was taking on a gigantic endeavor. There had been many attempts to organize migrant workers in the previous eighty-five years, and all had failed. There were no state or federal laws allowing farmworkers to organize, and the growers were running billion-dollar businesses and had banks, politicians, and law enforcement on their side. There was a need for decent living conditions, fair wages, health care, clean water, and toilet facilities at home and in the fields, good schools and day care centers for the children, a credit union, fair-hiring agencies, and pension plans.

Cesar began slowly and systematically, talking with foremen and workers and visiting the barrios at night to talk with families. In eleven months he covered eighty-seven communities to recruit new members. Workers were asked to pay $3.50 a month for membership and with this Cesar was able to set up a credit union and offer burial insurance as a start.

By 1962 the union had 250 members and was able to hold a convention in an abandoned theater. Three years later the numbers were up to 1,200 and the organization called a strike, asking for a raise of fifteen cents per hour (up from $1.25!). The growers immediately brought in scabs and some marched around with shotguns, firing at strike signs and car windows. Strikers were kicked, stomped, spit on, and sprayed with chemicals as the police stood by watching. The union headquarters was bombed and rammed by a truck, and Cesar's house was barraged with rocks and bottles. The Teamsters Union regularly sent their 'goons' to beat, intimidate, and even kill the strikers. At one point, Nan Freeman, a young college student, was deliberately run down by a truck as she was picketing, and on another occasion Nagi Daifallah, a twenty-four-year-old Arab farmworker, was chased and bludgeoned to death with a flashlight. Cesar deeply mourned the losses of these courageous people and spoke at their funerals, publicly condemning the murderers. At the same time, he always held his followers to the strict discipline of nonviolence. He trained his people to be confrontational, assertive, and determined, but to never retaliate with violence. Their weapons were to be tenacity, courage, love, prayer, and fasting. For his inspiration, Chavez turned to Jesus, Gandhi, Martin Luther King Jr., and St. Francis.

Aside from organizing strikes, Chavez led boycotts to put pressure on the state of California to pass laws for farmworkers. His boycott on grapes went nationwide and brought the industry to the bargaining table. He also led marches and was joined by powerful figures like Sen. Robert Kennedy and Walter Reuther. One march was three hundred miles long.

Much of Cesar's motivation came from his devotion to Jesus and his Catholic faith. He said: "I think Jesus really taught us to go and do something. We look at his sermons, and it's very plain what he wants us to do: clothe the naked, feed the hungry, and give water to the thirsty. It's very simple stuff." Cesar was extremely well versed in Catholic social teaching and applied its principles to his struggle for justice for migrant workers. He worked closely with Catholic priests as well as Protestant ministers and Jewish rabbis in his effort to improve the lives of workers, and he was eager to worship with them.

Cesar led countless strikes and more than fifty boycotts. He carried on long fasts to purify himself and to show his followers how to bear suffering and to urge them to nonviolence. His union remains a powerful force that has gained respect and increased justice for migrant farmworkers.

I remember meeting Cesar when he came to speak at our university in the late 1980s. He was a small, gentle man with great inner strength, and he spoke with the power of a prophet. At that time he was touring the nation, speaking out against the harm that spraying pesticides caused to farmworkers and to everyone through our food. My two children, Ami and BJ, were small then, and they wanted to meet him and give him some money they had brought. I remember how kind and loving Cesar was toward them and how grateful he was for their little offering.

Cesar died in April 1993. More than fifty thousand people gathered to march with the plain pine coffin. Many were bishops, labor leaders, politicians, celebrities, priests, and Sisters; but most were the simple "chavistas," migrant farmworkers who loved this man for giving so much of himself to them. Many recalled a prayer Cesar had written:

> "Show me the suffering or the most miserable, so I will know my people's plight. Free me to pray for others, for you are present in every person. Help me take responsibility for my own life, so that I can be free at last."

Conclusion

Catholic social teaching brings the gospel teaching of Jesus into modern times. It is the heart of the Church's mission to carry on Jesus' work for downtrodden and outcast people. It reminds Christians that salvation is not simply a personal concern but also a concern for others, especially those who are oppressed. This social teaching signals how Christians can better love others as they love themselves.

Activities

1. Plan a trip to a homeless shelter, where students might have the opportunity to help with a meal, eat with the residents, and hear some of their stories.

2. Have teams sign up to work at a soup kitchen where team members might help with cooking and talk with the staff and guests.

3. Teams of students can make presentations on such figures as Mahatma Gandhi, Dorothy Day, Nelson Mandela, Martin Luther King Jr., Oscar Romero, Mother Teresa, Corrie ten Boom, Jean Vanier, Harriet Tubman, Bernard Haring, or Susan B. Anthony. PowerPoint, clips from the many fine films available, and dramatizations can be used in such presentations.

Sources

Coleman, John, and Wm. Ryan, eds. *Globalization and Catholic Social Thought.* Maryknoll, NY: Orbis Books, 2005.

Curran, Charles. *Catholic Social Teaching.* Washington, DC: Georgetown University Press, 2002.

Hill, Brennan. *8 Freedom Heroes.* Cincinnati, OH: St. Anthony Messenger Press, 2007.

Mich, Marvin, and L. Krier. *Catholic Social Teaching and Movements.* Mystic, CT: Twenty-Third Publications, 1998.

Shiva, Vandana. *Earth Democracy.* Cambridge, MA: South End Press, 2005.

Tanner, Kathryn. *The Politics of God.* Minneapolis, MN: Fortress, 1992.

Thompson, Joseph. *Justice and Peace.* Maryknoll, NY: Orbis Books, 1997.

10 Christian Faith and the Environment

It is becoming increasingly evident that the earth's environment is in crisis. Nations around the globe are concerned and are searching for solutions. And world religions are reaching into their rich traditions of beliefs and values for ways to conserve the earth. In this country, many Christians, even those on the religious right that has usually dismissed the environmental movement, are now concerned and are becoming active in ecological efforts. In this chapter, we examine the Christian tradition to see what links there might be to move people to better appreciate the earth and act against its degradation. We will discuss the Old and New Testaments, the God question, Christology, sacraments, the voices of the churches, women's views, spirituality, and ethics.

The Old Testament

As we saw earlier, the Old Testament is a library of ancient theologies, in which one can study the human struggle and consider the mysteries of God and life on earth. These writings have shaped the religious thought of Jews, Christians, and Muslims for centuries. They have helped countless people live their lives and deal with the issues facing them. Today these Scriptures need to be studied and prayed over as a valuable resource for dealing with the degradation of the earth.

We might start with the biblical view of the human being, because we are not only the main perpetrators of environmental damage but also its most visible victims. The views on humans in the Bible come "from below," from everyday experience. Humans can embody great virtue and yet are capable of horrible evil. This contrast is explored in such biblical descriptions of humans as in the "image of God" or the "lowly worm." Humans are portrayed as being given dominion to preserve the earth and also as the authors of wanton destruction and injustice. In the Scriptures, humans can join the stars in praise of the Creator and also betray their covenant with God. In the Psalms, they can sing of love and also moan in desperate abandonment.

Made in the Image of God

One of the most dramatic images of the human being is that we are created in the "image and likeness of God." This description comes in 1 Genesis, a sophisticated story written six centuries before Jesus, just after the Babylonian exile, and one which echoes the Babylonian myth *Enuma Elish*. This highly artistic, liturgical story of creation is painted on a vast, cosmic canvas. The constant refrain is that God considers creation to be "good." Humans are created as the last and climactic creatures on the final day. God gathers his heavenly consorts and says: "Let us make man in our image." Then the author reports: "God created man in his image; male and female he created them" (Gen 1:26-27). God then gave humans dominion over all the living things in creation.

This idea has profoundly influenced the Jewish and Christian traditions regarding the sacredness of human life. At the same time, it has been used to oppress others, by saying that man's genesis didn't apply to certain people who were less than human. The conquistadores of the sixteenth century, for example, decided that the indigenous people of the New World were not made in the image of God, but were in fact subhuman and could therefore be enslaved and deprived of their rich resources. Slavery in America and even the savage Holocaust in Nazi Germany were justified by saying that certain people were subhuman.

What does it mean to be created in God's image? It helps to return to the original language of the text. The Hebrew word for *image* is *selem,* which means statue or icon. In ancient times, the kings and pharaohs were looked upon as gods and had images of themselves placed around their empires to represent them and their presence. Similarly, Genesis seems to indicate that humans are representations or symbols of the power and presence of God. Among the Hebrews, authentic kings and queens were supposed to be honorable and just. They were not to exalt themselves above others and were to be dedicated to the welfare of others. To represent a royal figure or a God was to act with these principles. To "stand for" the God who was loving, caring, and just was to live a life characterized by these virtues.

The implications for ecology are clear. All of creation comes from the hand of God and is "good." Humans represent God in the world and must care for the earth in the name of the Creator. At the same time, humans must respect and care for each other as images of God. They must share the earth's resources and not subject each other to conditions that are harmful or even deadly.

Dominion

The notion that humans have dominion over all living things on earth (Gen 1:28) has been subjected to intense debate, especially since historian Lynn White charged that this notion led to Western civilization's exploitation of the environment. Most today see White's thesis as an oversimplified explanation for the present crisis, but nonetheless his charge led to serious study of what *dominion* means in the creation story.

The original meaning of dominion does not seem to carry any connotation of exploitation or abuse. As mentioned earlier, as images of God, humans stand as representatives of the Creator. They are indeed co-creators who are to act with the same justice and care as the Creator. Humans are destined to share a personal relationship (covenant) with the Creator and represent God in sustaining order, peace, and harmony on earth. This obviously rules out plundering and destroying the earth and its resources. Instead, it commissions humans to be responsible for the welfare of the earth and each other.

The Hebrews did not interpret dominion as exploitation, nor did the Christians from the earliest period until the modern age. It was only with the "discovery of the New World," the coming of the Enlightenment, and the development of modern science and technology that dominion became synonymous with exploitation. The ecological crisis could be more accurately attributed to these movements, as well as to colonialism, secularization, nationalism, industrialization, capitalism, and communism. Seldom have these movements been driven by the Hebrew Scriptures, and if Scripture was used at all, its original meaning was distorted.

Humbler Images

Elsewhere in the Hebrew Bible, human beings are described in a more earthy fashion, with all their limitations and weaknesses, as fools, worms, and sinners. Humans are creatures of the dust, who can often make little sense of life and whose lives last but a brief moment.

We are perhaps most familiar with the human image in the 2 Genesis story. This is a myth written several centuries before 1 Genesis and it has parallels in Babylonian and Egyptian literature. The story begins on a barren stretch of soil, with a stream welling out of the earth and watering the ground. The Creator, a more rural and homey figure than the cosmic God of the first story, fashions a human being out of mud and then makes the figure into a living being by giving it the breath of life.

The word *adamah* in Hebrew means "earth," and thus Adam is an "earth man" who is forever linked to the other creatures of the earth, and like them he is destined to die and return to the soil from which he was made. The "breath of life" makes this human being wholly a person, with no question of a separation between the body and soul or the material and spiritual.

Then this "potter God" plants an exotic garden and places the "mud man" in it, asking him to cultivate it. This is a caring God, who walks with the human being in the cool of the evening and is concerned about his loneliness. After several failed attempts to provide a companion for Adam, God finally devises a suitable partner, one made from Adam's own rib. With Eve, paradise is complete. Eve is then deceived by the serpent, eats the fruit of the forbidden tree, and persuades Adam to do the same. Adam and Eve lose their innocence and are cursed with work, the pains of child-birth, and masculine mastery, and they are banished from the garden. Sin has entered the world! And yet the Hebrews maintain their hope in God's forgiveness and are able to pray: "When you send forth your breath, they are created, and you renew the face of the earth" (Ps 104:27-30).

The connections between this tradition and ecology are numerous. As humans are made from the earth, we are linked to it. All breath, all life comes from God and must therefore be held as sacred. Degrading the earth is in fact degrading us, because all creation is interrelated and finds its source in the Creator. Not only are people partners with each other, they are also interrelated with all living things and with the earth itself. We are commissioned by God to preserve and sustain the web of life. To betray this trust is sinful.

Our sinfulness in degrading the earth must be acknowledged. Through ignorance and greed, humans have ravaged the earth and disturbed its harmony and integrity. Most of this damage has occurred in the last two hundred years. Our air, water, and soil have been severely damaged. The earth's resources, given to us to share, are inequitably distributed to the

all breath, all life comes from God

point where many starve each day. Humans have disturbed the natural harmony of our ecosystems, destroyed countless species, and brought many others to the brink of extinction. Humans have seriously altered the earth's atmosphere, which controls our climate and protects us from deadly ultraviolet rays. People have morally offended the earth and its citizens, and through violence have forced many people to become refugees, who are in turn forced to inhabit small areas, which are then devastated.

Creation Theology

The creation theology of the Hebrew Scriptures can provide our motivation to care for the earth. We begin to see that creation is much more than human life—we are not at its center. Indeed, there is such a vastness to creation that it has in the past and could in the future continue without human life. But as the one free creature on earth, we can choose to destroy or sustain the earth. The love that we have for our God, our children, and future generations can move us to turn this devastation around and better sustain the good earth.

The Christian Scriptures

The New Testament is a treasured collection of Christian faith documents. Based on memories of the life, death, and Resurrection of Jesus, the Scriptures bear witness to the earliest faith in Jesus as Messiah and Savior of the world. These beliefs and values have inspired countless people in their daily struggles for two millennia. Most certainly these biblical beliefs can help Christians face the challenging environmental problems of our day.

The Teaching of Jesus

As we noted in chapter 1, Jesus of Nazareth was a Jewish reformer who attempted to restore the best of his tradition and help his people be faithful to their covenant with God. He taught that God is a loving parent (Abba) who attends to all of creation with concern and provides for the needs of all. This Abba cares even for the sparrows and the lilies of the field, and lets the sun shine and the rain fall on both the good and bad. For Jesus, all people are children of God. Jesus had "good news" for the people of his time. They were "the salt of the earth," "the light of the world." All were indeed "blessed."

 ## Student Reflection

> "I work at a homeless shelter, and I am always amazed that when I ask one of the residents how they are, they reply: 'I am blessed.' I have so much more than they, but I don't tend to answer that way. Their faith seems to tell them that whatever they have comes from their God, and they feel blessed to just make it through this day. This really seems to come from Jesus' beatitudes."

Jesus saw everyone as a child of God, but he seems to have been called to reach out especially to those least likely to realize their dignity: the sick and disabled, who were told that they were unclean and cursed; the prostitutes, whose poverty and abuse led them to sell their bodies; and the prisoners, who had been locked away from society.

Jesus taught that there is no need to have anxiety in our lives because the Creator provides in the same way for the birds of the air and the lilies and the grasses of the field as God provides for us (Mt 6:26). Jesus calls his followers to a detachment, a simple way of living. This is appropriate for today, when our present-day habits of accumulation and waste are in part responsible for the depletion of the world's resources and the degradation of our environment. John Paul II addressed this when he spoke of the "moral crisis" that exists today. He said that our need for instant gratification and consumption causes us to be indifferent to the suffering of others and to the damage we are inflicting on the earth. He calls for simplicity, moderation, and a spirit of sacrifice.

Jesus lived as an example of simplicity. He once remarked: "Foxes have dens and birds of the sky have nests, but the Son of Man has nowhere to rest his head" (Lk 9:58). He expected the same detachment from those who followed him, and when he sent his disciples on mission he instructed them: "Take nothing for your journey, no staff, nor bag, nor bread, nor money—not even a tunic" (Lk 9:3-4). The Acts of the Apostles describes how the early communities followed his instruction: "The community of believers was of one heart and mind, and no one claimed that any of his possessions was his own, but they had everything in common [...] There was no needy person among them" (Acts 4:32-34).

Jesus also warned of the dangers of greed, teaching that one's life should not consist in an abundance of possessions. He told his disciples not to store up treasures that can be consumed by moths and thieves, but instead to store up spiritual treasures. His words are powerful: "For where your treasure is, there also will be your heart" (Mt 6:21). In one of the most touching of the gospel stories, a rich young man can't follow Jesus because he can't give up his possessions. Jesus later says: "For whoever wishes to save his life will lose it, but whoever loses his life for my sake will save it. What profit is there for one to gain the whole world yet lose or forfeit himself?" (Lk 9:24-25). Jesus warns that it is difficult for the rich to enter the kingdom because they serve a "master" other than their God. He challenges the luxurious lifestyle, which usually ignores the dangers to the environment and deprives the poor of what is needed to barely exist.

The notion of the "reign of God" is central to Jesus' teaching. The "kingdom" is the loving, saving presence of God in all of creation. It goes back to the Hebrew belief that creation ultimately belongs to God and is offered to those who dwell here at any given time. This teaching about God's power and presence in the world can be a source of courage in resisting abuses to the earth. The presence of God in creation signals a "power with" and a "power for," rather than a "power over" the earth.

The parables of Jesus reveal how close he lived to nature and teach what he had learned of the Creator from his closeness to the earth. Jesus uses the sowing of seeds, vineyards, harvests, fruit trees, and shepherds to show the mysterious workings of the Creator, who works within creation to bless, protect, and save. In these stories he calls his disciples to be alert to the presence of God and to work in partnership with God to be a caring and saving presence in the world.

The miracles of Jesus also have relevance to taking care of the earth. Stories where Jesus saves disciples from a storm, heals many from disabilities, and even brings the dead back to life reveal a God of creativity and wholeness. This is a God who supports those who are compassionate and creatively active against the disorder and suffering in the world. This is a Savior who empowers those who choose to deal with the chaos and degradation to which we are subjecting the earth today.

The gospel feeding and table ministry stories where Jesus opens his life to people from all walks of life also reveal a Creator who provides for and shares with people. It is a God of bounty, a God who opposes the deprivation and even starvation that come from greed and indifference. The stories of miraculous catches of fish further emphasize that the power of God provides in amazing ways and stands with those who struggle to provide the poor with food and drink. These stories all teach the indomitable power of faith, which can overcome the deprivation that grips so many parts of the world today.

The stories of Jesus' birth are also applicable to our struggle to save the earth. In John's gospel, Jesus is identified with the Word, the creative principle in God. That Word becomes Flesh and a "new creation" comes about whereby God's presence is revealed in the most concrete way possible, in a baby. In the birth stories of Luke and Matthew, the Spirit of God comes miraculously upon the earth as a child and brings blessings to the earth. In Luke the angels proclaim the joining of heaven and earth: "Glory to God in the highest, and peace to those on whom his favor rests" (Lk 2:14). Later, Paul proclaims to the Corinthians: "So whoever is in Christ is a new creation: the old things have passed away; behold, new things have come" (2 Cor 5:17).

In the passion plays, the agony in the garden and the death on the hill reveal how oppression and suffering are so much a part of life and yet can be redemptive and saving if endured with courage and faith. The sweat, blood, and spit of life are real but can be overcome through a compassionate Jesus, who forgives his oppressors from the cross and brings the thief next to him into the kingdom. In Jesus, the power of sacrifice, even of one's own life, can heal the world.

Student Reflection

"A Sister of Notre Dame from our area was just shot to death for her efforts to serve the poor and save the rain forests in Brazil. She gave thirty years of her life there and became such a force for the logging companies that they had her murdered. Her death brought the world's attention to her remote area in Brazil and things have improved a great deal there."

Creation motifs also appear in the Resurrection stories. Images of darkness, sunrise, and lightning surround the "new creation" of Jesus' transformation into new life. Paul says that Jesus is the "first fruits" of the new creation and that those who belong to him belong to the kingdom (1 Cor 15:20-24). The Resurrection reveals the new life that is now brought to the earth and to all people. It reveals the ultimate goal of all creation—life with God. Paul teaches the Romans: "For creation awaits with eager expectation the revelation of the children of God" (Rom 8:19). The Resurrection is Jesus' victory over sin and death and stands over and against the sinful destruction of the earth and human life.

Christology and Saving the Earth

Pierre Teilhard de Chardin, the great Jesuit scientist-theologian, once pointed out that early Christianity's task was to link the Logos with the Incarnation and that in this era, there was a need to link Christology with evolution and the cosmos. Now it seems we are charged with seeing

in Jesus, sacrifice can heal the world

how the study of Jesus Christ can be relevant to our concerns about the environment.

The doctrine of the Incarnation is central to the Christian tradition. Unique among all religious beliefs, it teaches that God has entered creation as a human person. The Word, the divine creative Power, actually became part of creation. God has actually entered the DNA and genetic structures of materiality! Scotus taught that this Incarnation was not an afterthought of the Fall but was part of God's plan from the beginning. The Creator has from the beginning planned to enter creation as the Christ and through him re-create all reality. Now that the Christ has entered the world, he continues to direct and save the world. As the Russian Patriarch Alexy puts it, "The Incarnation of the Lord Jesus has originated the renewal of not only humans but of the whole of nature as well." In other words, Jesus as the Christ now works through those who strive to conserve the resources of the earth and deal with the many ways in which the health of the environment is being endangered. He helps us realize that we are one family with other creatures and are truly connected to and dependent on all of nature.

Jesus as Savior

Contemporary interpretations of Jesus' saving power expand the theology beyond the saving of souls to the salvation of the world and extend salvation beyond personal sin to social sin, including the degradation of the earth. If "being saved" is to be relevant today, it has to include the power of God's love over violence, nuclear threat, terrorism, oppression, and environmental harms.

It is proposed in today's theology that Jesus attempted to restore the best of the Jewish tradition of salvation. In his life and teaching, he revealed a loving and caring Abba who protected all of creation. He taught that God's saving power extended to all things. Jesus' own mission was to reveal and accomplish this salvation through his life, death, and Resurrection.

As the Gospel of John puts it: "For God did not send his Son into the world to condemn the world, but that the world might be saved through him" (Jn 3:17).

In the Christian tradition, Jesus has been seen as a conqueror of the demonic in the world. Jesus brought truth and freedom from sin: he liberated the world from sin past and present. Modern theologians suggest that if we are to be healed from the sins of the past, whether slavery, colonialism, or the Holocaust, it must be through the power of God. And they point out that if we are to free our children and ourselves from "sins against the earth," it must be through the grace of God moving us to struggle against these evils. As John Paul II pointed out, our environmental problems are due to a moral crisis, and only through God's power working within us can this crisis be amended.

Salvation as Liberation

Salvation is today often interpreted as liberation. People feel the need to be freed from the political and economic forces that are oppressing them and destroying the environment around them. Liberation is at the heart of the Judeo-Christian religion. The central event in Judaism is God freeing the Hebrews from slavery in Egypt. Yahweh then freed the chosen people from sin by giving them a covenant and a law of love. Many of the Jewish faith believe that God constantly forgives them and ultimately frees them from oppression by their adversaries, whether they be the Babylonians, Persians, Romans, or more recently, Germans.

Early in his ministry, Jesus identified himself with God's mission to free others, whether from hunger, disease, rejection, oppression, or sin. In John's gospel, Jesus tells his disciples: "The truth will set you free [....] If a Son frees you, then you will truly be free" (Jn 8:32-36). Paul proclaims this same good news to the Galatians: "Christ has set us free" (Gal 5, 1).

When salvation is viewed as liberation, religion goes beyond piety and good works and begins to struggle against the sinful structures that deprive countless people of their rights. People need to be liberated not only from personal sin but also from structures that oppress in government, prisons, the military, health care, industry, or even in the home. People also need to be freed to breathe fresh air, drink clean water, own land suitable for growing food, and live in areas protected from pollution and uncontrolled development.

Christian Sacraments

All religions are sacramental, in that they use symbols and rituals to get in touch with the sacred. Christianity is no exception. Christians have always been initiated and confirmed into the life of Christ and the Church through the symbols of water and oil. Using the symbols of bread and wine, they have been nourished with the Lord's presence in communal liturgy. Through symbolic rituals, they have been joined in marriage, designated as ministers, forgiven of their sins, healed of their infirmities, and prepared for death.

Environmental theology has taught us that sacraments can put us in touch with the sacred dimensions of the cosmos itself. They can transform us to resist the abuse of nature and work for its preservation. In the sacred waters, oils, breads, and wines, we can discover that God is indeed embedded within creation and thus see the world as a graced reality to be respected and honored.

Sacraments are symbolic events that draw us into God as Mystery and allow us to glimpse the secrets within our world and ourselves. At their center is the Spirit of the risen Jesus, showing us our place in the world and what we are called to do to make a difference.

Each sacrament can be linked to a better awareness of our earth and the reasons to conserve it. For instance, the central symbol in baptism is water, one of the most basic elements in the world. Life began in the waters of the deep, and a good portion of the earth—its elements and living things—is made up of water. Human life grows and is nurtured in the waters of the womb, and water is essential for sustaining all life. At the same time, water can be death dealing, as we learned so tragically with Hurricane

Katrina. And polluted water often carries disease and death to humans and other living things.

Water is a central symbol in the Bible. Both creation stories begin with it. In the flood story, water destroys the earth, and creation has to be started again. The Hebrews are saved by their journey through the Red Sea and cross the Jordan into the Promised Land; thus, the constant ritual washings and blessings in the Hebrew tradition.

The New Testament also features water stories: the baptism of Jesus, the calming of the storm, the walking on water, the miraculous catches, and the first miracle, where water is changed into wine at a wedding. Nicodemus is told that he must be reborn by water and the Spirit; Jesus offers to give the Samaritan woman "living water," and at another time invites others to come to him for drink. He cures a man in the waters of Siloam and washes the feet of his disciples at his last supper. In his last hours, Jesus cries out his thirst, and after his Resurrection he cooks breakfast for his followers on the beach of the Sea of Galilee. And he commissions his disciples to go forth and baptize all nations.

Baptism

From early times Christians have viewed the waters of baptism as a "new creation." In today's world this can remind us that our waterways and oceans are gifts from God and places where we can encounter the creation. At the same time, our experience with polluted water can strengthen our resolve to work for the restoration of our waterways.

Baptism also symbolizes the washing away of sin and the promise to live the gospel life of faith, hope, and love. The vows taken at baptism promise to see life as coming from God and to work to preserve it. Baptismal vows today might indeed include cherishing the earth, its resources, and its people. Imagine if the billion and a half baptized people in the world today resolved to work for a better environment. What a difference that would make!

Eucharist

The word *Eucharist* means "thanksgiving," a concept rooted in ancient Hebrew meals where God's people gathered to thank God for their blessings. The great harvest feasts were celebrated in Jerusalem, and Yahweh was praised and thanked for all of creation. Locally, Hebrews gathered in fellowship meals and shared bread and wine to strengthen their community bonds and give thanks to their God.

The Gospels describe a number of meals that seem to be based on memories of Jesus' fellowship meals and echo early Christian Eucharist. At Matthew's house, Jesus proclaimed the love and forgiveness of Abba as he ate with outcasts, tax collectors, and sinners. At the table of Simon the Pharisee, Jesus revealed the compassion and mercy of God as he raised up the prostitute. At Martha and Mary's table, Jesus pointed to God's treasured revelation. At the wedding feast, he manifested the creative powers of God; and dining with Zaccaeus, Jesus transformed a corrupt miser into a generous disciple. Through the stories of miraculous feeding and fish catches, we are taught about the abundance that Abba makes available. And finally, at his last supper, Jesus gives thanks and praise and then passes the bread and cup to his disciples to symbolize his sacrifice and encourages them to "do this in memory of me."

Paul's letter to the Corinthians (50 CE) and the Didache (ca. 60 CE) show that early Christians gathered for thanksgiving meals (Eucharist) to thank God for creation, for their material and spiritual blessings, and for sending the Son to them to save them through his life, death, and Resurrection. They believed the risen Christ was uniquely present in Eucharist, transforming their lives with the creative and saving power of God in their world.

The Eucharist and Ecology

The Eucharist has many levels of meaning and can easily be connected to environmental concerns. The symbols are material and natural: bread from wheat and wine from grapes. They point to the flesh and blood of Christ, who is the human Incarnation of the Creator. Eucharist is a time to thank the Creator for all of our gifts, a time to worship and praise the Christ. It is a meal wherein Christians celebrate God's bounty, remember the starving and deprived of the world, and resolve to see that these get their proper share.

The Eucharist is a renewal of the covenant God made through Moses with his people, and through Noah with all the earth, as well as the renewal of the new covenant God made through Jesus Christ. Eucharist is an occasion to deepen one's relationship with God and with all of creation. It is a time to repent our complicity in harming creation; a time to resolve to live more simply, share more generously, and act to better sustain the earth.

Pierre Teilhard de Chardin wrote *Mass on the World* when he was working on an archeological dig in the desert and did not have the means for a traditional Mass. It reads: "Since I have neither bread, nor wine, nor altar, I will raise myself beyond these symbols, up to the majesty of the real itself; I, your priest, will make the whole earth my altar and on it I will offer you all the labors and sufferings of the world [....] But the offering you really want is nothing less than the growth of the world borne onwards in the stream of universal becoming."

Penance

The sacrament of penance is concerned with repentance for sin, forgiveness, and reconciliation. Jesus called his disciples to imitate the love that he had shown all, and yet he knew well the sinful side of humanity. Jesus called his disciples to repent, which means to stop in your tracks, turn around, and allow God to lead you in the right direction. Jesus died forgiving those who had betrayed and crucified him. After the Resurrection he said to his disciples: "Thus it is written that the Messiah would suffer and rise from the dead on the third day and that repentance, for the forgiveness of sins, would be preached in his name to all the nations" (Lk 24:47).

The celebration of the sacrament of penance should include conversion in the area of environmental responsibility. A new direction is called for in the way we treat nature, relate to other living things, and share resources. The danger of perishing can take on a whole new meaning if we consider the damage that has been done to our air, waterways, and natural resources. Material things have become idols for many, and there is a hardening of heart toward the poor. Attitudes of use and abuse, consumerism, and runaway debt are creating social, political, and natural threats to life on our planet. Human complicity with or at least passivity to the degradation of the earth has become a moral issue and calls for repentance and reconciliation between our environment and us.

The Churches Speak Out

The Christian churches are gradually awakening to the environmental crisis and are searching their beliefs and values for solutions. Even many on the religious right in our country, who have in the past written off environmentalists as fanatics, are now seeing in the Bible grounds to appreciate and work for the preservation of creation. Let's now look at an overview of the relevant statements from the Catholic and Protestant churches. These views can help Christians in their effort to connect their faith to their concern for the environment.

John Paul II

John Paul's first substantial statement on ecology came in his message for World Peace Day in 1990. He pointed out that lack of respect for nature is linked to the nuclear arms race, war, and injustice—all threats to world peace. He warned that the ecological crisis is part of the insecurity and danger that surround us. The ecological crisis is in fact a moral crisis and serves as a "seedbed" for selfishness, dishonesty, and disregard for others.

The pope urged a new respect for life and maintained this to be an essential factor in the building of world peace. He suggested that we focus on sharing resources and that there be more solidarity between the industrialized world and the developing nations. The pontiff pointed to widespread poverty, unjust land distribution, and the dislocation of people, and how indebted countries are being forced to pillage their resources to pay their debts. And he emphasized that chemical and biological weapons pose a new threat to human life and the environment. John Paul urged people to live more simply and to better educate themselves and their families, schools, and churches with regard to this crisis. He urged all churches and religions to work together for the care of the earth.

The U.S. Bishops

In 1991 the U.S. bishops issued a powerful document on ecology, signaling that ecology presents serious questions of justice and profoundly affects the poor and the powerless of the world. The bishops surveyed appropriate biblical teachings on the sacredness of the earth and human life and connected these issues with Catholic social teaching on human dignity and concern for the common good.

The bishops warn that the environmental crisis has brought the United States and the world community to a crossroads that calls for conversion. Besides the central Christian virtue of love for all things, there is a pressing need for prudence, humility, and temperance. The bishops call for a commitment to sacrifice and a radical change in lifestyles. They urge more environmental education in schools and parishes and the use of environmental themes in Catholic worship and prayer.

Voices from Appalachia

One of the most extraordinary documents on religion and the environment has come from the Catholic churches in the Appalachian Mountains that run through thirteen states from Georgia to New York. Much of this beautiful area has been scarred, first by industry and mining, and now by clear-cutting, strip mining, garbage dumping, and new prisons. There is a plea here to preserve and sustain the forests, land, and aquifers so that the people in Appalachia can live in harmony with "the web of life." Residents recall when native peoples and new settlers enjoyed the hills and hollows and the fresh air and water, a time when they cared more for each other and worshipped the God of creation. Today's residents also believe that nature speaks of God's beauty, goodness, and love, and they feel called to sustain what they have left. Many of these folk are deeply in touch with nature, descendants of a great mountain people who lived freely and simply, close to land and kin.

These people see their communities aging and suffering from unemployment, and they often lack the political clout to withstand the further flattening of their mountaintops for coal. They too have come to a cross-roads: one path leads to devastation; the other, to building a sustainable community. In this document they reach into their biblical tradition and the principles of Catholic social teaching for a roadmap to sustainability. They accent human dignity and the common good and thus advocate an economy based on spiritual values, more power to local businesses, sharing and preserving God-given resources, rejecting materialism, and preserving the earth, lest they destroy themselves and steal the future from their children. Their hope is that their churches will become centers dedicated to the regeneration of their region. These are people truly in touch with their history and their environment, and they offer a role model for other Christians to become more active in ecological efforts.

Bishops from Poor Countries

Catholic leaders from poor countries are also addressing the environmental crisis.

The Guatemalan bishops echo the "cry for land" from millions of poor farmers who have been expelled from lands that had been theirs for thousands of years. They expose the extreme poverty of the peasants, while the privileged rich hold most of the property and live in luxury. They reveal how public funds are withheld from the peasants and how they are an exploited work force, laboring in unhealthy conditions for small pay. Those who complain are run off and often subjected to violence.

The bishops review the Catholic biblical and doctrinal tradition and cry out against greed and injustice. They censure the silencing of the poor with guns and disappearances. They criticize their government for preserving the rights of the rich while doing little to protect the poor. They call for solidarity among Guatemalans and entreat their people to see each other as children of God, as brothers and sisters with equal dignity and rights.

The bishops of the Philippines have written an extraordinary document on environmental issues. They recall how their country was once covered with lush trees and flowering plants, and was home to many species of animals, birds, and insects. They were surrounded with blue seas, wonderful coral reefs, and fish of every shape and color. Now ruthless exploitation of land and seas has robbed the area of most of this natural endowment. Only 3 percent of the forests are left, and many of the animal species have been relentlessly hunted as their habitats are rapidly destroyed. Most of the birds are gone. The chocolate-colored rivers have become running sewers carrying the islands' soil to the sea and killing the coral reefs, of which only 5 percent remain pristine. The air in the cities has become noxious and the lakes have grown heavy with silt. The bishops cry out: "We have sinned against God and his creation," and they call upon their people to continue their recent efforts toward environmental reform. The bishops propose a new vision for the Philippines, one grounded in creation theology, good stewardship, and the covenant that binds all of creation together.

The Protestant Churches

The World Council of Churches (WCC) has contributed mightily to linking Christianity to concern for the earth. The WCC links ecology to liberation theology. They point out that the many human cries for liberation must be joined with the cries of animals, plants, and the earth itself. They review how colonialism in Africa and Asia depleted the resources of these continents and brought untold suffering to their people.

Western development was accompanied by "division theologies," which were arrogant toward nature, reduced people to "cogs" in the labor force or military, and exploited women and poor people.

The WCC has called for a new theology of liberation to free all life from abusive domination, listen to the voices of the oppressed, and integrate the Christian faith with concern for the environment. They call for a new Christian ethic to honor the integrity of all things and move from a notion of conquest to a practice of reverence.

The latest effort by the WCC came in 2006, when its General Assembly in Brazil reviewed the environmental work done by Christian communities around the globe. They stress that even though churches are divided in beliefs, they can unite in their concern for the earth. Ecological witness and action are essential elements of ecumenism, and they urge churches and indeed all religions to embark on joint actions to protect the earth. They urge all their members to dialogue with scientists, politicians, economists, and corporate leaders for solutions to our environmental challenges.

The Presbyterians have been leaders among Christian environmentalists. They view creation as a "living reality" that cries out for justice for people and the earth. They have helped many realize that environmental problems are always also human problems, especially for poor people. They point out that deterioration of the earth and social disintegration feed on each other. Competitive individualism and the prosperity of the few continually contribute to ecological problems. And they confess that as a church they have been too uncritical, too unbiblical, and too self-serving in the area of ecology. They call upon their people to commit themselves to sustain the ecosystems of the earth, to work for equal distribution of resources, the common good, frugality, and solidarity with the earth and all its people, especially poor people. The Presbyterians have done their scientific homework and present many concrete strategies for improving agriculture, water purification, waste disposal, preservation of wildlife and land, and even for solving such complicated problems as ozone depletion and global warming. They are indeed leaders among those who attempt to integrate Christian faith with ecology.

Feminine Perspectives

The movement called *ecofeminism* seems to have grown out of the women's movement. In 1972, a French woman, Francoise d'Eaubonne, first used the term *ecological feminism*. She argued that the destruction of the planet was due to the profit motive inherent in male power and that women were needed to bring about an ecological revolution. As the movement grew, women theologians began to study the religious dimensions of ecological issues.

Ivone Gebara, a Brazilian theologian, maintains the feminist movement went through several stages before linking theology with ecology. First women became aware that they were oppressed. Then they began to realize that this oppression was linked with the degradation of the environment. Women are the prime sustainers in society. In poor countries it is usually women who get up before dawn, travel long distances for water, gather wood for cooking and heating, and feed their families. When wooded areas are stripped and waters polluted, they face malnutrition and disease. Often they watch sadly as their homes are bulldozed to clear land or as their husbands can no longer find game or fish.

Out of this suffering, many women began to suspect that their oppression was linked to the churches and certain interpretations of the Bible. They began to see that the predominance of male images for God and patriarchal structures were not only leading to the abuse of the earth, but also to the abuse of women, who were often seen as unclean, sinful, and identified with nature.

Ecofeminism began in Europe and the United States and then moved to the developing countries where the plight of women is much worse. The views of ecofeminists are diverse: some want to revise the Christian tradition, while others suggest the tradition is beyond repair and should be abandoned.

Women are often linked with the physical, natural, and material, and Christianity has held various views toward these aspects of reality. The philosophy of ancient Greece, which profoundly influenced early Christians, separated and denigrated matter: the soul mattered, not the body, and reality stood in a hierarchy moving from spirit (identified with male) down to matter (identified with female). Apocalyptic thinking saw an imminent end of the material, but an eternal existence for the spiritual. For Christians this meant that the soul left the body in order to enter heaven. Christian asceticism entailed leaving the sexual and physical behind to focus on the spiritual.

The medieval world was ambiguous about matter and spirit. On one hand, sacramental theology held that God and the Church nurtured the spirit through material things. Yet nature was often associated with demonic powers, which led to superstitions, witchcraft, and a bizarre preoccupation with skeletons and death. Women were often held to be associated with all of these. Misogyny or the hatred of women is said to have begun with the awareness that women are responsible for the life and death cycle. The execution of witches was closely connected with these views.

Much of the sacramental was lost during the Protestant Reformation. For instance, Calvin did not think that nature and the material world could be trusted to convey the experience of God. Much sacramental practice was written off as superstitious or pagan. This suspicion of nature often became a suspicion of women, who were associated with nature. Women were to be closely monitored at home and at church.

Holistic Thinking

Holistic thinking calls for respect for both the material (physical) and spiritual. It engenders respect for nature and the human body and sees male and female as equally expressing both. From this perspective, women are no longer singularly associated with the natural world or viewed as existing to be dominated by and serve the needs of men. The holistic approach perceives reality as one entity, with physical and spiritual dimensions. Both men and women have these two dimensions and are created to complement each other and to treat each other with respect. Domination and abuse are no longer acceptable.

holistic thinking calls for respect

Diversity among Ecofeminist Theologians

There is diversity among Christian feminist theologians who address environmental issues, and these differences seem to fall into three main approaches. The first approach maintains that the Hebrew-Christian tradition, with its patriarchal and hierarchical structure, has been too deeply implicated in the oppression of women and the earth to be of use any longer. This post-Christian perspective sometimes suggests a return to indigenous religions of the past for beliefs relevant to ecology. Often these religions honored goddesses who these theologians believe were more respectful of nature and life. At times this approach tends to romanticize these ancient religious traditions.

A second approach attempts to hold to the teachings of Scripture and tradition but to reinterpret them from the perspective of contemporary feminist experience. These theologians work within the framework of the theology of God, Trinity, Christ, and Church, but want to strip these doctrines of past patriarchal and hierarchical interpretations and begin anew with feminine interpretations. They often focus on feminine images of God, the restoration of the goddesses, the feminine aspects of the Trinity, and move away from focusing on the maleness of Jesus and his male saving power; they call for a reconfiguring of the male-dominated church. Usually the experience of women, especially that of oppressed women in developing countries, is the context for these interpretations. Often these interpretations are beyond the bounds of orthodoxy and threaten mainline Christian theology. Once the Christian tradition has been thus radically revised, these feminist theologians are ready to link their new perspectives to the environmental crisis.

Finally there are feminist theologians who are willing to work more closely within the orthodox tradition. They, of course, are aware of patriarchal and hierarchical distortions but are also willing to grant that there is much of value that can be retrieved from Christian beliefs in spite of these flaws. Once these theologians have revised and renewed the interpretations of the Christian tradition, they are prepared to link them to their concerns for the environment.

Ecofeminist theology seems to be gaining strength in developing countries, where many women experience oppression against themselves and their surroundings. In much of this writing, there is a strong political agenda, because the injustices find their source in the government and the military. Originally many of these theologians were influenced by liberation theology, but most have moved beyond it, believing it to be too male in its approach. Ecofeminist theology is generally down to earth, practical, and focused on meeting the needs of women. Ecofeminist theologians refuse to be dominated by their governments and are actively engaged in resisting the destruction of the local environment, on which they depend to sustain their families. They make strong demands for accessible and clean water, land rights, and reduced taxes. Vandana Shiva, a leading advocate for women's rights in India, is a good example of a woman who is making a difference in these areas. Her book *Water Wars* attacks the recent trend toward claiming water as private property and then selling it for profit, a new reality that is oppressing women and their families in many parts of the developing world.

An Environmental Ethic

A quarter of a century ago, Bernard Häring, one of the great ethicists of our time, prophetically placed environmental ethics at the center of his concerns. He observed that ecological issues touch on many areas of social living: health, economics, politics, even genetics. He realized that environmental issues reveal the interdependence of everything and call humans to accept serious responsibilities toward the world in which they live. He calls his Church to recognize its role in addressing these issues.

It is only recently that Christians have come to realize that waste and degradation of the earth are moral issues. Our list of sins simply has not included wasting resources, polluting waters, and destroying living things other than humans. This raises questions about our past morality. Was it too otherworldly, concerned more about getting into heaven than attending to our earth? Was it too much a private morality and not sufficiently concerned about such public issues as social justice and ecology? Were we perhaps too concerned about Church law and oblivious to the laws of nature? Possibly our morality was so human-centered that ironically we failed to realize how essential the health of the earth is to human life. We have often opposed violence, but looked the other way when violence was done to our earth. We might have been concerned about paying a fair price for goods, but oblivious to the fact that these goods were being made by poorly paid workers in an environment unprotected by laws.

As Christians, we have stressed love of God, self, and neighbor, but have spoken little about the love we should have for nature, for our earth. James Nash, in his book *Loving Nature,* shows us how many dimensions of love can be applied to ecology. He lists these dimensions as follows:

1. **Beneficence**, serving others and looking out for their interests. In ecology this can be expressed in the way we care for animals, have respect for bodies of water, and preserve endangered species.

2. **Esteem for Others**, which includes a respect for the integrity of all things. This could include avoiding the abuse and destruction of all living things.

3. **Receptivity**, which includes our recognition of our dependence on others, in this case nature. This includes having a certain awe about nature and a concern to protect and nurture living things.

4. **Humility**, which avoids arrogance or the feeling of superiority over nature. This implies the realization that we all come from and return to the earth and share in the finiteness of all things.

5. **Understanding**, which moves us to learn more about nature, its strengths and vulnerabilities, and the ways that nature can be repaired and sustained.

6. **Communion**, which moves us to be linked with nature, to be in solidarity with the earth and living things, and to act to prevent damage to all these things.

Justice and the Environment

In our discussion of Catholic social teaching, we have seen how the Church has connected justice with wages, unions, social conditions, the ownership of land, and human rights. Now the challenge is to link justice with ecology. John Paul II, in *On Social Concern,* points out the many human inequities and abuses in the world and singles out the abuse of the earth as a special concern. He notes that the uneven distribution of food, water, and resources and the lack of respect for life and nature are closely connected with the many threats to peace in the world. There is an increasing imbalance between the haves and the have-nots, and a building frustration and anger among the poor that could easily overflow into violence.

As mentioned earlier, the United Nations has reported that one-third of the world's people have much and are gaining more, while two-thirds have little and are losing that. This formula points to inevitable conflict and violence.

Justice demands we recognize that all people have a right to life and happiness and calls for a much more equitable sharing of resources. Justice challenges those situations where a few people live in opulence and glitter, while many more live in squalor and suffer from malnutrition or even starvation. Justice condemns the squandering of resources and the dumping that wastes, pollutes, and endangers health. The Christian tradition teaches that the earth and its bountiful resources are a divine gift to all and should be shared. Justice calls us to sacrifice time and goods so that those less fortunate can have the things they need. Justice demands that we preserve nature so that its beauty can be admired and so that it can be a source of contemplation of God's creation and presence.

A safe and healthy environment has now been added to the list of human rights. Not only do all humans have a right to food, shelter, health care, security, and work, they also have a right to clean water to drink, clean air to breathe, and an environment that is safe for their health and well-being. Justice cries out that we attend to the millions in our world who have been forced by war to wander as refugees on vast wastelands, who have been driven off their lands into urban areas, where they are subjected to contaminated water and dangerously polluted air. An image of this from one of my visits to El Salvador is forever etched in my memory. In front of us in traffic was a truck loaded with *campesinos* going to work. Few of the cars and trucks had catalytic converters, so black, poisonous fumes spewed out from all of the vehicles. Standing in the front of the truck bed was a young mother holding her baby. While sitting in traffic, the black smoke from the truck in front of them was pouring black exhaust into the face of this mother and child!

The Common Good

The common good has always been part of the Christian ethic. An environmental ethic is concerned about the common good because air, land, and water pollution affect the health and well-being of everyone. Global warming and the depletion of the ozone layer affect the global community and must therefore be the concern of all. So many environmental issues are connected. With Hurricane Katrina we saw how not only individuals but also an entire region of the United States was deeply affected by a storm that many fear is a harbinger of global warming. The destruction of a rain forest not only destroys a valuable and irreplaceable resource, it also displaces the indigenous people who live there and wipes out all the living organisms in that ecosystem. The destruction of these "lungs of the world" also increases pollution and deprives the earth and its people of oxygen.

We can see that an environmental ethic is still in the making. Only gradually will Christians begin to see that their Scriptures, traditions, and social teaching are applicable to the challenge of sustaining our environment. Persons of faith will have to shape their consciences toward concern and action on ecological issues. They will have to extend their love beyond their fellow human beings to include the earth and all living things. They will have to extend their sense of justice to the millions who are deprived of resources and subjected to unhealthy environments. They will have to live more simply, share more vigorously, and work harder for a cleaner and healthier world.

Conclusion

If Christians are going to be part of the solution for a better environment, they are going to have to reexamine their Scriptures, tradition, social teachings, and ethics to see the richness there and how it applies to the many environmental concerns of today. But, reflection and theology will not be enough to survive this crisis. Christians will have to be moved by their beliefs and values to take action to share their resources with the needy, and to conserve and sustain the earth, along with its beauty and bounty. Pope John Paul II has said: "God entrusted the whole of creation to the man and the woman, and only then—as we read—could God rest."

A Chart of Some Major Environmental Problems

1. Acid Rain: The burning of fuel releases chemicals and gasses that mix with water to form acid that falls with rain and snow. This "acid rain" results in the degradation of plants, forests, and crops, and the pollution of waterways, destruction of fish life, and erosion of buildings and infrastructures.

2. Pollution of Waterways: The Global International Waters Assessment reports serious environmental problems in the world's waterways, including those in the South China Sea region. This region comprises nine nations—China, Vietnam, Cambodia, Thailand, Malaysia, Singapore, Indonesia, Brunei, and the Philippines—and forms the global heart of tropical marine biodiversity. Although the region supports a fast-growing human coastal population, its marine ecosystems are rapidly deteriorating and the collapse of many of its coral reefs and fish populations is imminent. The Amazon Basin, an area of land surrounding the Amazon River in South America, is the largest basin on the planet, but it has been extensively damaged through deforestation, mining, hydropower generation, and agricultural activities.

3. The Water Crisis: More than one billion people do not have access to clean drinking water. More than two billion lack access to proper sanitation. As a consequence, millions of people die every year due to preventable water-related diseases. Water resources around the globe are threatened by climate change, wasteful use, and pollution.

(Continued on page 310)

(Continued from page 309)

4. Global Warming: Burning fossil fuels (coal, oil, and gas) releases gases including carbon dioxide, nitrogen, and methane into the atmosphere. These gases blanket the earth and trap in heat, causing the average global temperature to rise. This global warming results in climate changes that endanger many species and even ecosystems, including coral reefs. Consequences of these climate changes include a shift in the seasons; an increase in extreme weather events such as level-5 hurricanes, floods, cold snaps, droughts, and heat waves; melting polar ice caps and glaciers; rising sea levels; and an increase in wildfire due to more frequent droughts.

5. Depletion of the Ozone Layer: Our planet is shielded from harmful ultraviolet rays by a band of ozone in the atmosphere. The ozone layer has been depleted by the use of chlorofluorocarbons in products such as hairsprays, refrigerators, and air conditioners. As a result, more harmful radiation now reaches the earth's surface, which can cause skin cancer, cataracts, and skin infections in humans. This radiation also adversely affects plant life including plankton, the single-cell plant that forms the bottom of the world's food chain and produces most of our oxygen. The use of chlorofluorocarbons has now been banned around the world.

6. Destruction of the Rain Forests: Rain forests grow in areas of high rainfall and are mainly found in Central and South America, India, and other parts of the Near East. Rain forests supply oxygen, provide habitat for millions of species, and are key sources of medicines. These forests are rapidly being destroyed and are now half of what they were two hundred years ago. At the present rate of destruction they could disappear in forty years.

7. Extinction of Species: Human-caused pollution, poaching, legal hunting, habitat fragmentation and destruction, and other actions have caused the actual or near extinction of thousands of species. Some scientists estimate that within thirty years about 20 percent of the world's species will no longer exist. This could have devastating effects on the web of life that sustains all species.

these forests are being destroyed

Activities

1. Make team presentations, using PowerPoint and film clips, on outstanding environmentalists, such as Steve Irwin, Jacques Cousteau, Sr. Dorothy Stanger, John Muir, Aldo Leopold, Rachel Carson, Julia Butterfly Hill, Dian Fossey, and Jane Goodall.

2. Do a survey on the Internet of environmental groups and discuss their concerns and goals in class.

3. Hold a debate on the topic: Global Warming: Fact or Myth?

4. Show Al Gore's film, *An Inconvenient Truth*, and discuss his presentation.

5. Do a study of what your university does to conserve energy, recycle, and promote ecological awareness. Discuss your results with an administrator.

Sources

Bassett, Libby, ed. *Earth and Faith*. New York: UNEP, 2000.

Berry, Thomas. *Dream of the Earth*. San Francisco: Sierra Books, 1988.

Boff, Leonardo. *Ecology and Liberation*. Maryknoll, NY: Orbis Books, 1995.

Gebara, Ivone. *Longing for Running Water: Ecofeminism and Liberation*. Minneapolis, MN: Fortress Press, 1999.

Glazer, Walter, and Drew Christiansen, eds. *"And God Saw that It Was Good": Catholic Theology and the Environment*. Washington, DC: USCC, 1996.

Gottlieb, Roger. *This Sacred Earth*. New York: Routledge, 2004.

Haught, John. *The Promise of Nature*. New York: Paulist Press, 1993.

Hill, Brennan R. *Christian Faith and the Environment*. Maryknoll, NY: Orbis Books, 1998.

Rasmussen, Larry. *Earth Community, Earth Ethics*. Geneva: WCC Publications, 1996.

Smith, Pamela. *What Are They Saying about Environmental Ethics?* New York: Paulist Press, 1997.

INDEX

A

Aaron, 130

Abba, 14, 20, 24, 27, 28, 29, 33, 73, 185, 187, 262, 287, 291, 295

Abel, 40

Abimelech, 22

Abraham, 17, 39, 40, 60, 129
    and Sara, 40, 129

Abrahamic religions, 129

Abu Bakr, 136

Abu Talib, 137

acid rain, 309

Acts of the Apostles, 52, 183, 184, 188, 288

Adam and Eve, 59, 219, 239, 285

Aelia Capitolina, 43

Afghanistan, 143

Africa
    Christianity in, 81

Agni, 144

ahimsa, 145

Alban, 75

al-Banna, Hasan, 142

Albigensians, 104

Alexander the Great, 43

Alexandra, 220

Alexandria, 71, 99

Alexy, 291

Algonquins, 162

Ali, 136, 138

Allah, 139, 264

almsgiving, Islam, 142

al-Qaeda, 143

Amazon Basin, 309

American Canon Law Society, 230

American Indians, 78–79

Anabaptists, 112, 200

Andrew, 19

Anglicans, 118–119, 200, 215–216
    Eucharist, 215
    women and, 216, 229

Annas, 65

Annunciation, the, 61
    Luke's nativity story, 61

anointing of the sick, 187–189

Anthony, Susan B., 227

Antioch, 70, 71, 99, 102, 195, 206, 225

anti-Semitism, 91, 133, 155, 156

apologists, 72

apostles, 69, 81, 223–224, 233, 243.
    See also disciples

Appalachia, 298–299

Aquinas, Thomas, 140, 155, 167, 188, 249, 256

Arianism, 98, 99, 208

Aristotle, 140, 209, 210

Arizona, 79

Asclepius, 187

Ashtar, 236

Asia Minor, 70

Aslan, Rez, 140

Assyrian Church, Eucharist and, 216

Assyrians, 46, 130
    conquest of Israel, 42